• WAR IN THE INFORMATION AGE •

War in the Information Age

...

NEW CHALLENGES FOR U.S. SECURITY POLICY

War in the Information Age

...

NEW CHALLENGES FOR U.S. SECURITY POLICY

Edited by
Robert L. Pfaltzgraff, Jr.
Richard H. Shultz, Jr.

BRASSEY'S

WASHINGTON/LONDON

Brassey's Editorial Offices: Brassey's Order Department:
22883 Quicksilver Drive   P.O. Box 960
Dulles, Virginia 20166   Herndon, Virginia 20172

Brassey's books are available at special discounts for bulk purchases for sales promotions, premiums, fund-raising, or educational use.

Library of Congress Cataloging-in-Publication Data

War in the information age: new challenges for U.S. security policy /
edited by Robert L. Pfaltzgraff, Jr., Richard Shultz, Jr.:
foreword by Dennis Reimer.
p. cm.
  Includes bibliographical references.
  ISBN 1-57488-118-3 (alk. Paper)
1. Military arts and science—Forecasting. 2. Information technology.
3. United States—Military policy. I. Pfaltzgraff, Robert L.
II. Shultz, Richard H., 1947– .
U104.W37   1997
355.02—dc20
[B]
                                                          96–22516
                                                          CIP

10 9 8 7 6 5 4 3 2
Printed in the United States of America

 AN AUSA INSTITUTE
OF LAND WARFARE
BOOK

The Association of the United States Army, or AUSA, was founded in 1950 as a nonprofit organization dedicated to education concerning the role of the U.S. Army, to providing material for military professional development, and to the promotion of proper recognition and appreciation of the profession of arms. Its constituencies include those who serve in the Army today, including Army National Guard, Army Reserve, and Army civilians, the retirees and veterans who have served in the past, and all their families. A large number of public-minded citizens and business leaders are also an important constituency. The Association seeks to educate the public, elected and appointed officials, and leaders of the defense industry on crucial issues involving the adequacy of our national defense, particularly those issues affecting land warfare.

In 1988, AUSA established within its existing organization a new entity known as the Institute of Land Warfare. ILW's mission is to extend the educational work of AUSA by sponsoring a wide range of publications, to include books, monographs, and essays on key defense issues, as well as workshops, symposia, and since 1992, a television series. Among the volumes chosen as "An AUSA Institute of Land Warfare Book" are both new texts and reprints of titles of enduring value. Topics include history, policy issues, strategy, and tactics. Publication as an AUSA Book does not indicate that the Association of the United States Army and the publisher agree with everything in the book but does suggest that AUSA and the publisher believe the book will stimulate the thinking of AUSA members and others concerned about important defense-related issues.

table of contents

Foreword   ix
   Dennis J. Reimer

Preface   xvii

Section I The Emerging Security Environment   1

Introduction   3

1: Future Actors in a Changing Security Environment   9
   Robert L. Pfaltzgraff, Jr., Richard H. Shultz, Jr.

2: The Revolution in Military Affairs and Military Capabilities   29
   Michael J. Vickers

3: An Introduction to Information Warfare   47
   Winn Schwartau

4: The Threat of Information Operations: A Russian Perspective   61
   Timothy L. Thomas

Section II Technology and Human
Understanding for War in the Information Age   81

Introduction   83

5: Managing Battlespace Information: 87
The Challenge of Information Collection, Distribution, and Targeting
   James P. McCarthy

6: Tactical Situational Awareness: The Human Challenge   99
   Frederic J. Brown

7: Transition into the Information Age: 121
Opportunities, Lessons Learned, and Challenges
   John R. Wood

8: Exploiting Battlespace Transparency: 143
Operating Inside an Opponent's Decision Cycle
    John W. McDonald

Section III The Operational Issues   **169**

Introduction   171

9: Operations in the Information Age   175
    William W. Hartzog, Susan Canedy

10: Integrating Offensive and Defensive Information Warfare   187
    Richard P. O'Neill

11: Maneuver in the Information Age   203
    Huba Wass de Czege

12: Force XXI: U.S. Army Requirements,   225
Priorities, and Challenges in the Information Age
    John P. Rose, Robert M. Evans, Mark J. Eschelman, Jack Gerber,
    Jo-Ann C. Webber

Section IV The Information Age and   **241**
Nontraditional Military Issues

Introduction   243

13: The Impact of Information Age Technologies   247
on Operations Other Than War
    Christopher Jon Lamb

14: The Role of the Internet in International Politics: 279
Department of Defense Considerations
    Charles Swett

15: PSYOP and the Revolution in Military Affairs   307
    Carnes Lord

16: Public Affairs, the Media, and War in the Information Age   321
    Douglas Waller

Conclusion   **331**
A Framework for Discussing War in the Information Age
    Gregory J. Rattray, Laurence E. Rothenberg

Contributing Authors   **355**

Index   363

Foreword

Dennis J. Reimer

WE ARE PRESENTLY EXPERIENCING a revolution in military affairs. This is not the first such revolution in history. Generally, they occur whenever a major technological, political, or social innovation fundamentally alters the character and conduct of conflict. However, new technologies or weapons cannot be truly effective unless an organization adapts and develops a doctrine so that soldiers on the battlefield can maximize the potential inherent in such developments. In short, revolutions occur when military organizations adapt – and military organizations adapt because people make change happen.[1]

In the past two hundred years, six revolutions in military affairs have radically altered the conduct and character of war. The first was the French Revolution of 1789. With the institution of universal military obligation, France was able to raise mass armies, allowing Napoleon to overwhelm the military forces of his opponents for twenty years. Next came the Industrial Revolution of the mid-nineteenth century. This revolution enabled a modernizing nation to arm, equip, and transport large armies conscripted under universal military obligation. New weapons increased the lethality and scope of the battlefield. The telegraph and railroad dramatically altered the speed and ferocity of operations.[2]

The third revolution was the managerial revolution of the late nineteenth century, which enabled the rapid assembly and deployment of large military units. Nations developed general staffs, composed of trained technical experts, to integrate their industrial, civilian, and manpower resources. Unfortunately, the lag between industrial development and managerial change resulted in the costly stalemate of World War I.[3] The price of this misunderstanding was the loss of a generation on the battlefields of Europe. The fourth revolution in military affairs, the mechanized revolution, occurred between 1919–1939. The innovative use of the internal combustion engine dramatically changed both air and ground warfare; it replaced trench warfare and with fluid, fast-moving operations, characterized by deep penetrations and huge encirclements.[4] The swift ground advances of World War II epitomized this revolution.

Even as the effects of mechanized warfare were first being felt in World War II, they were outpaced by a fifth revolution. The scientific revolution harnessed the intellect of the scientist, engineer, and technical expert to win the war. The culmination of this effort was the design, construction, and employment of the atomic bomb. After the dawn of the nuclear age, the character of war remained virtually unchanged for the next thirty years. Then, in the early 1970s, the introduction of precision-strike weapons and computers ushered in a new era. The present information revolution centers on the concept that the ability to collect, analyze, disseminate, and act upon battlefield information is the dominant factor in warfare.

In today's Information Age, time and technology blur the line between planning and execution. The Army of the twenty-first century must be prepared to deal with threats across a broad spectrum; it must be equipped to handle, in Alvin Toffler's words, Agrarian and Industrial Age foes even as it prepares to face Information Age adversaries. As in the past, the primary challenge of this revolution is to leverage emerging technologies to maximize the inherent capabilities of the American soldier. The interface between technology and the individual soldier is at the heart of the Army's plan to adapt itself to twenty-first century demands.

Two recent events underscore the importance of clearly understanding the full spectrum of future challenges, and quickly adapting to meet them correctly. In early September 1995, celebrations were held to mark the fiftieth anniversary of the end of fighting in the Pacific. The previous summer, a ceremony was held in Washington to dedicate a memorial to soldiers of the Korean War. Though separated by less than five years, the contrasts between these two wars are astounding. From the end of World War II to the outbreak of the Korean War, the U.S. Army changed drastically. In August 1945, the U.S. Army was the largest and most powerful army in the world. Its eighty-nine divisions were instrumental in destroying the military might of the Axis powers – a tribute to both the millions of brave men and women who served and the tremendous capabilities of industrial America. However, by June of 1950, America's Army had shrunk to a shell of its former self, reduced from twelve million to less than 600,000 soldiers.

In the summer of 1950, the U.S. Army was not prepared. Poorly equipped and untrained soldiers were hastily sent into battle to buy time for the Army to respond. The setbacks in Korea were not the fault of these soldiers, or their leaders – the system let them down. Once again we were surprised and, once again, we paid a very steep price. As General Creighton Abrams said in 1973, "We paid dearly for our unpreparedness during those early days in Korea with our most precious currency – the lives of our young men. The monuments we raise to their heroism and sacrifice are really surrogates for the monuments we owe ourself for our blindness to reality, for our indifference to real threats to our security, and our determination to deal in intentions and perceptions, for our unsubstantiated wishful thinking about how war could not come."[5]

History has demonstrated time and again that technological superiority alone is not the decisive factor for success. The right balance of quality people, training, leadership, doctrine, and equipment is critical. Evidence that the lessons of history are indeed being learned can be seen in the changes instituted over the past six years. The Army has been dramatically reshaped, yet remains trained and ready. The successes of the Gulf War make it tempting simply to rest on our laurels, but we recognize that course as a luxury which cannot be indulged. The Army of tomorrow, one that will meet the needs of a vastly different world, has yet to be built.

The vision of the twenty-first century Army is a direct legacy of the bloody battlefield lessons of the past. Sacrificing the nation's youth is not the solution to tomorrow's challenges. We need no more monuments to our blindness to reality. Instead, we envision the world's best Army – a total force of quality soldiers and civilians, trained and ready for victory. The Army must be a values-based organization that can perform as an integral part of any team. It must be equipped with the most modern weapons the country can provide, enabling it to respond effectively to today's needs while continually adapting to meet future challenges.

The Army's vision is set in an environment in which missions are expanding both in terms of quantity and diversity. At the same time, it acknowledges decreased resources, reflected in a purchasing power loss of 34 percent since 1989. It recognizes, as President Clinton has noted, a world in which the line between domestic and foreign policy is increasingly blurred. It emphasizes a modernization program that is currently at the irreducible minimum and badly in need of more resources. Today the Army is allocated only 13 percent of the Department of Defense modernization budget, the smallest piece of an already small defense pie. The Army remains trained and ready, but our ability to dominate land warfare is eroding. And our modernization plan does not forecast filling the gap quickly enough.

The plan developed by the Army to make this vision of the future a reality has been given the title "Force XXI." Simply stated, Force XXI provides quality people with the right doctrine and organizations, the most realistic training, an adequate sustainment package during both peace and war, and the best equipment and weapons systems, given the resources available. Technology will be leveraged to arm U.S. soldiers with the finest, most lethal weapons systems in the world. The power of information will allow the ultimate weapon – the individual soldier – to meet successfully the challenges of the twenty-first century and achieve decisive victory. Force XXI provides the framework for the decisions we must make to ensure that tomorrow's force will remain as prepared as today's.

Force XXI is more than a series of charts. Using a systems approach to technology infusion coupled with organizational redesign, the Force XXI process translates into the Army XXI product, both on time and on target. The plan includes the Force Protection Tactical Operations Center to apply the technology associated with theater missile defense command, control, communications, computers, and information (C^4I) system already available for deployment. Advanced warfighting experiments gauge the potential of technology to reduce training costs through a combination of live and simulated training techniques. Yet, as organizational specialist Peter Senge states, "New technologies are only as effective as the people working with them."[6] Soldiers must continually improve their ability to use technology to fight the enemy, day or night, rain or shine, twenty-four hours a day, seven days a week.

Decisions made today regarding force structure, equipment modernization, and doctrine must carry through the next fifteen to twenty years. The senior leadership of the twenty-first century Army can be found among the majors studying today at Fort Leavenworth. Through the power of simulation they are currently training to fight an opponent that does not yet exist, equipped with weapon systems not yet in the inventory. Tomorrow's brigade commanders are running today's companies, batteries, and troops; the next battalion commanders lead today's platoons; and future company commanders and their soldiers are still in primary school.

These future soldiers and leaders must be capable of assimilating a rapid flow of information and performing diverse missions across the spectrum of war in a multinational environment. The soldier of the next century must be comfortable with technology, culturally aware, a good information processor, adaptable, tenacious under stress, and sound of judgment. Today, throughout the battle labs of the Army's Training and Doctrine Command, models and simulations are used to study the traits that future leaders and soldiers must possess in order to win on tomorrow's battlefield. In training, for example, U.S. advancements in mission planning through the use of rehearsal systems are unparalleled, allowing forces to prepare for combat in a near-live environment, literally creating "virtual veterans." These life-saving techniques can only be achieved by effectively leveraging current information technology to anticipate tomorrow's challenges better.

In the future, the range of adversaries confronted by the United States will no doubt be similar to their historical predecessors. In addition to conventional forces, there will still be thugs that burn frightening images of genocide and ethnic cleansing into the media; narcotics traffickers who put future generations at risk; and terrorists who threaten a peaceful and stable world. Force XXI must maintain the advantage over such ill-defined, "don't play by the rules" competitors. An enemy still living in an agrarian world will readily defy an Information Age force that can fly, shoot, and sail with unmatched speed, accuracy, and impunity but cannot contend with thugs armed with machetes and AK-47s. Quality soldiers are key to bridging that gap, ensuring that the Army is relevant across the full spectrum of conflict. They must be able to defeat an enemy armed with spears and blowguns well as one armed with weapons of mass destruction. As General Raoul Cedras of Haiti discovered, nothing helps focus the mind faster than knowing that the 82nd Airborne is en route.

The vision of Force XXI is crystal clear. However, its attainment is not preordained. The basic challenge is to adapt to change while successfully remaining anchored to our rich tradition and history. To do so, we must balance near-term readiness, quality of life, and future modernization. Internally, resources must be allocated effectively. In this regard, the Army will not be bound by traditional approaches. A range of profound changes in the way the Army operates will be considered as long as they increase efficiency and do not degrade core competencies. Important new techniques – such as velocity management, total asset visibility, integrated sustainment maintenance, and improved force management – offer critical advantages in our effort to become more effective.

Many people talk about the essential tenets of the revolution of military affairs – precision strike, information warfare, space warfare, and dominating maneuver. Yet, to ensure success in this revolution, the Army must embrace an additional tenet: efficiency. War's traditional reputation as a wasteful, consuming necessity must be overcome. In preparing for war, we must leverage technology and modern management techniques to get the most bang out of every buck. We owe that to the taxpayer, but, more importantly, we owe it to our soldiers.

As always, the key to building a cutting-edge force is high-quality soldiers. Quality soldiers are the essence of the Army. Complex equipment serves no purpose unless it is crewed by capable soldiers. Less than a decade ago, a company commander's driver was responsible for maintaining and operating a jeep and radio. The radio was simple to operate; it had only a power switch and a frequency dial. Today that same company commander's driver is responsible for a much more capable, yet complex, command vehicle. The HMMWV (highly mobile multipurpose wheeled vehicle) is equipped with a sophisticated frequency-hopping radio with electronic counter-countermeasures, a global positioning system, a secure mobile telephone linked to a mobile subscriber system, night-vision goggles, and a chemical agent alarm. These are sophisticated devices that take considerable intelligence and technical know-how to master. Once these skills are mastered, developmental technology can even be inserted directly on the battlefield. The last-minute decision to modernize the *Abrams* and *Bradley* fleets in the desert on the eve of combat during the Gulf War was taken primarily because exceptional combat crewmen were able to exchange the equipment quickly without any loss in fighting ability.

For the past two decades we have demonstrated that a volunteer army can be the world's premier fighting force. The state of readiness of the Army is more than its weapons, equipment, and doctrine. A critical but intangible element of success is the spirit of our soldiers. As General Patton said, "It is the cold glitter in the attacker's eye, not the point of the questing bayonet that breaks the line. It is the fierce determination of the drive to close with the enemy not the mechanical perfection of the tank that conquers the trench."[7] His words still ring true. Survivors of the Bataan Death March still have a glint in their eye, reflecting the indomitable spirit that steeled them to press on against overwhelming odds. The same spirited gleam can be found in the eyes of soldiers at combat training centers today.

To some, the idea of war in the Information Age conjures images of bloodless conflict, more like a computer game than the bloody wars of the past. Nothing could be further from the truth. Warfare may change, but its impact on nations, armies, and soldiers will not. The fates of nations and armies will still be decided by war, perhaps more rapidly than in the past. Losers may still spend generations recovering from the consequences of defeat. And soldiers will always be the key to victory. Technology, and the ability to master it, may be increasingly important; but it will always be soldiers who win or lose wars. The battlefield will always be a dangerous, frightening, and lonely place. Only soldiers of character and courage, well trained, ably led, and properly equipped, will survive and win tomorrow — as they have in the past.

ENDNOTES
1. Andrew Krepinevich, "Cavalry to Computer: The Pattern of Military Revolutions," *The National Interest* (Fall 1994), p. 30.
2. Walter Millis, *Arms and Men* (New York: Capricorn Books, 1956), pp. 115 and 205.
3. Millis, pp. 205-6 and 282-3.
4. Millis, pp. 293,295.

5. General Creighton Abrams in an address to the Association of the U.S. Army, 16 October 1973.
6. Peter Senge in videotape for the Association of the United States Army Convention, 16–19 October 1995.
7. George S. Patton, cited in Peter Tsouras, *Warriors' Words: A Dictionary of Military Quotations* (London: Arms and Armour Press, 1994), p. 401.

Preface

Robert L. Pfaltzgraff, Jr.
Richard H. Shultz, Jr.

THE PROLIFERATION OF INFORMATION TECHNOLOGIES — computers, faxes, modems, the Internet, satellite communications, etc. — has important implications for national security that have yet to be fully understood. Successful integration of information systems into a sophisticated conventional force proved decisive for the U.S. victory in the Gulf War. The power of the global media to influence policy was highlighted during the conflict in Somalia; CNN coverage of starvation and strife helped propel President Bush to intervene in the crisis for humanitarian reasons. However, less than a year later, CNN broadcasts of Somalis dragging the corpses of U.S. soldiers through the streets of Mogadishu inflamed public outrage and heightened pressure to withdraw from an increasingly problematic situation. The threat of computer attacks against crucial information-dependent institutions — such as air traffic control, the banking system, and the Department of Defense itself — has increased concern that, while the United States may be safe from conventional military assault, a new national security threat may be emerging. Rogue states and terrorists may be able to wreak havoc on the information superhighway through computer-based assaults. Clearly, war in the Information Age is a growing and pressing concern for those concerned with national security. It encompasses several different but related concepts – the ability to use information-enhanced systems to create lethal precision weapons; the political impact of military operations in a world linked by real-time, visual media reporting; and the new challenges and opportunities created by the wide use of computers for financial, political, and military purposes.

All of these aspects of war in the Information Age affect national security planning. Admiral William Owens, the former Vice Chairman of the Joint Chiefs of Staff, argues that a "system of systems" approach will allow U.S. forces to achieve "dominant battlespace knowledge" and precision, stand-off weapons, enabling the United States to fight and win the wars of the next century. Each of the military services is working to incorporate Information Age technologies into doctrinc and operations, and are establishing new organization and units to do so. Protecting military and civilian information systems from attack has become a priority throughout the government. The Defense Department, the law enforcement community, and the intelligence community are defining their roles in defending America from information warfare, and interagency coordination is a key element of this process. Cooperation between government and industry is also a focus of attention. At the same time, Washington decisionmakers are clearly becoming more sensitive to the influence of the media on public opinion as it affects the military operations of the United States.

In an effort to promote dialogue on the issues surrounding the impact of the Information Age on national security, the Institute for Foreign Policy Analysis (IFPA) and International Security Studies Program of The Fletcher School of Law and Diplomacy, Tufts University, in association with the Deputy Chief of Staff of the Army for Operations and Plans, the Louisiana Maneuvers Task Force, and the Army War College, organized and hosted a conference entitled War in the Information Age on November 15, 1995. The conference featured participants from the Department of Defense, and the military services, as well as civilian academics and commentators. The collection of articles in this volume expands on the themes discussed during the conference. The common thread throughout the book is the emphasis on the need to examine the manner and extent to which information technologies alter our basic assumptions about the nature and conduct of war. What, for example, are the effects on national security of increasing dependence on computers in military and civilian life? What new vulnerabilities does this create, and how can we build a defense structure that meets changing needs? How can the United States leverage its advantages in high technology to craft strategies for victory in the Information Age? What are the vulnerabilities of advanced societies to information warfare? How will information technologies affect those who fight our wars and operate our weapon systems? What does this mean for training, tactics, and procedures in the military? Finally, what kind of intellectual framework will help us tackle the policy issues posed by Information Age technologies? The contributors set forth a range descriptions and prescriptions regarding these pressing issues.

The conference and this volume could not have been produced without the sustained support of the sponsoring agencies. In particular, we benefited from the continued interest and commitment of General Dennis Reimer, the Army Chief of Staff, as well as his immediate predecessor, General Gordon Sullivan, under whose auspices we planned the conference on which this volume is based. Dr. Jacquelyn K. Davis, Executive Vice President of the Institute for Foreign Policy Analysis, and Dr. Charles M. Perry, Vice President and Director of Studies of the Institute, offered valuable intellectual input into both the development of the conference and this volume. Special thanks are also due to Ruth Citrin, Project Research Coordinator of the International Security Studies Program (ISSP) at the Fletcher School of Law and Diplomacy; Roberta Breen, Staff Assistant at the ISSP; Larry Rothenberg, Research Associate at the Institute for Foreign Policy Analysis; Major Gregory Rattray, USAF; and last but not least, Freda Kilgallen, ISSP Administrator, whose superb managerial and organizational skills, as always, contributed to the success of the proceedings.

SECTION

I

The Emerging Security Environment

The Emerging Security Environment

THE END OF THE COLD WAR has brought vast changes in American defense planning, as the assumptions that drove strategy, doctrine, force structure, and procurement for fifty years have become outdated or irrelevant. The emerging security environment is no longer dominated by the prospect of two armed camps engaging in a cataclysmic war, but rather is characterized by ethnic conflict, attempts at hegemony by regional states, and the actions of sub-state actors such as terrorists, separatists, and international criminal organizations. The writers in the first section of this volume argue that this security environment will also be radically affected by an explosion of information technologies that will alter both the nature and conduct of warfare. Indeed, a new way to wage war is developing, termed information warfare. The concept of information warfare covers a range of issues, from the use of computers to attack vulnerable civilian information systems and the integration of advanced technology into weapons platforms to the manipulation of the media for propaganda purposes. In fact, to many analysts, information warfare is the latest in a series of revolutions in military affairs (RMAs) that have occurred throughout history.

In the first essay, Robert L. Pfaltzgraff and Richard H. Shultz offer an overview of the emerging security environment. They characterize it as *bifurcated* – that is, conflicts will occur at both the state level and at the level of sub-state and trans-state actors. Next, they identify the impact of information technologies on this new security landscape. Given the capabilities of computers and other information-processing technologies, such as cellular phones and the Global Positioning System, future conflicts will occur in a battlespace that covers not only physical geography, but cyberspace as well. As economic, financial, psychological, and political sectors of society become contested ground, traditional distinctions between military and economic security, or between domestic and foreign security, are blurred; U.S. information systems and infrastructures, such as the New York Stock Exchange or the Federal Reserve System, become potential targets for attack.

In this environment, Pfaltzgraff and Shultz argue, the increasing availability of basic Information Age technologies makes information warfare possible across a spectrum that encompasses the major regional conflicts that U.S. force structure currently is designed to fight, as well as low-intensity conflicts against sub-state or low-technology actors. Advanced societies, especially the United States, will be particularly vulnerable to information warfare attacks because of our vast reliance on information systems, in both the civilian and military sectors. Thus, the authors suggest the United States needs simultaneously to consider the impact of Information Age technologies on offensive operations both on the battlefield and in the electronic battlespace – and take necessary measures to minimize vulnerabilities.

In his essay, Michael Vickers makes some predictions about the nature and scope of the emerging RMA. First, Vickers defines an RMA as a *major discontinuity in military affairs* brought about by changes in militarily-relevant technologies, concepts of organization, and/or resources, which relatively abruptly *transform the conduct of war and make possible order-of-magnitude* (or greater) *gains in military effectiveness*. Second, he reviews the history of RMAs and describes their effects on the conduct of warfare in the past. Finally, he presents his conception of the new RMA. Vickers contends that it will result in overlapping battlespace and multidimensionality – that is, integrated air, land, sea, space, and information operations. As this happens, theaters of operations will lose their strategic autonomy because the outcomes of naval battles will depend on space warfare, land battles on the outcomes of sea battles, and so forth. In addition, established boundaries between levels of war will no longer be applicable; we will no longer be able to talk about strategic versus tactical assets, but instead will need to focus on the purposes to which they are applied.

Significantly, Vickers disagrees with the prevailing third wave concept of the emerging RMA that Alvin and Heidi Toffler promote in their writings. In contrast to the Tofflers' belief that history is divided into three waves of development – agrarian, industrial, and post-industrial – Vickers says that there have been at least nine RMAs based on technological developments. And, most importantly, the adversaries the United States is likely to face during the new RMA do not correspond to the three waves. Instead, he argues that there are at least five types of competitors to the United States, ranging from large peer competitors to non-state actors, who will be empowered by the trickle-down effects of this RMA. Nevertheless, Vickers believes that the United States will still dominate the strategic environment if it can avoid self-obsolescence.

Winn Schwartau examines a type of warfare that may transform the security environment because of its disassociation from traditional bombs and bullets operations. He views information warfare as the use of information and information systems as offensive weapons in a conflict that does not require military presence or even state sponsorship, only desire and will. The key to this type of warfare, Schwartau writes, is that the economic structures of our society will become its targets. This creates a serious problem for those responsible for American national security. How, asks Schwartau, can we define an aggressive act in cyberspace? How can we even trace responsibility for what happens in cyberspace, when computer capabilities are generally invisible and anonymous? Most importantly, how do we protect ourselves from such attacks? Is the military to be responsible for defense, or the FBI? Schwartau ends by urging the development of a comprehensive government strategy to answer these questions and prepare for information warfare against the United States.

Finally, Timothy Thomas reminds us that while the United States is leading the way, the Information Age will affect many other countries as well. Thomas's analysis demonstrates that Russian commentary on war in the Information Age is similar to that in the United States. Like American thinkers, the Russians are concerned about issues such as the blurring of civilian and military targets, the possibility of information terrorism, and the use of information resources and technologies for strategic psychological campaigns. Likewise, they agree with American analyses that information technologies have applicability in both enhancing current weapon systems and in creating a whole new means of attack against information-dependent infrastructures. Most significantly, Russian commentators, like their American counterparts, believe that the best response to the challenges of the Information Age is a comprehensive government information strategy that integrates military, political, and economic resources. However, the key difference between the two countries, Thomas writes, is context: the Russian attitude toward the Information Age is characterized by fear and vulnerability in both the technological and psychological sense. Russia does not have the technical capabilities to compete in the Information Age. At the same time, Russian society is undergoing a period of psychological turmoil because of the end of the Soviet Union and the rise of lawlessness. In such a situation, Russian fears of vulnerability are real and intensifying.

chapter one

Future Actors in a Changing Security Environment

Robert L. Pfaltzgraff, Jr.
Richard H. Shultz, Jr.

SUPERIMPOSED ON THE EMERGING GEOSTRATEGIC ENVIRONMENT is the impact of information technologies, with their implications for the nature of conflict and the conduct of military operations. As a result, policymakers and strategists are confronted with a series of critical issues, including whether – and to what extent – information technologies represent simply an additional means to achieve strategic objectives, or actually spur the creation of new missions. Traditionally, wars were fought for geographic dominance. Henceforth, national power may be measured by the ability to attain information dominance and the capacity to deprive enemies of information. In short, we must now ask: To what extent will information dominance hold the key to military success?

The advent of information technologies expands physical battlespace and the area of military operations far beyond traditional boundaries to include economic, financial, psychological, and political sectors. The battleground is no longer defined merely along geographical boundaries – it extends to cyberspace. As Information Age technologies make state frontiers increasingly permeable, the historic distinction between foreign policy and domestic politics becomes obsolete. Strategic arenas once considered to be either off limits or irrelevant, such as stock exchanges and banking systems, assume increasing significance. To the extent that information technologies shape the conduct of warfare, we must think less of geographically bounded theaters of operations, and look toward trans-theater operations. Spatial relationships are being transformed to the extent that actions in one theater can cause an unprecedented spectrum of responses in other arenas. Equally important, whatever distinctions that may have existed between economic and military definitions of security collapse in cyberspace. The sterile argument that military and economic security can somehow be examined separately has no relevance in an age of information warfare. The battlespace is multi-dimensional. The response to military operations on the battlefield can come in the form of an attack on such critical U.S. information systems as the New York Stock Exchange or the Federal Reserve System. Thus, we may be in the midst of a paradigmatic transformation that changes the very substance of state interactions – even as Information Age technologies offer non-state actors unprecedented capabilities to enter the arena of conflict. Taken together, these issues help structure the geostrategic context in which Information Age technologies and future actors must be considered.

Increasingly, the study of war has focused on the roles of states as well as non-state actors. What Martin van Creveld has termed the Clausewitzian *trinitarian* concept of warfare – centering on the state, the government, and the population – has been supplemented, though not replaced, by a concept in which the state is either weakened or has disintegrated.[1] In the late twentieth century we have witnessed not only the breakup of existing states, but also instances in which states have, at best, only nominal control over the territory they claim to govern. Thus we are said to live in an era of political fragmentation and ungovernability.

The emerging post-Cold War paradigm can be contrasted with its predecessors by observing the transition, currently under way, from a state-centric system to one marked by a greater number of destabilizing sub-state and trans-state actors. To be sure, states will continue to be the primary actors in the post-Cold War system. Furthermore, those states that seek to dominate key regions of the world through military force – as did Iraq in the Gulf War and as North Korea still does on the Korean peninsula – will continue to threaten post-Cold War stability and U.S. interests. However, within the new bifurcated international environment, destabilizing sub-state and trans-state actors will demand increasing attention. Policymakers will confront such sources of state and regional conflict and fragmentation as radical nationalism and religious extremism, international criminal organizations, non-state weapons proliferation, and societal breakdown.

The transition to the post-Cold War paradigm coincides with the increasing availability of basic Information Age technologies – and, most notably, computers and modems – to nearly anyone who seeks to join the era of global interactive communications. For most people, electronic information networks are used merely for research, entertainment, and correspondence. However, the global access conferred by cyberspace also empowers actors with less benign objectives in mind. Therefore, discussion of the geostrategic setting of the Information Age must account for a wide variety of individuals and groups whose goals may have little direct connection with conflict in the physical battlespace.

Cyberspace also adds a new dimension to warfare, one that is relatively cheap both in monetary terms and in the risk of casualties. The initiator of an information warfare attack can often be anonymous — and therefore largely invulnerable — and can cross national boundaries with impunity. As a result, the spectrum of state and identifiable non-state actors is now being supplemented, if not replaced, by a growing number and diversity of actors whose identity may be difficult to establish, but whose ability to shape the nature and magnitude of conflict may be formidable indeed. Even without Information Age technologies, we face major forces of political fragmentation; when combined with the possibilities offered by the Information Age, we confront a volatile mixture of factors that fuel conflict and instability.[2]

In at least one respect, Information Age technologies may become a great equalizer to the extent that pre-industrial, agrarian societies, in addition to industrial and post-industrial societies — to use the Tofflers' framework — each have access to the basic instruments needed to wage information warfare.[3] Less-developed societies are increasingly able to obtain the latest technologies. Although a country can be considered largely agrarian, or poor, by post-industrial standards, a substantial part of its population may possess televisions and fax machines as well as other means of communication. This is explained by the tendency of technology, as it diffuses from its point of origin and progresses from one technological generation to the next, to become more accessible and less expensive. Societies that are backward in one phase can leapfrog over existing technologies to obtain state-of-the-art systems. For example, the telephone networks that such societies acquire will be based, not on wire lines, but on cellular technologies. Thus, we are likely to encounter societies that retain traditional sociopolitical and cultural dimensions, but which possess an increasing number of advanced technologies. While whole populations may not necessarily be avid users of the Internet, such societies will nevertheless be able to make substantial use of Information Age technologies for political-military purposes. As a result, the differentiation between the types of warfare waged by agrarian societies and post-industrial societies, respectively, will be blurred by their equal access to the basic Information Age technologies of the computer and modem.

The post-industrial society is likely to be the object of relatively inexpensive information warfare attacks waged against its sophisticated military and civilian infrastructure by less-developed societies and groups. To the extent that future conflicts will be the result of the clashes between and among agrarian, industrial, and post-industrial societies, as posited by the Tofflers, such conflicts may be waged less on the traditional battlefield than in forums and with strategies made possible by Information Age technologies. In fact, given the likely dominance of the United States in a potential regional conflict, societies with inferior military forces have every incentive to exploit its post-industrial vulnerabilities. The analogy to the strategies developed by guerrilla forces and leaders, such as Mao Tse-Tung and Ho Chi Minh, to defeat a technologically superior Western force comes to mind. Conversely, Information Age technologies, in the hands of post-industrial societies, may be most effective against societies that make use of Industrial Age technologies, as was the case with Saddam Hussein. Information Age technologies wielded by post-industrial societies may be less useful in conflicts with agrarian societies, where the penetration of technology is not as pervasive. The result may be the creation of an information warfare asymmetry that actually favors the agrarian society over the post-industrial society; an agrarian society may lack the systems against which Information Age technologies can be used most effectively, while a post-industrial society will have an abundance of such targets.

Information Age technologies shape the geostrategic landscape to the extent that they offer unprecedented capabilities for information dominance even as they create unparalleled vulnerabilities. The greater the importance that is attached to information dominance, the greater the need to deny information dominance to an adversary becomes. This means that the post-industrial societies most dependent on information will be the most vulnerable to information warfare. Thus, post-industrial societies must simultaneously consider the effects of Information Age technologies on offensive operations, while taking necessary measures to minimize vulnerabilities. As the most advanced Information Age society, the United States will be both the most capable Information Age military force and, at the same time, the most vulnerable to the effects of information warfare, especially in battlespace remote from the immediate theater of operations. Potential adversaries will extend across a spectrum that includes industrializing as well as agrarian societies, and both state and non-state actors. These societies, although they will not possess capabilities that can match those held by the United States, will nevertheless be in a position to take steps to counter, if not nullify, many of the advantages conferred on the United States by advanced technologies.

THE NATURE OF MILITARY MISSIONS
IN THE INFORMATION AGE

As we assess the changing geostrategic landscape and Information Age actors, it is essential to consider the extent to which Information Age technologies will affect the conduct of existing military missions, or fundamentally transform the nature of military missions. In the first category, we can examine the effects of Information Age technologies on the ability of the United States and its coalition partners to operate in future regional conflicts. If the Gulf War represented the most extensive use, thus far, of Information Age technologies, how will such systems affect future wars in regions such as Southwest Asia or Northeast Asia, as depicted in the contingencies and scenarios set forth in the Bottom-Up Review completed by the Clinton administration in 1993? Alternatively, to what extent will conflicts be waged with cyberspace weapons, in which the objective will be neither the control of territory nor the killing of combatants or noncombatants, but rather the destruction or disruption of the information systems on which the post-industrial society is heavily dependent? Or, we may face a situation in which, given the increasing numbers and types of actors, the geostrategic landscape will feature a combination of contingencies within and between the categories set forth above. Prudent national security planning dictates an emphasis on exploring and understanding the effects of information technologies on military operations, including the digitized battlefield, while at the same time examining the range of other uses to which Information Age technologies can be applied. These may include the utilization of such technologies to counter advanced U.S. systems in the immediate theater of military operations or an effort to carry the conflict to another theater of operations.

Information Age technologies confer unprecedented capabilities on the United States and other post-industrial societies for the achievement of what is termed battlespace transparency or situational awareness in real time. The ever-increasing ability to collect, process, and distribute information is unprecedented. At the same time, such capabilities create new vulnerabilities. For example, in the absence of effective protective countermeasures, U.S. systems at sea and on the ground could be attacked by computer hackers thousands of miles away. To demonstrate such vulnerabilities, a U.S. Air Force captain – using a personal computer and modem – reportedly penetrated the command and control systems of U.S. Navy ships operating in the Atlantic Ocean, providing tangible evidence of the formidable offensive capability of information warfare.[4]

In recent years there has been extensive discussion of counterproliferation as a major component of the post-Cold War geostrategic landscape. The advent of Information Age technologies gives new meaning to counterproliferation strategies and their requirements. On the one hand, the dual-use technologies of Information Age warfare, initially developed in the civilian sector before they are adapted for military purposes, become increasingly difficult for governments to control. Information, whatever its nature and content, is becoming more widely accessible as a result of cyberspace. We are in the midst of a communications revolution whose effect is to intensify the difficulty of preventing technology transfer. Boundaries protecting what is classified (and classifiable) are likely to become more porous. On the other hand, we are in the midst of an era in which weapons of mass destruction – nuclear, biological, and chemical – are becoming more widely available. Such capabilities offer a relatively inexpensive means to counter the Information Age technologies of a post-industrial society. In fact, a nuclear capability in the hands of a regional actor such as Iraq, Iran, or North Korea, whether or not it is actually used, would have profound implications for the ability of the United States and its coalition partners to operate in the digitized battlespace during a potential conflict. A single nuclear warhead, detonated above the battlespace, could have devastating consequences for the Information Age technologies deployed by the United States. If information warfare includes the ability to disable an enemy's electronic information system, it follows that such systems – in an era of weapons of mass destruction (WMD) proliferation – will need to be protected from the effects of an electromagnetic pulse.

DEFINING CHARACTERISTICS OF
INFORMATION AGE CONFLICTS

The battlespace of information warfare, we have noted, extends wherever cyberspace permits the strategist to take warfare in time, place, and object. Because cyberspace cannot be defined exclusively in geographic terms, there are no sanctuaries – the front is everywhere. Consequently, the distinction between international politics and domestic politics becomes less relevant and perhaps even irrelevant. Air traffic control systems, the routing of high-speed trains, bank transfers, telecommunications networks vital to civilian and military traffic, and electric power grids are vulnerable to a variety of disruptions with major economic, political, and psychological effects. The actors able to wage such information warfare include individuals and groups based within or outside the country. In the case of Western Europe and North America, the major influx of immigrant populations in recent decades provides the basis for a large number of diasporas containing, in some cases, individuals or groups prepared to act on behalf of a government or non-state actor seeking to influence U.S. policy. In a future Gulf War-type of operation, it is not difficult to envisage a series of simultaneous efforts, emanating from remote locations, to disrupt the economies of the United States and its coalition partners. Such operations could form a component of a crisis-escalation strategy on the part of an adversary bent on shaping public opinion in the open societies of North America, Western Europe, and Japan. The intended effect of such strategic warfare would be to demonstrate the socioeconomic cost to post-industrial societies of continuing military operations in regions such as Southwest Asia or Northeast Asia – a cost that might not be deemed acceptable to highly vocal and mercurial public in such societies, and which could be voiced by broadly-based opposition groups within them.

Although information warfare can be expected to form an integral part of future regional conflicts, for which the United States will need to be prepared, it is quite possible that most confrontations will fall below this threshold. There may be a proliferation of low-intensity conflicts (LICs) and an increase in the number of sub-state and trans-state confrontations. Furthermore, those groups and movements initiating unconventional challenges to existing states will have an opportunity to execute new and diverse forms of indirect attack. During the Cold War, LIC proved exceedingly difficult for industrialized societies to counter because of the indirect strategies and tactics employed by sub-state actors, such as guerrilla forces. As we have noted, the future prospects for post-industrial societies facing LIC challenges will be even more complex due to the availability of basic Information Age technologies to a broader range of sub-state and trans-state actors.

The post-Cold War geostrategic landscape already features a rising number of destabilizing sub-state and trans-state actors. Some of these entities are new; others have reemerged from dormancy during the Cold War. They include, among others, ethnic factions, extreme ethno-nationalist movements, religious radicals, militias, international criminal organizations, and terrorists. These groups and movements sometimes evade, sometimes undermine, and sometimes act in concert with, the governments of existing nation-states. In recent years, they have sometimes gained significant influence or control over parts of states and their governments. The cumulative effect of these activities is the growing crisis of state ungovernability and political fragmentation taking place within several states and, in turn, contributing to regional and broader international instability.

The conflicts precipitated by such actors can take one or more violent forms. They include civil unrest, urban violence, state and trans-state level terrorism, guerrilla insurgency, and various levels of quasi-conventional warfare. While these conflicts can be divided into discrete categories, individual situations often comprise a complex mix of several forms of violence. For example, ethnic conflicts tend to be protracted, experiencing prolonged phases of escalation and de-escalation. Terrorism can evolve into insurgency and subsequently extend into conventional warfare or lapse back to terrorism. These were the basic strategies and tactics of the groups and movements who conducted LIC during the Cold War. In the future, sub-state and trans-state actors will be able to add to these strategies of LIC the technologies and tactics of information operations.

While most sub-state and trans-state actors do not pose a direct strategic threat to U.S. interests today, over time their cumulative impact could undermine regional stability in areas of vital U.S. interest. Furthermore, such groups will be able to put at risk vulnerable aspects of post-industrial American society. A brief catalogue of the indirect challenges posed by non-state and trans-state actors to U.S. interests ranges from terrorism and international crime to secession and religious radicalism.

The Problem of Terrorism and Subversion. The end of the Cold War did not bring an end to terrorism. Adherents to transcendent religious ideals and burning ethno-nationalist passions are just as likely to ignore moral scruples concerning the use of terrorist tactics to achieve desired ends as were many followers of the radical Cold War ideologies. The United States has been the target of such violence, both at home (in the World Trade Center bombing and other diaspora violence) and abroad (Lebanon). Key allies of the United States have also been the targets of such violence, including Turkey, Egypt, and Israel.

Cooperation Between Ethnic and Religious Groups. Terrorists and Insurgents, and Organized Crime. A second category of indirect threat to U.S. interests centers on the expanding linkages between organized crime and ethnic and religious groups using terrorist, insurgent, and other indirect forms of attack. Examples of conflicts in regions where the United States has important interests and allies include the Kurdish Workers' Party (PKK) in Turkey, Hezbollah in Lebanon, and the National Liberation Army (ELN) and the Colombia Revolutionary Armed Forces (FARC) in Colombia. Additionally, the faltering position of various governments fosters state disintegration and lawlessness. In the subsequent power vacuum, criminal organizations flourish and become involved with ethnic and religious movements, as in Russia and Eastern Europe. These developments slow, and may even reverse, the process of democratization in the former communist countries, endangering European security interests.

Domestic Impact of International Organized Crime. The dramatic changes in the number, size, sophistication, and activities of international criminal organizations also have a significant impact on U.S. domestic security. These groups often carry out their activities in the United States through ethnic diasporas (e.g., Chinese Triads and Tongs). The annual economic cost and the number of lives lost as a result of these criminal activities in the United States are significant. Moreover, international criminal activity fuels violent crime and places serious stress on the

U.S. judicial system, intensifying the heavy societal costs to the United States.

Proliferation of Secessionist Movements. Secession is the demand by an ethnic minority for political and geographical separation from an internationally recognized state. Secessionist movements employ significant armed violence in pursuit of their cause. In many cases, third-party involvement in the form of outside arms, funds, training, sanctuary, or political-diplomatic support is common. With the end of the Cold War, a new chapter on secessionist violence has opened. It is a major contributor to nation-state disintegration and regional instability. There are currently fifteen to twenty ongoing secessionist challenges. Exacerbating this upsurge in secessionist violence has been the increase in external state support to these movements. Secessionist challenges are taking place in key regions of the world where the United States has identifiable interests and allies. Recent examples include the former Yugoslavia, Russia, Turkey, and India.

Escalation in Transnational Islamic Radicalism. Religion as a source of violent political conflict was supposed to have disappeared with the emergence of the modern nation-state system. This has proven incorrect. A case in point is Islamic political radicalism. It has come to serve as a powerful vehicle for expressing a commitment to tradition and opposition to secular regimes, as well as resistance to Western, and in particular, U.S. influence in Southwest Asia. As a result, radical Islamist political groups are able to compete, often effectively, for political power. As the confrontation sharpens between radical political Islamists and secular governments, there is a corresponding escalation in the tactics employed. The violence and terrorism in Algeria and Egypt are illustrative. Other world

religions are also experiencing the emergence of radical political factions that will use terror and violence, as demonstrated
by the assassination of Yitzhak Rabin by a Jewish ultra-nation-
alist in Israel.

*Repercussions on U.S. Allies and Alliances of Ethnic and Reli-
gious Conflict.* Another long-term challenge is the repercussions
on U.S. allies and alliances caused by internal ethnic and religious conflict. In particular, there are situations where local
political upheavals could engage the United States through
alliance relationships or through existing security concerns and
interests, as in Bosnia. These situations could take several forms,
including the escalation of an existing ethnic or religious conflict into a wider regional conflagration. Potential threats of this
type now exist in Egypt, Israel, and Algeria.

State Disintegration and Ungovernability. An indirect threat to
U.S. interests could emerge from the cumulative effect of several
of the sub-state and trans-state challenges described above. The
aggregate impact of these developments will be the continued
and perhaps widespread process of political fragmentation, in
which states split apart and existing governments lose their
authority and the wherewithal to function effectively. So far,
we have seen the collapse of marginal states. However, there
are other important states that, if they collapse, could destabi-
lize entire key regions, such as Pakistan, India, Egypt, Algeria,
Iraq, Indonesia, Nigeria, and perhaps even Mexico. In the
twenty-first century, one of the major challenges facing the
international system will be growing global ungovernability —
the inability of governments to govern, to provide domestic
security, or to maintain the integrity of their boundaries and
institutions. There are multiple security implications from such
developments for the United States.

As we have noted, a variety of states, or stages, of development – Agrarian, Industrial, or Information Age – are likely to characterize both sub-state and trans-state actors. While many of the post-Cold War low-intensity conflicts can be expected to take place in agrarian and industrializing societies (of course, these conflicts frequently extend into post-industrial Europe, Japan, and North America through diasporas and terrorism), it would be a mistake to assume that actors challenging such regimes will have access only to agrarian and limited industrial-level capabilities. The resources available to particular groups and movements will vary, especially in light of state support and new approaches to resource acquisition. Information Age technologies will empower these actors through access to major disruptive capabilities. As noted above, these technologies will allow such groups to devise new strategies and tactics for indirect attack. Below are a few examples of how sub-state and trans-state actors may take advantage of Information Age capabilities.

In the past, terrorist groups have used crude but effective capabilities against the United States, such as those employed in the World Trade Center and Oklahoma City bombings. They have also utilized more sophisticated timing devices. Recently, Algerian Islamic radicals in France conducted a terrorist bombing campaign reminiscent of similar operations executed in Europe in the 1980s. Terrorists continue to rely on both crude and modern conventional explosives and weapons. The exception can be found in Japan, where a fanatical religious cult employed crude unconventional capabilities. However, these and similar groups opposed to the policies of a post-industrial society will be able to expand their target list to include vital elements of the domestic infrastructure that are dependent on information and Information Age technologies. As stated earlier, banking systems, telecommunications networks, transportation systems, electric power grids, and other vital information-based nodes of post-industrial societies are inadequately protected from electronic manipulation and disruption. It may not be long before sub-state and trans-state actors attempt to exploit these weaknesses.

Likewise, ethnic factions, extreme ethno-nationalist movements, and religious radicals challenging existing states have thus far relied on older Industrial Age conventional weaponry. There is no guarantee that this will continue to be the case in the years ahead. For example, sub-state and trans-state actors have the potential for acquiring weapons of mass destruction. The conditions that once controlled the spread of nuclear capabilities have seriously eroded. The danger of clandestine sales and theft amid political turmoil and a dire economic crisis in Russia is very real. Russian nuclear warheads or enriched uranium could find their way into the hands of radical ethno-national or religious movements seeking a nuclear capability. There are now several documented cases of attempted clandestine sales of fissionable material. Other WMDs, or the materials and technologies to construct them – including chemical and biological substances – may likewise find their way to radical sub-state and trans-state actors. Because we are in the midst of a technological revolution driven by dual-use technologies, these technologies will become more widely available in various forms to those executing LIC operations.

Sub-state and trans-state actors with access to resources will also be able to acquire existing Information Age weapons systems. These include small precision-guided capabilities, highly lethal munitions, and night-vision equipment, to name only a few. Challengers to modern industrializing societies, such as Turkey and India, will be able to disrupt economic and other societal structures of these states, playing upon their vulnerability to the basic Information Age technologies of the computer and modem.

Thus, the PKK or Sikh separatists will be able to attack the Turkish and Indian states through several indirect economic and societal paths previously inaccessible to insurgents.

The forces of fragmentation, including secessionist movements, will also be able to employ Information Age capabilities for psychological operations (PSYOP) that, until recently, were not available to such groups. We now live in a global interactive communication system that secessionists can utilize for international PSYOP campaigns aimed at gaining international legitimacy and support for their cause and at discrediting the state from which they seek to break away. Imagine if Hanoi, which conducted an impressive international PSYOP campaign against the United States during the Vietnam War, had possessed Information Age capabilities at that time. Likewise, such communications capabilities can be used to mobilize ethnic elements of the population to support and fight for secession. This is a quantum leap from the cassettes used during the Iranian revolution in the late 1970s to mobilize massive opposition to the Shah.

International organized crime (IOC), in several cases, has extensive resources available for conducting activities across state frontiers. It already makes use of sophisticated Information Age technologies to operate transnationally. Likewise, transnational criminal groups employ these capabilities for defensive counterintelligence purposes to prevent governments and other international agencies from detecting their operating procedures and taking effective steps to disrupt them. Examples can be seen in the secure communications and cryptographic capabilities that have been employed by drug cartels. In coming years, IOC groups could go on the offensive to disrupt governments and create the conditions and environment in which criminal organizations flourish. The end result could be that an IOC or coalition of IOCs could gain significant influence or control over parts of nations or even regions.

In sum, Information Age capabilities will be available not only to post-industrial states but to various sub-state and trans-state actors. These actors include ethnic factions, extreme ethno-nationalist movements, religious radicals, militias, international criminal organizations, and terrorists. They will utilize Agrarian, Industrial, and Information Age capabilities to initiate ethnic and ethno-nationalistic violence, radical religious turmoil, secessionist and irredentist strife, terrorism, assassination, narcotics trafficking, money laundering, counterfeiting, fraud, alien smuggling, and other criminal activities.

If Information Age technologies can empower these sub-state and trans-state actors, they also confer on the United States a formidable capacity to respond to the indirect challenges posed by such actors. This is true of new technologies for collection, assembly, analysis, and distribution of information on these actors, their operational profiles, and the geographic space in which they operate. Likewise, Information Age weapons will be available, when adapted, to disrupt those non-state and trans-state actors that threaten U.S. interests. The challenge facing the United States, in this emerging geostrategic landscape, will be to press its advantage in information technologies to remain at the forefront of innovation. At the same time, we will need to develop a security strategy that takes as full account as possible of the threats posed by a broadening spectrum of actors applying information technologies. Within an appropriate strategic framework, the United States faces the formidable task of maximizing the opportunities and minimizing the vulnerabilities conferred by, and resulting from, information technologies in the changing geostrategic landscape.

ENDNOTES

1. Martin van Creveld, *The Transformation of War* (New York: The Free Press, 1991), esp. pp. 33-63.

2. For extended discussion of such issues, see Winn Schwartau, *Chaos on the Electronic Superhighway: Information Warfare* (New York: Thunder's Mouth Press, 1994), esp. pp. 215-248.

3. Alvin and Heidi Toffler, *War and Anti-War: Survival at the Dawn of the 21st Century* (Boston: Little, Brown and Company, 1993), pp. 18-25.

4. Pat Cooper and Frank Oliveri, "Hacker Exposes U.S. Vulnerability," *Defense News,* 9-15 October, 1995, p. 1.

chapter two

The Revolution in Military Affairs and Military Capabilities

Michael J. Vickers

OVER THE NEXT TWO TO THREE DECADES, an emerging revolution in military affairs (RMA) could have profound consequences for global strategic balances. Driven by a broader information revolution, the emerging RMA could transform war on land, in the air, and at sea, and bring war into two new dimensions – space and the information spectrum.[1] Although the nuclear revolution can be expected to have a continuing, truncating effect on the strategic scope of the emerging RMA, the advent of a post-RMA military regime would complicate planning and result in increased stratification of military capabilities. The United States will almost assuredly enter this period of transformational change well in advance of other competitors, but others inevitably will follow. Asymmetries in strategic requirements, moreover, should cause some competitors to emphasize significantly different aspects of the post-RMA regime.

Military revolutions are major discontinuities in military affairs. They are brought about by changes in militarily relevant technologies, concepts of operations, methods of organization, and/or resources available. Relatively abruptly – most typically over two to three decades – they transform the conduct of war and make possible order-of-magnitude (or greater) gains in military effectiveness. They sharpen the advantage held by the strategic/operational offense and create enormous intertemporal differentials of capability between military regimes. A hierarchy of change links these revolutions with broader social, economic, and scientific transformations.[2]

Beginning with the rapid rise of the chariot to battlefield dominance in the eighteenth century B.C., the historical record provides evidence of at least a dozen cases of revolutionary change in the conduct of war. The modern period in general, and the past two centuries in particular, have witnessed the greatest rate of change. Since the early fifteenth century, the conduct of war has been radically altered eight times. Six of these transformations have occurred within the past two hundred years alone, making this in effect an age of military revolutions.[3]

These eight cases of modern transformational change in the conduct of war have several potentially important implications for a prospective revolution in military affairs. The artillery revolution of the fifteenth century – and its naval counterpart, the guns and sails revolution, approximately a century later – were central developments underwriting the West's rise to global dominance. The Napoleonic revolution at the end of the eighteenth century underscored the potential catalytic importance of political and social change. The railroad, rifle, and telegraph revolution of the mid-nineteenth century marked the initial industrialization of war, and was brought about by developments from outside the military sphere. The dreadnought and submarine revolution at the turn of the twentieth century illuminates the problems of technological flux, self-obsolescence, and non-hierarchical changes in power relationships. The interwar revolutions in armored warfare, air superiority, and naval air power underscore how differences in concepts of operation and methods of organization can result in large disparities in military capability between similarly equipped adversaries. Finally, the bifurcation of warfare into nuclear and conventional regimes induced by the nuclear revolution will likely limit the strategic scope of a prospective RMA for some time to come.

THE EMERGING REVOLUTION IN MILITARY AFFAIRS
Since the early 1980s, Russian military planners have foreseen an impending revolution in military affairs that would give extended-range conventional weapons a level of effectiveness equivalent to nuclear weapons.[4] Over the past several years, the notion of an impending transformation of war has increasingly influenced U.S. military thinking as well.[5] By no means, however, is there unanimity of agreement within the U.S. military establishment about the rate, scope, or even existence of this prospective revolution. Current views range from those who believe that all ongoing change is evolutionary to those who foresee an extended period of continuous change. For some, the revolution has already occurred; or it is based on air power, and the Gulf War was its defining event. For others, the revolution is at hand and the United States will be its sole participant. For still others, the real revolution is two or more decades away and the identity of its participants remains an open question. Some see the revolution as largely limited to land warfare; others see greater dimensional scope. Some see the emergence of new platforms; others see the essential irrelevance or even absence of them.[6]

What follows is one vision of the prospective revolution in military affairs and its potential consequences for the conduct of war and the international distribution of military power. It views the prospective military revolution as deriving from a broader information revolution. It foresees the emergence of new platforms, new concepts of operation, and new forms of organization. It anticipates the emergence of a large peer competitor to the United States – who will participate fully, albeit somewhat asymmetrically, in the transformation to a new military regime – as well as the rise of niche competitors and non-state actors who would participate in selected areas of the revolution.

Evidence abounds that an information revolution is underway. Over the next few decades, the capability of military organizations to acquire, process, and move information over wide areas will increase exponentially. As information increases in military importance, further advances in information denial and manipulation could follow. There is little indication that even the U.S. military, currently at the forefront of this change, has progressed much beyond the very early stages of this process.

The emerging revolution in military affairs might comprise several components, which major competitors could pursue asymmetrically depending on their strategic requirements. Driven by a broader, societal information revolution, the RMA might encompass, for example, deep-strike dominated, non-linear ground operations; unmanned, system-dominated, stealthy air operations; land- and space-based defense of the sea and submersible power projection; space warfare; and independent and integrated information warfare. In its disaggregate effects, this emerging revolution could transform war on land, in the air, and at sea, while bringing war into the two new dimensions of space and the information spectrum. The principal impact of the RMA, however, will be in its aggregate or integrated theater effects, leading to the emergence of multidimensional warfare. The conduct of war could be transformed in several fundamental ways:

- The boundaries among the dimensions of war, the levels of war, and the orientation of military operations could become substantially eroded.
- Military operations will likely be dramatically expanded spatially and compressed temporally. Geographically defined theaters could lose much of their strategic autonomy, with out-of-area operations increasingly influencing the outcome of operations in-theater. Within a theater, a non-linear battlespace could become the norm.
- Integrative technology could dramatically enhance the ability to coordinate the actions of widely dispersed and dissimilar units, establishing the "system of systems" as the dominant military architecture of the new era.
- The proliferation of smart, long-range missiles and developments in signature reduction could shift the balance in favor of offensive systems. Fixed sites and high signature targets – airfields, ports, centralized command and control facilities, surface amphibious task forces, large field armies, non-stealthy aircraft, and low earth-orbit satellite constellations – could become extremely vulnerable to destruction or denial. Dimensional control could become far more difficult to attain.
- The lethality of multidimensional warfare could empty the battlefield, with unmanned systems assuming many of the critical warfare functions heretofore performed by manned systems.
- Operational and tactical maneuvers on "information terrain" could become central to maneuver on physical battlespace. A paradigm shift could occur in which tra-

ditional notions of physical protection are supplanted by information-based protection.

- The 500-year dominance of chemical propulsion in war could be significantly eroded as electromagnetic guns, electric drive, and war in the electromagnetic spectrum become increasingly prominent.

Transformation of Air, Land, and Sea Combat. Post-RMA ground forces will likely be significantly smaller and far more stealthy, with much of their combat power exported offshore.[7] These forces will be required to enter a theater clandestinely using dispersed, transitory entry points, and will probably fight from non-contiguous positions with a 360-degree orientation. Network forms of small unit organization and tactics centered around the individual soldier or combat system are likely to emerge to take advantage of the enhanced coordination and information protection capabilities offered by advanced information technologies.

Multidimensional deep-strike capabilities – stealthy intercontinental bombers, arsenal ships, long-range, land-based missiles, and space-to-ground attack satellites – could impose significant costs on ground force operations, through both reduced operating efficiency and virtual attrition, as forces are withheld from combat in order to avoid being destroyed. Nonlinearity and increasing stealth and mobility could enable small, dispersed ground forces to decline battle, causing conventional ground operations to resemble high intensity guerrilla warfare. While dramatically reduced force-to-space ratios might substantially enhance opportunity for maneuver, lack of enemy force concentrations could also limit its effects to the tactical level. Air-ground close-combat forces, on the other hand, might provide enormous operational leverage against an enemy's deployed, land-based, deep-strike systems or protected information systems.

The inability to protect friendly forces from deep attack by residual, long-range strike systems will complicate the traditional occupation function of ground forces. Under the new military regime, seizing territory may become easier to accomplish than physically holding it. Indirect land control, through an interlocking network of deep-strike systems, coupled with the indirect presence of close-combat forces, might be the most that can be attained.

Future close-combat operations will likely require a new tactical cycle of converging on enemy forces and then dispersing to avoid enemy counterfires. Close combat can generally be expected to be conducted only during periods of low visibility and with extensive operational and tactical deception. Multidimensional warfare will need to be planned in terms of time as much as space. Commanders will increasingly need to think in terms of exploiting and protecting time flanks instead of traditional spatial ones. Lines of operation and culminating points could come to be viewed predominantly in terms of time as well. Maneuver forces, however, will likely often not be the supported arm in ground combat. Friendly movement might be used, for example, to force the enemy to make tactically disadvantageous attacks, thereby making the opponent more vulnerable to destruction by fires.

Several new types of ground force organization could emerge. A deep-strike brigade might comprise a long-range missile regiment, a stealthy attack helicopter regiment, and an information warfare regiment equipped with unmanned aerial vehicles (UAVs). Exoskeleton-equipped light infantry units, with organic stealthy, loitering, weaponized UAVs for information warfare and close-air support, together with robotic helpers for surveillance and logistics, might operate as a network of air-droppable, information warfare-intensive, mobile, armored infantry.[8]

Air power could be transformed by the increasing substitution of unmanned for manned systems and the wide application of signature-management technologies. Broadly conceived, air power will likely be fundamental to the operations of almost all military organizations in a post-RMA regime. However, it could also be less and less the sole province of air forces.

The major operational challenge for air power in a stealth- and missile-dominated world will likely be the vulnerability of in-theater bases. Aircraft will likely be most vulnerable when on the ground; hence, those without intercontinental range or the ability to operate from bases within a strategic sanctuary will likely be forced to operate from dispersed, unimproved, transitory airfields during periods of limited visibility, with the active support of multispectral information-warfare deception operations. Information protection for aircraft on the ground – and for other ground-based forces as well – might be provided by portable electrothermochromatic shelters.

Stealthy intercontinental bombers, manned or unmanned, should dominate the airborne component of deep-strike forces. The widespread use of ballistic and stealthy cruise missiles launched from sea- and land-based platforms (and perhaps the advent of space-to-ground attack satellites) should allow stealthy intercontinental bombers to play a more specialized (albeit reduced) role in long-range strike. Stealthy, weaponized, loitering UAVs, on the other hand, will likely dominate the close-strike mission. The combination of high mobility, low observability, and extended loitering capability may be so powerful that weaponized UAVs displace short-range artillery from the battlefield.

The meaning of the term air superiority could be fundamentally altered in the stealth- and missile-dominated world of multidimensional warfare. As a result, there could be far fewer fighter aircraft in combat air orders of battle. Moreover, the application of stealth to fighter aircraft could bring back renewed emphasis on visual engagement or *dogfighting* skills.

The application of stealth to air mobility operations, both inter-theater and intra-theater, will likely be essential if forces are to be inserted safely into a theater and sustained once there. Deployed forces will probably not be inserted directly into combat, but rather into remote operating areas. Power-projection forces will also most likely have to move from CONUS directly into the area of operations without the benefit of in-theater basing. Operational and tactical mobility systems would then be used to enable inserted forces to move and fight at the place and time of their own choosing.

War at sea could be transformed by the ability to dominate extended sea areas using land- and space-based assets, and by the replacement of manned aircraft with missiles as the basis for naval strike.[9] Long-range, stealthy, weaponized UAVs could, by themselves, become a major anti-navy capability. A complete reconnaissance-strike system of satellites, unmanned aerial vehicles, and mobile, land-based, terminally-guided, long-range missiles could enable formerly second- or third-tier naval powers to contest control of the sea for extended distances from their borders. This land-based defense of the sea could even have fewer barriers to entry, in terms of cost and learning, than traditional carrier battle-group operations. Integration of brilliant mines, sea-based sensors, and stealthy attack submarines would substantially enhance land-based sea denial, with the result that most naval operations could be driven below the surface.

The future capital ship of the fleet might be a missile-firing, submersible arsenal ship, armed with cruise and conventional ballistic missiles. Warheads could include cluster munitions for information warfare, minefield generation, and multiple attack of concentrated targets. Depending upon the degree of concentration desirable in strike platforms, arsenal ships might be armed with a few hundred to a few thousand missiles. A distributed power-projection navy might include several classes of arsenal ships and other submersible power projection forces in its fleet.

Naval warfare will remain highly asymmetrical. Navies whose strategic environment requires them to project power over intercontinental distances against a formidable adversary will likely require far more arsenal ships and other forms of submersible power projection in their fleets. Those interested in sea denial could elect to rely instead on land- and space-based defense of the sea and anti-submarine warfare forces.

The Emergence of Space and Information Warfare. The military importance of space could be transformed from a supporting medium to an integrative theater of operations. Counter-space operations could become to twenty-first century warfare what sea battles were for war in the seventeenth and eighteenth centuries. Counter-space operations might include direct ascent and space-based anti-satellite (ASAT) systems, as well as soft kill systems to spoof or temporarily disable enemy space-based capabilities. Space-to-ground attack capabilities could also appear in the next few decades, particularly for use against fixed, hardened targets, adding a new dimension to global precision-strike capabilities.

Increasing satellite vulnerability will likely force a search for operational methods of escaping from Kepler's laws of orbital paths, perhaps through the application of low-observable technologies or the development of transorbital maneuver capabilities. Given the difficulty of defending many space-based assets, however, rapid relaunch capabilities will prove critical. Moreover, against an opposing force with robust counter-space warfare capabilities, space systems (non-lethal ASATs, space-to-ground, direct-attack satellites, and multipurpose, rapid launch lightsats) may have to be sequentially deployed in order to minimize an opponent's incentive to launch a disarming first strike.

The emergence of war in the information spectrum would add a new means of destroying enemy targets and disrupting enemy operations. Independent information warfare operations could include covert attack with adaptable, time-phased computer viruses. These could be followed by overt attack using anti-satellite and media override operations, conventional electromagnetic pulse weapons for area effects, and high-power microwave beam attacks to disable specific targets. Integrated information warfare operations could be used to mislead an opposing force as to the size, location, and orientation of friendly forces, in addition to temporarily or permanently disabling an opponent's sensor and information-processing systems.

Integrated information warfare operations could be shaping or paralyzing. Shaping operations will likely be central to force mobility and operational effectiveness. Shaping maneuvers could be used to deceive enemy information systems as to force locations (including theater entry points and close combat dispositions) or force posture (including force-baiting operations to induce an enemy to move or fight). Paralyzing operations could be used to overload the enemy's command and control system during periods of heightened friendly signature, or as a key component of an endgame strategy.

Information warfare at the strategic, operational, and tactical levels could be the principal means of maximizing relative frictional advantage over an adversary. It may well be that greater operational advantage will accrue from making the enemy's environment more opaque – through destruction or deception – than it will from making one's own environment more transparent. The ultimate goal of information warfare will be not only to desynchronize and disable enemy operations, but actually to make the system turn against the enemy. This is seldom likely to be achievable, however, against protected systems.

The hider-finder balance could well be the central determinant of how theater warfare is conducted during the first quarter of the next century. If information systems become capable of rendering the battlefield transparent, operational movement could be completely stymied. Conversely, if advances in information denial outpace advances in information acquisition, long-range strike systems could become ineffectual and highly vulnerable to attack by mobile, stealthy forces. Rather than either extreme dominating, it is likely that stealth and deep strike will coexist uneasily. The resulting tension could produce a battlefield in which deep-strike systems dominate but, as low-observable technologies and information warfare capabilities are applied to more military systems, substantial scope could also be provided for force concealment and movement. If this turns out to be the case, the information aspects of war – such as information acquisition and denial, information strikes, information-based protection and information-based movement – will likely permeate post-RMA military operations at all levels.

Implications for Force Structure. While RMA capabilities could be expected to be diffused throughout the total force, the post-RMA component of future force structures will not likely be dominant in terms of relative size. An army of six deep-strike brigades and twelve exoskeleton and UAV-equipped light infantry regiments, for example, might comprise as few as

25,000 soldiers. Accordingly, given the likely requirement for substantial dismounted infantry strength and special operations forces for many other contingencies, the non-RMA component of a future ground force organization could well be several times that size. The post-RMA component of a fleet — attack submarines, arsenal ships, and other submersible power projection forces — could number fewer than 150 naval combatants.[10] Stealthy transport aircraft could be the dominant platform in the post-RMA component of future air forces. Stealthy fighters might number as few as two hundred, while the bomber fleet could number under one hundred. The non-RMA (non-stealthy) air force, by contrast, could include far more air superiority aircraft as well as short-range manned attack and traditional air mobility aircraft.

THE RMA, MILITARY POWER, AND THE INTERNATIONAL SYSTEM

The prospective revolution in military affairs is a central driver shaping the future security environment. Maintenance of the United States' dominant position in military affairs could well depend on the relative ability of our armed forces to adapt to the demands of transformational change. Similarly, the rise of new great powers, such as China, could also depend upon their ability to leapfrog the current military regime and change the rules of military competition in their favor.[11] In general, the rate at which the conduct of war is transformed from the current regime to the next will be a function of the intensity of strategic rivalry extant in the international system, the political purposes military power is asked to attain, the rate and scope of militarily-relevant technological change, the economics of defense in the Information Age, and the ability of military institutions to adapt to discontinuous change.

The dynamics of military regime transformation will likely be driven by the development of increasingly sophisticated, long-range, precision-strike capabilities. As systems become more advanced, increasingly discriminate military targets could be held at risk. At first, only fixed facilities, such as theater airbases and ports, might be vulnerable to destruction or denial. Subsequently, distributed, mobile ground targets and surface naval platforms could be held at risk.

While increasingly sophisticated long-range, precision-strike capabilities are likely to be the central technological force for regime transformation, the transition to new ways of war will also likely turn on other related developments. Dramatic increases in integrative technologies, connecting dissimilar systems to wide-area operational networks, will almost certainly be central to regime transformation. The substitution of unmanned for manned systems and the robustness and breadth of stealth will likely be key drivers as well, as will the emergence of new capabilities in information warfare and, perhaps, in space warfare.

Rather than following Agrarian, Industrial, and Information Age waves of development, military capabilities in the aftermath of the emerging military revolution will likely span several warfare regimes. The bifurcation of nuclear and conventional warfare regimes that has endured since the end of World War II will be made more complex by the emerging RMA. Military capabilities will be differentiated not only according to their relative modernity, but also with respect to their political affiliation, purpose, and relative quantity. Strategically, military capabilities might be differentiated hierarchically – from large RMA peer and niche competitors down to non-RMA, non-nuclear powers, and non-state actors.

Asymmetries in strategic requirements, moreover, should cause some competitors to emphasize significantly different aspects of the post-RMA regime. While the development of long-range, precision-strike, information-warfare, and space-warfare capabilities might be common to all large RMA peer competitors, other warfare areas may be pursued asymmetrically. A competitor that is interested in a keep-out strategy of regional denial might pursue land- and space-based defense of the sea.[12] A competitor whose strategic situation stresses global power projection, on the other hand, might emphasize submersible power projection, stealthy air operations, and non-linear ground operations.

The nuclear revolution can be expected to have a continuing, truncating effect on the strategic scope of the emerging RMA, even though the RMA could expand the menu of strategic warfare options. There could, for example, be some substitution of conventional long-range, precision-strike capabilities for nuclear weaponry in strategic war planning, and a few new means of carrying out strategic attack – including independent information warfare, genetically specific biological warfare, and space warfare. But the presence of robust strategic nuclear deterrents would still mean that nations possessing nuclear weapons would likely be granted status as strategic sanctuaries in any general war between large peer competitors.

The emerging revolution in military affairs may also be unique historically in its potential impact at the lower end of the conflict spectrum. Subnational groups could become increasingly formidable as they gain access to precision weapons, advanced communications systems, information warfare capabilities, and perhaps even weapons of mass destruction.[13] While the emerging RMA should also increase the state's ability to intervene in or counter subnational conflict, it is by no means yet clear whether the impact of the RMA will be greater for the forces of integration or disintegration.

The emerging RMA could also have several important consequences for alliance relationships and coalition warfare. The value of visible forward presence could, for example, be sharply diminished. Given the difficulty of controlling territory, occupation requirements could fall to host nation coalition partners, with RMA power-projection forces engaging in indirect land control only. Independent information warfare capabilities could provide a state with new means of deterring the formation of hostile coalitions against it.

The implications of the current RMA for the international distribution of power could be no less profound than the revolutions associated with the rise of the West more than half a millennia ago. East Asia appears to be developing many of the initial conditions for an RMA: rising powers, dynamic economies, and the proliferation of information and dual-use technologies. Several potential future East-Asian strategic and operational requirements – regional denial, extended distance power projection, and defense without depth – could spur RMA-inducing military innovation with the result that global capabilities become more concentrated along the Pacific rim.

At present, the United States is the best positioned to exploit the emerging revolution in military affairs, and will almost assuredly enter this period of transformational change well in advance of other competitors. The United States faces a dilemma, however, analogous to that faced by the British Navy at the turn of the century: dominance in the existing regime and a commanding lead in an emerging one. Early pursuit of the RMA will inevitably mean self-obsolescence in today's dominant capabilities as well as demand management of technological flux inherent in many of the new systems.

The challenge of successfully meeting the requirements of near- and long-term strategy, and striking the proper balance between self-obsolescence and organizational innovation within the current domestic political environment, should not be underestimated. However, if those who see an impending transformation are correct, a fundamental rethinking of our future military capabilities is mandatory. One can only hope that we as a nation are up to the task.

ENDNOTES

1. The term "revolution in military affairs" should be considered interchangeable with military revolution or military-technical revolution.

2. See Michael J. Vickers, *The Structure of Military Revolutions,* Ph.D. dissertation, The Johns Hopkins University, forthcoming.

3. See Geoffrey Parker, *The Military Revolution: Military Innovation and the Rise of the West 1500-1800* (Cambridge: Cambridge University Press, 1988).

4. See Notra Trulock et al., *Soviet Military Thought in Transition: Implications for the Long-Term Competition* (Arlington, Virginia: Pacific-Sierra Research Corporation, 1988).

5. See, for example, the article by the former Vice Chairman of the Joint Chiefs of Staff, Admiral William A. Owens, "The Emerging System of Systems," *Proceedings,* 121:5 (May 1995), pp. 35-39. The intellectual center for American thinking on the emerging RMA has been the Office of Net Assessment in the Office of the Secretary of Defense.

6. For a more complete description of competing views on the RMA, see Michael J. Vickers, *Perspectives on the Revolution in Military Affairs* (Washington, D.C.: Defense Budget Project, April 1995).

7. This section is drawn from Michael J. Vickers, *A Concept for Theater Warfare in 2020* (Washington, D.C.: Office of the Secretary of Defense/Office of Net Assessment, 24 November 1993).

8. Exoskeletons might allow protected cross-country movement at speeds approaching forty miles per hour and permit individual soldiers to be equipped with a powerful suite of weapons, sensors, information warfare capabilities, and communications systems.

9. Arsenal ships will initially emphasize surface designs, and become undersea platforms only as the anti-navy threat evolves. The U.S. Navy's experience with the arsenal ship concept to date has even been slightly regressive. A double-hull, low profile design was initially proposed, but the concept was subsequently modified to incorporate the more traditional DDG-51 hull. "Industry Gears Up for New Arsenal Ship Con-

cept," *Navy News & Undersea Technology* (30 October 1995), p. 1, and John Robinson, "Navy Taps CG-48 As Smart Ship: Arsenal Ship to Use DDG-51 Hull," *Defense Daily* (20 December 1995), p. 400.

10. This figure does not include support ships. Given the importance of undersea control for submersible power projection, such a fleet would likely be attack-submarine heavy.

11. For the argument that twenty-first century military capabilities will be differentiated according to waves of economic development, see Alvin and Heidi Toffler, *War and Anti-War: Survival and the Dawn of the 21st Century* (Boston: Little, Brown and Company, 1993).

12. Development of extended-area, land- and space-based defense of the sea could also have significant political effects on trade flows. Traditional naval forces, moreover, will likely provide little protection against this threat.

13. Among potential WMD threats, biological weapons pose perhaps the greatest danger in the hands of non-state actors. The ongoing revolution in molecular biology, which, unlike nuclear physics, is a decentralized discipline, could make this situation substantially worse, with ethnically selective weapons just one of the possibilities.

chapter three

An Introduction to
Information Warfare

Winn Schwartau

AT SOME POINT, if not already, you will become the victim of
information warfare. If not you, then a member of your family,
a close friend, or perhaps your company will become the designated target. If not yesterday or today, then definitely
tomorrow. In short, the United States is at war, a war that few
have bothered to notice. The twentieth-century information
skirmishes that are the prelude to global information warfare
have begun.

As citizens of both the United States and cyberspace, Americans must come to terms with their electronic destiny to lead
the world into the twenty-first century and the Information
Age. Some tough choices must be made; the information revolution is not an easy transition, and the proposed national
information infrastructure illuminates the complexity of the
next generation of American dreams. But the opportunities are
too great and the alternatives too grave to be ignored. This

chapter is an overview of where we are today, where we are going, and what issues must be directly confronted if we wish to design our future and not be consumed by it.

As the specter of global warfare recedes into the history books, a collective sigh of complacency is replacing bombshelter hysteria. Despite the fact that nearly 175 million people were killed in the twentieth century from the effects of war and politics, Strangelovian predictions thankfully never came to pass. However, as equally dangerous international economic competition supplants megatonnage intimidation, offensive pugnacity will be aimed at the informational and financial infrastructure upon which Western economies depend.

The Cold War is over; it has been replaced by economic warfare. Competition is shaping up between three major trading blocks: North America, Europe, and the Asia-Pacific Rim. Richard Nixon was fond of saying in the 1970s and 1980s that World War III had already begun and that it was an economic war, perhaps one that the United States was destined to lose. In retrospect, the United States might have been more attentive to his prescience. These three huge economic forces account for about one quarter of the population, and 80 percent of all economic production on planet Earth. The stakes are enormous and everyone wants a piece.

Modern society is based on information. Access to information can drive a thriving economy upward, or propel a weak one into a position of power. In today's electronically interconnected world, information moves at the speed of light, is intangible, and is of immense value. Today's information is the equivalent of yesterday's factories. Yet, at the same time, it is considerably more vulnerable. The United States leads the way toward a globally networked society, a true Information Age where information and economic value become nearly synonymous. With over 125 million computers inextricably tying the world together through complex land- and satellite-based communications systems, a major portion of the United States' domestic economy depends upon the consistent and reliable operation of computer systems.

Information warfare is an electronic conflict in which information is a strategic asset worthy of conquest or destruction. Both computers and information systems become attractive first-strike targets. As reported to a congressional committee on June 27, 1991, "Government and commercial computer systems are so poorly protected today, that they can essentially be considered defenseless. An electronic Pearl Harbor is waiting to happen. As a result of inadequate security planning on the part of both the Government and the private sector, the privacy of most Americans has virtually disappeared."[1] These sentiments were echoed by *Computers at Risk,* a report published in October of 1990 by the National Research Council. "The modern thief can steal more with a computer than with a gun. Tomorrow's terrorist may be able to do more damage with a keyboard than with a bomb."[2] In a recent study, two-thirds of Americans polled said that computer usage should be curtailed if personal privacy was at risk. As a country, we are only now beginning to recognize and accept the fact that personal and economic interests are indeed merging with national security interests.

Information warfare is an integral component of the new economic and political world order. Economic battles are being fought and will continue to be fought, ultimately affecting every American citizen and company as well as the national security of the United States. As terrorism now invades our shores, we can expect attacks not only upon airliners and the water supply, but upon airwaves and the money supply – a sure way to strike terror in millions of people with a single keystroke.

Cyberspace is a brave new world that only such luminaries as Marshall McCluhan and Arthur Clarke glimpsed in their mind's eye. But not even they could presage the uncertainties unleashed in the last two decades. Imagine a world where information is the commodity of exchange and cash is used only for pedestrian trade. A world where information, not English, German, Japanese, or Russian, is the common language. A world where the power of knowledge and information usurp the strength of military might. A world totally dependent upon new high-tech tools to make information available instantaneously to anyone, anywhere, at any time; one where those who control information control people, and where electronic privacy is nearly nonexistent. Now imagine a conflict between adversaries where information is the prize, the spoils of war. It is a conflict with a winner and a loser. It turns computers into highly effective offensive weapons and defines computers and communications systems as primary targets, forced to defend themselves against deadly, invisible bullets and bombs.

In this conflict, rival economies battle for a widening sphere of global influence over the electronic financial highways where no expense is spared to ensure victory. Companies settle disputes and compete by regularly bombarding each other's information infrastructure. Electronic and competitive espionage are the expected manner of conducting business. In the future, Information Age weaponry will replace more bloody means of warfare. The weapons of information warfare will no longer be restricted to the government or the CIA or KGB. Computer and communications weapons are available from catalogues, retail store fronts, and trade shows. Many can be built from hobbyist parts at home. And, of course, the military is developing its own arsenal of weapons to wage war.

Information warfare is about money. It's about the acquisition of wealth, and the denial of wealth to competitors. It breeds information warriors who battle across the global network in a game of *CyberRisk*. Information warfare is about power; those who control information control money. Information warfare is about fear; those who control information can instill fear in those who want to keep their secrets. It is about the fear that the Bank of New York felt when it found itself $23 billion short of cash in only one day. Information warfare is about the arrogance that stems from the belief that one is committing the perfect crime. And information warfare is about politics. When the German government sponsors intelligence agency hacking against U.S. computers, the concept of an ally needs to be redefined. Or, when Iran takes aim at the U.S. economy by statesponsored counterfeiting, it should become clear that conflict is not what it once was.

Information warfare is key to survival. France and Israel expanded industries and strengthened their respective economies by stealing American secrets. With the help of their governments, Japan and Korea purloin American technology as it comes off the drawing boards and computer screens. Information warfare thrives on defiance and the disenfranchised masses in both modern and Third World societies. These range from inner-city hackers, who have nothing to lose, to gangs and organized crime. Such fringe elements recognize quite early the cost benefits of waging information warfare.

Information warfare currently costs the United States an estimated $100 to $300 billion per year, and the financial impact on our economy increases every year. Almost two percent of United States GNP slithers through the global network, thereby hurting deficit reduction efforts, impacting the U.S. export base and the current trade imbalance. With billions less in commerce, lower taxable revenues and taxable assets deprive the government of its fair share of profits. As a country, more than our image is tarnished by our constant place as victim in the information wars. U.S. credit is undermined and its ability to buy and trade suffers; in addition, our political and diplomatic impact is reduced because, in economic terms, we are no longer the unquestioned leader. Most importantly, over $200 billion in lost revenue affects three to eight million Americans who might be working if they were not also victims of information warfare. Information warfare takes advantage of the reliance on, indeed the addiction to, automation and modern computerized niceties. Information warfare attacks our very way of life.

CLASSIFYING INFORMATION WARFARE

The threat of a future computer Chernobyl is not an empty one. It is only a question of who and when. Waging information warfare is available to anyone with an agenda and an attitude, and can be conducted at three distinct levels of intensity, each with its own goals, methods and targets.

Class 1: Personal Information Warfare. There is no such thing as electronic privacy. The essence of who we are is distributed across thousands of computers and databases over which we have little or no control. From credit reports to health records, from DMV computers to court records and video rentals, from law enforcement computers to school transcripts and debit-card purchases, from insurance profiles to travel histories and our personal bank finances, everything we do and have done is sitting somewhere in a digital repository.

The sad fact is that these records which define us as individuals remain unprotected, subject to malicious modification, unauthorized disclosure, or out and out destruction. For $25 per name, Social Security Administration employees have sold our innermost secrets.[3] Worse yet, there is still no way to protect your "digital self." You are not given the option or the opportunity to keep you and your family protected from electronic invasions of privacy. Life can be turned upside down if your digital self ceases to exist; it is the equivalent of electronic murder in cyberspace. Try proving you're alive in a world where computers don't lie. Or, if a digital picture is electronically redrawn in just the right manner, a prince can become a pauper in microseconds.

Class 2: Corporate Information Warfare. Corporate management has little feel for just how weak and defenseless their assets have become. While the wealth of corporations is measured in the timeliness and value of their information, no company lists information assets on its balance sheet. Yet, without that information, the economic stability of a company is called into question. Putting a company out of business by attacking its information systems may soon become a common method of economic competition, political retribution, or social commentary. The weapons and techniques of information warfare are as common as spreadsheets and calculators.

Corporate boardrooms often take elaborate precautions to protect themselves against the statistical probability that a tornado will blow away their operations centers. The one in a million chance that a flood will rage through downtown Denver prompts companies to dig into nearby mountains to build underground vaults expected to survive a direct fifty megaton hit. What companies have not prepared themselves for, however, is a well organized offensive assault against their information systems – not by mother nature, but by man.

We shall discover that it is difficult to indict corporate America alone on all of these counts. The last fifteen years of spiraling growth in information processing has been a worldshaking revolution driven by heady technical successes and evangelical visions. Meanwhile, diligence in weighing the risks associated with placing our entire faith on a technical infrastructure is in short supply. Much of the blame for our current posture lies with the federal government. In fact, it is often not in the government's best interest to assist us in protecting our computers and networks. The contradictory policies of denial have harmed efforts now under way to enhance personal privacy and commercial national economic security. Nonetheless, inane antiquated policies continue unabated, and in some cases, overt attempts on the part of the federal government have further undermined the electronic privacy of every American citizen. Even President Clinton's proposal to address personal privacy and protect American businesses was met with near-universal derision, suspicion, and doubt.

Class 3: Global Information Warfare. Collective Capitol Hill and White House wisdom has not yet realized that information is a vital national asset. Still thinking in terms of military throw-weight, oil reserves, Japanese cars, and illegal aliens, they miss the fundamental concepts behind the New World Order, the national information infrastructure, and our place in the global econo-technical network.

Outside of a forward-thinking few within the bowels of the Pentagon and related intelligence services, national security assets are viewed as those tangible items with a concrete, quantifiable, and replaceable value. Information, on the other hand, is intangible and does not have an immediately quantifiable monetary worth – unless it is lost. Then it costs a great deal more than ever calculated.

As we move into cyberspace, we must avoid the temptation to ignore the possibilities that an unknown future may bring. We must take off the blinders and accept that the New World Order is full of bad guys as well as good guys. We must make preparations for contingencies that we might prefer not to consider, but that are nonetheless necessitated by the need to protect our national well being. We have to accept that, as the wealth of our nation shifts from smokestack to cybercash, our once well-defined borders are now ethereal concepts with hazy delineations at best. We will find that it is our job to prepare ourselves and future generations for a world filled with hope and with possibilities we could not have envisioned a decade ago, but also fraught with dangers and obstacles never considered. Both will be as commonplace and normal for our descendants as running hot water is today.

To cope with these challenges we must understand the sources of information warfare. Given our place in history, information warfare has clearly become inevitable. The incredibly rapid proliferation of high-quality, high-performance, electronic information systems that created the global cyberspace network have redefined the way we conduct business. Not only did business and government buy into technology, but tens of millions of us, within less than a decade, were suddenly empowered with tools and capabilities previously limited to a select few. The comparatively simple technology for information warfare is universally available. Technical anarchy is the result. The global network is a historically unprecedented highway system that defies borders and nationalism. It places the keys to the kingdom, to our wealth and our digital essence, within equal reach of everyone with a computer.

As the bipolar stand-off recedes, we unexpectedly find ourselves joined by dozens of new nation-states, each competing for its own identity. The failure of communism does not mean that democratic capitalism will automatically triumph, and be adopted by every newly created nation-state. There are other alternatives, and not all are compatible. The rules of the game – the global economic and political influence games – aren't the same for everyone. Americans play by an old rule-book, where goodness, mom, and apple pie define the competitive ethos.

Others are less likely to stick to the outmoded Puritan ethic by which we won the Industrial Revolution. Some groups will willingly beg, borrow, or steal to obtain what they want. Others will resort to physical violence in pursuit of their agendas. The United States and Americans are still often viewed as spoiled brats in a self-indulgent land where instant gratification counts for everything – an image that makes us inviting targets.

Only 25 percent of the planet can be considered economically developed, leaving several billion inhabitants in the unenviable position of being the have nots. The haves are the comparatively rich countries in Western Europe, Japan, some of the Pacific Rim, and, of course, North America. The have nots are everyone else. With the global network pouring an avalanche of information across borders in the form of text, sound, and especially pictures, the have nots are increasingly determined to become haves. Through CNN, "Dynasty," and global programming, they see for themselves how the other half lives, and they want their share of the pie. When there's nothing to fear, nothing left to lose, and the only way is up, going after the king of the hill – the United States – is an obvious tactic.

Greed is in no short supply, and few individuals, businesses, or countries are exempt. Businesses and governments constantly strive for advantage over each other, often relying on less-than-legal techniques to gain an edge. With the global network in place, and the proliferation of technology available for everyone, greed has found its way into the fingers and keyboards of people who might otherwise never commit a crime. Greed operates at all levels; most information systems oblige by providing ample opportunity to exploit their vulnerabilities for stupendous profits.

The effects of information warfare are unique in the annals of conflict. Information wars can be fought by remote control, the ringleaders invisible behind a keyboard ten thousand miles away. No longer is it necessary to intrude physically upon the intended victim's turf. The global network offers a million points of entry. Furthermore, the computer terrorist mentality allows indiscriminate damage to affect millions of people from a single strike, sowing fear, suspicion, and doubt. Information warfare provides a low budget, high-tech vehicle for mass destruction. The odds of getting caught are low, of being prosecuted lower still, and of being convicted almost nonexistent. On the international front, countries cannot agree on what to do with nuclear weapons, much less an information warrior sitting behind a keyboard.

Most importantly, information warfare will be waged because it can be waged. History clearly shows that any new technology, regardless of its original intentions, soon finds its way into the arsenals of warriors. In this case, computer technology has fallen into the hands of information warriors. Information warriors come in all shapes and colors. Hackers have been waging mild information warfare against corporate America and the telephone companies for years, but the newest generation of young cybernauts is more aggressive – patently echoing the ills of society as a whole.

The Soviets, of course, were information warriors par excellence. Now, tens of thousands of ex-Iron Curtain intelligence agents seek to ply their trade to the highest bidder; some having gone so far as offering their services in the classified sections of daily newspapers. Power-hungry dictators, radical fundamentalists, and a score of international political sects are investigating the use of cyberspace as a means of achieving their goals. The narcoterrorists are well financed, well armed, and enjoy a bevy of technical advisors; they have already taken aim at the Drug Enforcement Agency with information weapons. Environmental groups have also shown the willingness to be physically provocative, and information warfare offers them the ability to strike out at logging camps or oil companies in a new, imaginative, and less-dangerous fashion. Information brokers and data bankers will cheerfully sell your name, zip code, and the date you last bought underwear to anyone with a floppy disk – all without your permission. Banks and credit bureaus allow computers to make decisions that affect our lives and livelihoods based upon computer records containing as much as 30 percent erroneous data with virtual impunity.

Anyone can be an information warrior. Publications such as *2600: The Hacker Quarterly, Phrack*, and others provide the basic training for inductees.[4] Cyberspace itself offers safe havens for information warriors to build, develop and deploy their armies and weapons. An unhappy worker can suddenly turn against an employer with little chance of prosecution. A government employee may moonlight as an information warrior, or a teenager may live in cyberspace twenty hours a day, rising only for Coke and pizza. Potentially, a hundred million information warriors are poised, and honing their skills while they wait.

But information warfare also provides hope, a way out of the technocratic quagmire. The first step is to admit the problem and summon the willingness to apply available solutions. Personal electronic privacy can be achieved, and national economic security is possible, if these issues are deemed important enough to address. Cyberspace is a new place to live, and one way or another, everyone is moving in. We might as well figure out how to get along, since both our individual success and national strength depend upon it.

OUTLINING A NATIONAL INFORMATION POLICY

The solution that will enable us to control our electronic destiny is a national information policy. At present, life in cyberspace is subject to few rules or common sets of accepted behavior that delineate right from wrong, good from bad, or legal from illegal. We really don't even know what information is, yet our economy is based upon it. We vainly attempt to juryrig existing old and sometimes archaic guidelines that simply will not work in cyberspace. Most people – certainly most people in Washington – don't even know what questions need to be asked to create a national information policy. Cyberspace is technical anarchy in its purest form, and anarchists traditionally reject government control, preferring self-restraint. Unfortunately, self-restraint and moral responsibility are not hallmarks of the last twenty years and, as technology and information further intertwine with our existence, rules are required. But even before the rules must come the ethos and morals; and before the ethos must come the thesis.

A national information policy is not a specific legislative proposal for Congress to debate, but instead is a series of substantive issues and questions that must be asked, considered, and answered satisfactorily before we can live in the Information Age with any sense of security, stability, or trust. Who will own and operate cyberspace and the national information infrastructure? How will government and industry coexist during the birth and growth of this infrastructure? Will they or should they function as partners in the economic interest of the United States, or is that too socialistic for our taste? Then, we must decide if an attack against U.S. industrial or economic interests is the same as an attack against the country itself. On the international front, how isolationist a stance should we adapt as part of the global electronic village? Should personal electronic privacy be preserved as we progress into this country's third century?

The answers to these and other questions will determine how we live during the next ten to one hundred years. They will tell the world what kind of country we are and want to be. The answers may well define the long-term success of the U.S. economic system. Indeed, the answers will tell us who we are. A national information policy provides an outline by which to create a foundation for the future.

ENDNOTES

1. Submitted testimony, Subcommittee on Technology and Competitiveness, Committee on Science, Space, and Technology, U.S. House of Representatives, 27 June 1991.
2. *Computers At Risk: Safe Computing in the Information Age* (Washington, D.C.: National Academy Press, 1991), p. 7.
3. Jeffrey Rothfeder, *Privacy for Sale* (New York: Simon & Schuster, 1992), p. 124.
4. *New York Post*, 2 July 1992, p. 1.

chapter four

The Threat of Information Operations: A Russian Perspective

Timothy L. Thomas

OVER THE PAST FIVE YEARS, the United States Department of Defense has focused much of its research and development efforts on attaining parity, if not superiority, in the application of information-related systems and technologies. For example, the U.S. National Military Strategy, published in February of 1995 noted that "winning the information war"[1] was one of the priorities of flexible and selective engagement. The Army has also written an entire field manual on information operations.[2] This effort has touched levels of U.S. military thinking from the strategic to the tactical, primarily due to the effective use of information technologies in the Gulf War.

For countries trailing in the race to join the Information Age, especially a former superpower like Russia, the U.S. emphasis on, and early lead in, information technology breeds suspicion and fear. The very nature of information operations – their ability to strike another system invisibly, and with lightening speed

— is particularly threatening. Even many U.S. planners find the possibilities inherent in these technologies unnerving. In consequence, it is essential to avoid underestimating the reactions of those without similar capabilities. According to Russian analysts, their nation's responses may range from the use of information viruses or terrorism to potential nuclear strikes. The current lack of international legislation governing both attacks and responses merely heightens the fear and distress, encouraging consideration of such tactics. Russian military and civilian analysts are concerned about the conduct of information operations under these conditions.[3] Their evaluation of potential threats highlights the level of disordered ferment over the contours of future conflict. To counter growing concerns, the international community should seek mutual understanding and control over technologies that leverage information, especially when used strategically for weapons applications.

The Importance of
Information Operations to Russia

When Russian specialists discuss information operations, they readily identify information warfare as their greatest concern. Russians recognize that information warfare will soon be an essential element of warfighting. Those who ignore this stage of combat development risk being virtually defenseless. Information operations, in their view, must lie at the heart of any nation's military reform and modernization effort for the twenty-first century. For Russia, this applies in particular to the scientific-technical aspect of reform. Russian theorists understand that yesterday's technology will not serve the armed forces in five years, especially at the pace of military development of information technologies world-wide.

Foreign experience in this area is studied closely, not only for its purely technical importance but also its geopolitical significance. For example, several Russian specialists underscore the technical and geopolitical importance to the United States of powerful information-based operations. They assert that its lead in information-related technologies maintains U.S. status as the preeminent world power, assuring dominance over the potential nuclear club of Iraq, Iran, Libya, and North Korea. Information operations also enhance U.S. strategic interests in regard to Russia, making it more a superior than an equal power. Finally, Russian analysts note the extent to which development of information technology can support U.S. domestic industries, as well as bolster public support and confidence during wartime by ensuring that fewer lives will be lost in combat.[4] In their assessment of U.S. technical superiority, Russian specialists conclude that the United States has developed a variety of offensive information measures such as computer viruses to use against communication nets; logic bombs capable of disrupting military and civilian information infrastructures; and the means to suppress the exchange of information in telecommunications nets, or to falsify exchanges of information in military nets.

An analyst from the Russian Ministry of Defense offered one definition of information war. The definition indicates that some Russian security specialists believe information war concepts apply equally to both peacetime and wartime:

> Both a broad and narrow sense are inherent in the existing concept of information warfare. In the broad sense, information warfare is one of the varieties of the Cold War – countermeasures between two states implemented mainly in peacetime with respect ... not so much to the armed forces ... as to the civilian population awareness, to state administrative systems, production control systems, scientific control, cultural control, etc.... In the narrow sense, information warfare is one of a variety of military activities ... and

has as its goal the achievement of overwhelming superiority over the enemy in the form of efficiency, completeness, and reliability of information upon its receipt, treatment, and use, and working out effective administrative decisions and their purposeful implementation....[5]

This analyst believes that safeguards against information warfare must be worked into the constitutional requirements of the Russian Federation, its basic laws, the national economy, and the mission of the armed forces. In his view, Russia must consider the following in developing its capabilities under modern conditions:

- Perfection of equipment and capabilities to counteract an enemy equipped with information-warfare capacities.
- Assessment of how information-warfare capabilities will correspond to the current concepts of military construction and the military-technical policy of Russia.
- International participation and cooperation in both military and technical areas on problems of information warfare.[6]

RUSSIAN VIEWS OF THE INFORMATION THREAT

Russian military specialists are unnerved by the information operations capabilities witnessed during the Gulf War. This war was the capstone of a series of information operations developments that underscored several new threats to Russia. The Russians were particularly impressed with the electronic warfare aspects of the conflict, and with the ability of highly accurate, information-dependent cruise missiles to allow coalition forces to fight in a stand-off mode. The Russians also discussed rumored U.S. plans to use high-technology psychological operations systems to project hologram images of Muslim martyrs in the sky. Russia's perception of threat affects not only the future of Russian military art and strategy but also the technical components of Russian military doctrine and international law. The following review of potential threats and concerns from the Russian perspective covers a range of areas, and indicates the importance they ascribe to attaining parity in information capabilities.

Information resources must be guarded with the same care given to nuclear weapons. Attacks on strategic information resources, whether military or civilian, are as serious as attacks on military or economic targets – and will demand severe military responses. Information resources have become a strategic asset and demand a state policy of information security. According to one Russian general, "the greater the information capacities a state possesses, the more likely it can achieve strategic advantages with other conditions being equal."[7] As a result, suspending information flows for even a short period of time can cause a crisis no less significant than an economic or military one. Information resources and assets are thus identified as national interests similar to natural resources. Attempts to disrupt information exchanges, illegal use and collection of information, unsanctioned access to information resources, manipulation of information, illegal copying of data, or outright theft from databases require a serious response.[8]

Information operations destroy parity. New criteria, which include intelligence and information collection, are needed for determining parity among strategic forces, in place of existing nuclear and conventional norms.[9] This fact was recognized soon after the conclusion of negotiations on conventional and strategic weapons systems. Intelligence, command and control, early warning, communications, electronic warfare, "special software engineering effects," and disinformation assets are measures that assure one side superiority on the battlefield. These systems upset parity by shifting the correlation of forces to the side possessing such weapons.

Information operations blur understanding of the initial period of war. Since information attacks may be silent and hidden, the determination of crucial factors in planning for, or responding to, an initial period of war become treacherously complicated. It becomes difficult to pinpoint the commencement of an offensive information attack, or to determine with accuracy who delivered it. The question then centers on how to respond. Information actions may be taken against all probable enemies or only the most likely. Furthermore, questions arise regarding how long response can be delayed before the entire information infrastructure is under attack and a reaction is no longer possible. One alarmist noted that "the growing role of information-technology warfare is rapidly lowering the barrier between war and peace. The armed forces of likely adversaries are in a state of constant information warfare...."[10]

Precision information operations limit ecological damage and are therefore more likely to be used than nuclear weapons. One leading official of the General Staff Academy recently noted that "research results permit asserting that the enemy is planning, preparing, and waging a permanent information war, in which the beginning of armed aggression acquires the form of a large-scale special operation within the scope of a strategic offensive aerospace operation."[11] These actions, as several Russian specialists note, may not involve any physical damage or loss of life, and therefore may become more acceptable. Entire economies can be destroyed and yet, to use an old phrase from the age of neutron weapons, "leave the buildings standing." Such operations could take the form of an information blockade, intervention, or confrontation. The most serious form of an information operation, however, is an attempt to control the decisionmaking process in state structures by using special information or disinformation.[12] In every case, the Russians note, attacks may go unnoticed, cause no obvious physical damage, and may already have started.

Information operations are designed to destroy the Russian economy. According to some Russian analysts, the U.S. Strategic Defense Initiative was an attempt to exhaust the Soviet Union economically by causing it to spend money it didn't have on systems it couldn't use or took years to develop – a process known as reflexive control. Now some Russian analysts are viewing the U.S. interest in information warfare in the same way.[13] This implies that information war is, in fact, a Potemkin village that does not deliver an effective tool but only threatens to do so.

Information operations can debilitate the national psyche of a nation. Information, in its purest form, presents a threat to society, the individual, and state institutions. The struggle for control over the mass media leads to a condition in which "information totalitarianism" in international relations has become a method for capturing and manipulating a nation's psyche. If the target of an information operation is the individual mind, state secrets could be disclosed, agents recruited, or tongues loosened through the use of special chemicals or other agents. There are also threats from the introduction of false information into security systems. Special assets are required to prevent the manipulation of public opinion through the use of disinformation, to counter electronic eavesdropping, and to minimize the effects of computer attacks.[14]

Information operations can cause nations to make incorrect judgments and decisions. One of the dangers of the Information Age is that one nation can enter a decisionmaking cycle of another nation via information technologies. They can then deliver a false picture of a situation and force a country, working against the clock, to come to incorrect conclusions or follow a disadvantageous plan of action.[15] By entering a decisionmaking cycle, a nation can affect several sub-systems indirectly, yet instanta-neously, thereby generating confusion in the system-of-systems approach to information war.

Information operations and technologies greatly enhance the mil-itary effectiveness of weapons systems. Russian planners are extremely concerned about the "information component" of high tech weapons.[16] They recognize that this component rais-es the combat potential of precision weapons. Most importantly, it significantly raises the effectiveness of any weapon or system possessing modern information processing technologies. Russia currently lags beyond Western progress in these areas.

In addition, information operations, as proven by the coali-tion forces during the Gulf War, enable some countries to engage in a new sphere of military confrontation – stand-off weapons, electronic warfare, and electronic countermeasures – in which strategic objectives may be obtained without seizing enemy territory in the traditional manner.[17] In response, Russia and other countries may consider a permanent mobilization of defensive information systems.

INFORMATION OPERATIONS INCREASE
THE LIKELIHOOD OF "INFORMATION TERRORISM"
For the first time, technologically advanced small states can pre-sent as big a threat as superpowers once did. The ability of hackers to destroy command and control systems, or to wreak havoc on banking or military systems alike, demonstrates both the internal and external components of the threat. Non-state actors can inflict transnational damage with carefully selected target sets. Undoubtedly this threat can only be thwarted if adequate defensive measures are developed.

Information operations can involve the use of viruses and electronic warfare. According to one Russian analyst, the United States is spreading computer viruses and similar devices and has established a special office known as Computer Virus Countermeasures to combat attacks. Noting that the United States spends nearly $5 billion on information security methods each year, the analyst added that the threat to Russia, which is extremely short of funds, is much greater since it cannot adequately protect itself.[18] Four types of computer viruses were noted:

- Trojan horse virus: Remains idle for a certain period of time, then causes catastrophic destruction of the system.
- Forced quarantine virus: Knocks out the program of the unit into which it was planted. If components are not separated, the entire system network is destroyed.
- Overload virus: Quickly spreads throughout the entire system and gradually slows computer operations.
- Sensor virus: Penetrates a preplanned sector of a computer's data-storage area and, at a critical moment, destroys the data bank and its information.[19]

The Russians also claim to have developed a "stealth virus." This virus does not act in the normal manner – that is, it does not expose itself in the form of an enlarged file. Instead, the stealth virus conceals itself within a file, while the file retains its original size and shape. The Russian military has developed a complicated mathematical procedure to uncover the stealth virus, one that compares the files on a disk with file structures and virtual free space within the system.[20] Each virus, Russian analysts realize, possesses some collateral damage potential that could reveal itself via secondary infections. Therefore it is necessary to keep any virus confined to the system targeted in order to limit unintended consequences.

Russian scientists envision the need to confront distance virus weapons by the turn of the century. These computer viruses will be introduced through radio channels or laser communications directly into computers. They also pose a threat to command and control of the strategic missile force.[21] A final threat to Russia is the use of microwave weapons. These are electromagnetic pulses designed for use against electrical components of Russia's space-, air-, land-, and sea-based means of combating information warfare.[22] That is, an information warfare threat may simply be an electronic attack on the command and control system. In Russian opinion, the U.S. information command and control system, as well as new variants of lethal and non-lethal weapons, can now deliver timely, flexible, and universal means of destruction in both peacetime and wartime. Both electromagnetic pulse and distance virus weapons were being researched by the Russians before the collapse of the Soviet Union.

RUSSIAN RESPONSES TO THE THREAT OF INFORMATION OPERATIONS

Continual reassessment of emerging capabilities. Many Russian specialists believe that the assessment of information operations and weapons must be undertaken on a continuous basis. Otherwise, not only parity, but also Russia's military strategy, may be broken before a war even begins. Russian experts note the usefulness of information technologies not only in the military-technical sense, but in politics and law enforcement as well. They recognize that information technologies can help defuse local conflicts and contradictions, and locate criminals through eavesdropping or surveillance. They also understand how information capabilities can be used as a scare tactic or a tool to leverage military-political pressure on a country.[23] Thus

periodic reassessments must serve a watchdog role of overseeing all vital information processes related to the conduct of
information warfare.

Develop new systems and a "state information security policy."
Defensive and early-warning systems must be developed to
counter information weapons or technologies directed at Russia. This requires a government information security policy that
encompasses the correlation of information weapons and technologies on the military, political, and economic levels. The
economic level must account for the government's scientific-
technical policy, as well as imports and exports. The benefits
of joining the information superhighway, to the same extent as
the rest of the world, must also be weighed. Serious informa-
tion-security questions regarding national information
resources, telecommunications, and computer hacking, among
others, must be answered. Ironically, these considerations return
Russia to the problems of the old order – the balance between
censorship and control with efficient communication and information flows.

One recent step forward was the introduction of an information security policy at the state level. Public debate on
information accessibility began in 1988 with a groundbreak-
ing article in the journal *Kommunist* by a specialist in
information security, Vladimir Rubanov. His article, "From the
'Cult of Secrecy' to An Information Culture," called for an over-
haul of the pervasive Soviet system of secrecy. Rubanov, a KGB
colonel, asserted the superiority of economic systems that
quickly mastered large volumes of information. He was appalled
by the cult of secrecy of the Soviet system and its consequences
for the country. This obsession with secrecy often led to bizarre
arrangements, in which more military secrets were provided to
foreigners during arms control negotiations than to members
of the Soviet industrial complex. In turn, secrecy led to mas-

sive economic losses for the Soviet Union. Before the collapse of the Soviet state, Perestroika required the reform of the Soviet classification system, security agency system, and information policy in general to speed reform,[24] Rubanov argued. He noted:

> The country's information resources and intellectual potentialities remain shackled by deformed information security measures reproduced as ends in themselves ... intellect and knowledge are choked by a bureaucratic system disguised as a system "combating espionage." The situation is reminiscent of the case of the man who took offense and gouged his own eye out to make the son-in-law of his mother-in-law one eyed because he disliked her.[25]

Rubanov admired the availability of information in the West and sought to rehabilitate the information-control system in the Soviet Union. He wrote that "an equally important aspect of the problem of computerizing society and mastering information technology and sophisticated techniques is to raise the nation's culture, to build up its intellectual potential. And this is something you can never buy anywhere at any price."[26] Today, Rubanov is now the Deputy Secretary to the Security Council of the Russian Federation. In early 1995, his desire for an information policy became a reality with the publication of a new Russian Federation law on "Information, Informatization [computerization], and the Protection of Information."[27]

Passing this law was no simple matter. In April of 1994 it appeared within reach, however, when the Security Council's Interdepartmental Commission on Information Security considered the fundamentals of such a concept. Rubanov also gave due consideration to information property rights, noting that it was necessary to "register information as a commodity." He called for protectionism in the production and distribution of information, and cautioned that not all firms specializing in databases and other information assets were acting in conformity with Russia's vital interests.[28] In a later interview with ITAR-TASS, Rubanov called for the creation of a "general defense space" to protect the country against computer crimes aimed against controlling energy systems, the production of dangerous substances, the use and control of troops and weapons, and the defense of personal information rights and intellectual property."[29]

International networking and education. The Russians have developed a fascinating information networking system throughout the world. Designed to unite international information specialists everywhere and spread information throughout Russia, the system is called the International Information Academy. It has more than 250 departments in Russia, the Commonwealth of Independent States, and worldwide. Nearly five thousand of its full and corresponding members work abroad, while full-time staffs work in Moscow, Riga, Kazan, New York, Washington, and San Diego. Its members are drawn from the Russian Academy of Sciences and other prestigious national academies around the world. The Academy in Moscow is composed of institutes that study computer and information sciences as well as mathematics, linguistics, philosophy, management, law, and social issues. Its conferences and meetings cover a wide range of topics on information, business, society, medicine, human rights, and even parapsychology. Through such forums the Academy has called for international cooperation on issues of information technology, the regulation of cross-border information exchange, and the protection of information rights.

To educate and further train Russians, information warfare and security classes are now taught at the General Staff Academy and the Academy of Government Service, among other institutions. This should quickly help to raise the consciousness of leadership in the military and society on information issues.

Promote New Concepts of Deterrence and Parity. Finally, Russian theorists have called for the creation of an "information deterrence" concept, similar to the concept of nuclear deterrence of the past but now addressing information-attack systems and technologies. The goal of such a concept would be to alleviate mutual concerns among countries over attacks on C^4I systems, the use of computer viruses, and the ability of one side to affect the psyche of another nation by manipulating the mass consciousness of a people through new information technologies. There is equal desire to restore parity among both conventional and nuclear systems, altered by asymmetric information capabilities.

CONCLUSIONS

At first glance, the list of threats posited by Russian analysts to their country's national security appears to resemble U.S. concerns closely. Information resources, computer technologies, highly effective precision weapons, and terrorism all coincide with U.S. perceptions of threat. What differs is the national context within which the assessment is being made. For Russia, the situation is measured from a position of fear and vulnerability. From a technology perspective, Russia does not possess the military-industrial complex to field state-of-the-art information operations technology that can protect state secrets or conduct army operations efficiently with little loss of life. This increases concern over their ability to thwart or even detect an information strike. In addition, technologies that leverage information represent a direct assault on the Soviet-era legacy of secrecy and compartmentalization.

The Information Age has dawned in Russia at a time of intense psychological trauma. The present transition from a centrally planned economy to an economy showing signs of capitalism has created economic and social instability. According to Russian analysts, the populace is vulnerable to manipulation and penetration by other forms of thinking, generating concern among many Russians over control of and access to information. Furthermore, Russia, despite its huge nuclear arsenal, is hardly computerized. Many cashiers still compute on an abacus. Juxtaposed against this is the younger generation, who tend to think in terms of firewalls and information overloads. Rapid change has created a dichotomy in society: older-generation decisionmakers do not completely understand the power of the information revolution, while younger-generation operators have little say over its use. Another consequence is that insecure senior leaders turn to stock answers to national security problems in response to the information assault. Clearly, if Russia is to compete, it must shift its emphasis to those who are computer literate.

The perception of threat is so great among some Russian military analysts, that they believe an information operation has already been initiated. For example, Admiral Baltin, the former commander of the Black Sea Fleet, noted that:

> We have every reason to talk of a third world war that broke out, and has almost died out, before our very eyes. It was not a classic but a "velvet" war. For the third time this century, the leading world powers have divided up spheres of influence. This war can be deemed to have begun physically with the destruction of the Berlin Wall. The essence of the "velvet" third world war is an information-strategic offensive in which the main role is played by well-honed psychological operations.

The result of this war exceeded all expectations. The first is that NATO's political objectives have been secured: the socialist system with its once powerful economy and military potential has been destroyed. Moreover, as a result of the effects of the false values and convictions that were introduced into the minds of socialist countries' citizens, the territorial collapse of some of those countries, among them the Soviet Union, was achieved.[30]

A Russian security specialist, retired General-Major Shershev, president of the National and International Security Foundation of Russia, considers that four wars have occurred during the twentieth century: World Wars I and II, the Cold War, and now a world information war. He cautions that "... if we are unable to halt this war, we will see a racial [cultural] war. The mass media are being exploited in the Chechen problem, and Russia is being moved away from democracy toward criminality. If Russia is destroyed, it will be a catastrophe of global significance."[31]

Another serious disadvantage for Russia's national security elite is that some young computer operators are linked with criminal elements, and have begun to attack the country's information, insurance, and banking industries both at home and abroad. They represent a new internal threat to the state, one that an already overworked police apparatus has difficulty controlling. The countries of the West, on the other hand, have strong technology bases and have already adapted to the Information Age. Personal computers are available at affordable prices and are present in many homes. Even so, the West shares with Russia the difficult task of tracking down computer criminals, and to date has registered only moderate success.

To Russian specialists the threat is real, and intensifying. They believe the Russian state and society are now or potentially could be the target of information operations from many countries. Russia's inability to keep pace with rapid developments is strengthening this fear. Russia needs reassurance that an attack is not planned or even considered. The likely Russian reactions to the perceived threat, as outlined here, must be heeded by the West. Russian apprehensions must be addressed by international attendance at conferences on information warfare and discussion of information operations at high-level meetings of scientists and state leaders.

In the meantime, Russia's state and military confront the threat by developing its information technology infrastructure and by monitoring for internal and external signs of manipulation of the Russian psyche. One Russian analyst warned that Moscow's only retaliatory capability at this time is the nuclear response, certainly a strong deterrent to many nations. Unlike attack options of the Cold War, information operations leave little room for flexible response. The consequences of an information operation against Russia, or the U.S., are fraught with risks of escalation that could far exceed the geographic boundaries intended by a perpetrator. To reduce these risks, the West must alleviate Russian concerns by actively pursuing a policy of openness, transparency, and cooperation.

ENDNOTES

1. Chairman of the Joint Chiefs of Staff, *National Military Strategy* (February 1995), p. 15.

2. Headquarters, Department of the Army, Field Manual 100–6, *Information Operations* (8 July 1995).

3. The opinions expressed in this article are based on discussions with Russian military and civilian analysts. They may not represent official positions of the Russian government or the Ministry of Defense.

4. Georgiy Smolyan, Vitaliy Tsygichko, and Dmitriy Chereshkin, "A Weapon That May Be More Dangerous Than a Nuclear Weapon: The Realities of Information Warfare," *Nezavisimoye Voyennoye Obozreniye* 3 (supplement to *Nezavisimaya Gazeta*) (18 November 1995), pp. 1–2, as reported in FBIS-UMA-95-234-S (6 December 1995), pp. 32–33.

5. Professor V.I. Tsymbal, "Kontseptsiya 'informatsionnoy voyny'" [Concept of Information War], paper received at conference with the Russian Academy of Civil Service in Moscow, 14 September 1995.

6. Tsymbal, p. 4.

7. "New Trends in Power Deterrence," *Armeyskiy Sbornik* 9 (September 1995), pp. 12–19, as reported in FBIS-UMA-96-011-S (17 January 1996), p. 11.

8. "New Trends in Power Deterrence," p. 11.

9. "New Trends in Power Deterrence," p. 12.

10. Alexander Pozdnyakov, "Information Security," *Granitsa Rossii* 33 (September 1995), pp. 6–7, as reported in FBIS-UMA-95-239-S (13 December 1995), p. 41.

11. "New Trends in Power Deterrence," p. 3.

12. "New Trends in Power Deterrence," p. 11.

13. Smolyan, et al., p. 35.

14. Pozdnyakov, pp. 42–43.

15. M. Boytsov, "Informatsionnaya voyna" [Information Warfare], *Morskoy Sbornik* 10 (1995), p. 70.

16. For further explanation of this concept, see Timothy L. Thomas, "Russian Views of Information-Based Warfare," in a special issue of *Airpower Journal* (Summer 1996).

17. "Need For a New Collective Security System," *Krasnaya Zvesda* (5 December 1995), p. 3, as reported in FBIS-SOV-95-234 (6 December 1995), pp. 28–29.

18. "Need For a New Collective Security System," p. 43.

19. "Need For a New Collective Security System," p. 43.

20. R.M. Yusupov and B.P. Pal'chun, "Obespecheniye bezopasnosti komp'yuternoi infosfery" [Safeguarding the Security of the Computer Infosphere], Vooruzheniye, Politika, Konversiya [Armaments, Policy, Conversion] No. 3 (1993), p. 23.

21. Boytsov, p. 72.

22. Boytsov, p. 72.

23. Smolyan, et al. See also Russia Press Service (Minneapolis: East View Publications, 9 February 1996) for translation of an article in *Nezavisimaya Gazeta* (9 February 1996), p. 2. The unattributed report is a reassessment of the Russian situation during a recent conference among all the power services in Moscow. It states that " ... the continuing informatization and dissemination of computer technology in all spheres of our society naturally encompasses special services, the activity of which is inconceivable without scientific-technical and information support. In this connection the great interest in the conference's subject on the part of Russian special services is far from accidental. Leading scientists and specialists from the FSB, FAPSI [Federal Government Communications and Information Agency], GUO [Main Protection Directorate], FPS [Federal Border Service], and the Defense Ministry – in effect all power departments and special services – took part in the conference."

24. Vladimir Rubanov, "Ot 'Kul'ta Sekretnosti' - K Informatsionnoy Kul'ture" ["From the 'Cult of Secrecy' to an Information Culture"], *Kommunist* 13 (September 1988), pp. 24–36.
25. Vladimir Rubanov, "Defense Gets the Best, Economy the Rest," *International Affairs* (January 1991), p. 10.
26. Rubanov, "Defense Gets the Best," p. 10.
27. "Law: Russian Federation Federal Law on Information, Informatization, and the Protection of Information," *Rossiyskaya Gazeta* (22 February 1995), pp. 15–16, as reported in FBIS-SOV-95-048-S (13 March 1995), pp. 29–36.
28. Dmitry Volkov, "Security Council Takes a Closer Look at Information," *Sevodnya* 26 (April 1994), as printed in FBIS-SOV-94-080 (26 April 1994), pp. 25–26.
29. ITAR-TASS (April 25, 1994), as published in FBIS-SOV-94-080 (26 April 1994), p. 26.
30. Edward Baltin, interviewed by Zhanna Kasyanenko, "Russia Has Lost the Velvet War," *Sovetskaya Rossiya* (31 October 1995), p. 3, as reported in FBIS-SOV-95-211 (1 November 1995), pp. 18–20.
31. From the author's discussion with General-Major Shershev in Moscow, September 1995.

Technology & Human Understanding for War in the Information Age

Technology & Human Understanding for War in the Information Age

ALTHOUGH TECHNOLOGY MAY BE CREATING A NEW REVOLUTION in military affairs, the authors in this section point out that war will remain a human endeavor. Soldiers and their commanders need to understand how they can benefit from information but not be overwhelmed by it. Technology cannot simply be placed in soldiers' hands with the expectation that they will immediately have the skills to employ it. Rather, information-enhanced weapons systems and command and control networks will need to become part of operational doctrine. The military will need to train its members to deal with the capabilities and limitations of such technology. It is not enough to have technological capabilities; they must become part of military procedures and be integrated with the human elements of warfare that are still crucial to battlefield success.

In the first essay in this section, James P. McCarthy describes an operational concept for using information technology to achieve "battlespace awareness" for warfighters. As outlined by McCarthy, this concept, called the "WarNet," is an information dissemination system that can take vast amounts of information and transmit it to warfighters in a manner that is instantly comprehended and applied. Information derived from a multitude of sources on location of forces, weather, logistics, commanders' intent, and similar considerations, will be layered on top of a "geospatial, temporal, reference system" – a sophisticated map – that is transmitted to warfighters through "direct publishing" over the airwaves. Warfighters will then be empowered by dominant battlefield knowledge.

This system, according to McCarthy, will fundamentally change wartime operations. Warfighters will have a new set of tasks to account for the wider availability of information, such as the need to prioritize, edit, and filter the flow of information. Knowledge-enhanced soldiers will be better able to understand their commanders' intentions, even as a situation rapidly changes. Soldiers will be able to exploit initiative without direct tasking from the commander, thus increasing the tempo of operations and the potential for success. Simultaneous and parallel operations on the battlefield will become possible – in place of merely sequential ones – and decision-cycle times will be reduced. These developments, in turn, will lead to organizational change as units become less hierarchical.

Frederic J. Brown addresses the "human challenge" that systems such as the WarNet may bring. Even with technological advances, effective situational awareness, he writes, still requires three "legs" that depend on human abilities: the art of battle command; mastery of the tactical control of forces; and the ability to put together a high-performance organization that can communicate under combat stress. When information technologies are added to the battlefield, two issues cut across these three legs: determining how much information is required to accomplish a task, and ensuring that the military has people capable of handling the information. Thus, training and education must be adapted to the Information Age, as well as the division of responsibility between officers and NCOs. Brown goes on to suggest several ways to integrate the use of information capabilities into military cultures, such as developing "filters" for the flow of information that can aggregate information from various sources and disaggregate useless or redundant data. Second, both doctrine and tactics, training, and procedures need to be redesigned and streamlined. Individuals can handle only a few tasks, and the information provided to them must be matched to those tasks. Finally, training should focus on worst-case scenarios so that commanders are prepared for times of "digital default" – periods when information systems fail.

John R. Wood describes in practical terms the effects of integrating Information Age weapon systems into his unit, the 3rd Infantry Division (Mechanized) Artillery at Fort Stewart. Wood suggests that advanced systems, such as the *Paladin* howitzer, have broad implications in three areas – doctrine, training, and leader development. In the area of doctrine, he argues, battle command is now far less regimented and centralized, the battlespace has expanded and become more complex, and deep and simultaneous attack of the enemy, while easier on the battalion level, is increasingly difficult to synchronize on the division level. For training, the challenge is to develop and sustain the technical skills that allow soldiers to use the new equipment, while also enabling them to apply information without suffering "information overload." Wood identifies leader development as the greatest challenge for military operations in the Information Age. Senior enlisted men or officers will need to be reeducated to apply new weapons systems and doctrine. Wood comes to a conclusion similar to Brown's: officers will need to maintain their manual, tactical, and command skills in order to be able to deal with digital default.

In his essay, John W. McDonald addresses the effects that information may have on achieving decision-cycle dominance, generally considered the key to military success. McDonald argues that it is difficult to assess the exact impact of information technologies in terms of advantages and disadvantages for U.S. forces. When the United States has the monopoly on battlefield awareness, friendly forces may be able to operate inside the enemy's decision cycle. On the other hand, low-technology enemies might not deploy the sort of forces that would emit signatures for U.S. systems to track, thus actually slowing the U.S. decision cycle. In addition, low-tech forces may use built-up areas and close terrain as force multipliers, degrading the utility of U.S. sensors; and they may operate defensively, leading to difficulties in identifying patterns of activity.

McDonald points out that the United States may not have a monopoly on battlefield awareness. Against an opponent with similar capabilities, the United States will have to leverage its advantages in leadership, training, longer-range precision fires, joint operations, and special operations; conduct physical attacks on enemy visual capabilities; and use deceptive measures, including suppressing friendly signatures. These caveats lead McDonald to conclude, like the other authors in this section, that effective doctrine and training are crucial to managing the information revolution and enabling individuals to take advantage of it.

chapter five

Managing Battlespace Information: The Challenge of Information Collection, Distribution, and Targeting

James P. McCarthy

WE STAND ON THE THRESHOLD OF A REVOLUTION in military affairs. Together, the synergistic incorporation of new technologies in military systems, innovative operational concepts, and organizational adaptation will alter the character and conduct of military operations. At the heart of this revolution is the role of information and knowledge in warfare. This chapter discusses one element of information warfare, the battlespace infosphere – the situational awareness made possible by the information systems supporting combat forces. Given the breadth of the subject, this discussion does not include offensive or defensive warfare, though these are an integral part of information warfare.

The basis for integrating new technologies is the "system of systems" concept described by William A. Owens, the former Vice Chairman of the Joint Chiefs of Staff.[1] This concept links advanced sensors, such as unmanned aerial vehicles (UAVs), and

JSTARS,[2] to advanced command, control, communications, computers, and information systems (C^4I), providing the information flow to support the use of precision force. The focus here is on the development of advanced C^4I capabilities, for which "WarNet" is a shorthand name. WarNet comprises an information dissemination system conceived during a 1994 Defense Science Board Summer Study, called "Information Architecture for the Battlefield,"[3] and is consistent with the Joint Staff's publication, *C^4I for the Warrior*.[4]

The most important task for WarNet is the compilation of vast amounts of information for presentation to the warfighter in a form that can be understood and used instantly. An analogy may be made to the way weather forecasts are presented on cable television's weather channel. The techniques to convey information quickly, such as cloud patterns and radar images, provide instantaneous comprehension of weather patterns. A warfighter's quick assimilation of information can be enhanced using simi-

FIGURE I: *Warfighters' Picture of the Battlespace*

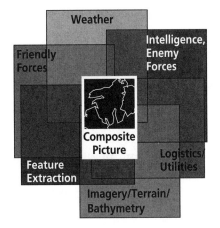

lar techniques, based on a geospatial, temporal, reference system – the foundation for a sophisticated map display that can be selectively modified to depict the battlespace infosphere. In the past, an intelligence analyst was mandated to search and analyze all possible sources of information, drawing conclusions that would later be presented to the operator, commander, or decisionmaker. The information revolution streamlines this process by creating a foundation – the geospatial temporal reference – upon which information can be continuously referenced and correlated. Today's technology also enables quick communication of information to the warfighter, thus improving situational awareness.

FIGURE 2: *The Visual-Operational Implementation*

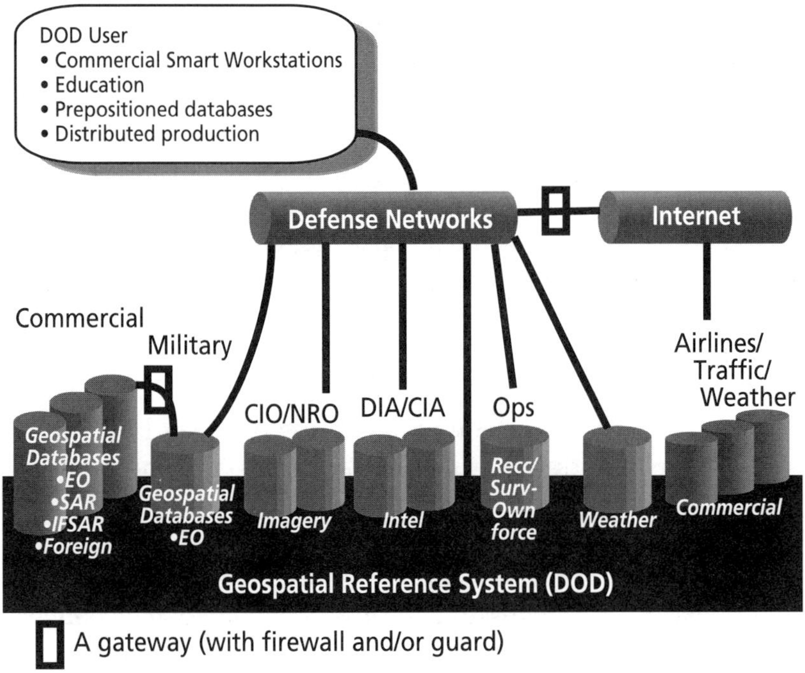

A gateway (with firewall and/or guard)

Figure 2 illustrates how the warrior's picture of the battle-space can be achieved. The geospatial temporal reference system creates the foundation, using data collected by numerous types of satellites. Ten other nations are also putting up satellites that will make imagery with one-meter accuracy available to any-one who wants to buy it. The Iraqis, for example, could buy capability close to what the U.S. publicly acknowledges it has today. Another part of the system is the Department of Defense's use of commercial activities – such as airline schedules, traffic, weather, and radar input from the Federal Aviation Adminis-tration – and its use of the Internet. During preparation for the Haiti and Somalia operations, for example, university experts around the country were consulted using the Internet. To guard U.S. databases within the defense information infrastructure, gateways and firewalls that limit access are essential.

By accessing information from the databases distributed along this network, the user of classified local area networks is able to create a picture of the battlespace. For example, the location of a particular hotel in Baghdad may be obtained from Fodor's travel guide. Sensors may then detect unusual activity at the hotel, such as a heat plume emanating from its south side. In addition, there might be unusual communications in certain bandwidths. It would thus be possible to conclude that this is no ordinary hotel but a command post. The empowerment that accompanies this type of information access is termed domi-nant battlefield knowledge.

However, this data network lacks a concept of information architecture to match the understanding of warfighting archi-tectures. Warfighting architectures are the operational concepts that commanders develop to accomplish their mission. An infor-mation architecture is required to translate the commander's concept of operations into information dissemination require-ments, based on the mission and forces involved. The concept of defining information needs to meet warfighting functions is new; it will require unique expertise not yet available within the military. A structure of communications systems is needed that can be altered to meet changing information needs. In fact, it is now recognized that the ability to "kluge together" information systems to support operations – as indeed happened in the Gulf War – is a national asset.

CREATING AN INFORMATION ARCHITECTURE

There are several classes of communications, not all of which are new. On one level there are interpersonal communications, such as video conferencing. There are also the traditional methods of messaging, epitomized by the flashlight flickering between two people who understand Morse code. More recent innovations include query-response techniques, developed during the Gulf War. There are not, however, enough servers in the world to satisfy a half-million people deployed to the Gulf, sitting at computer terminals, and accessing national databases. The most effective method for enhancing information distribution is through "publishing." The components of communications architecture of the future will then include the current tactical command and control nets; high-capacity systems for distributing information, like the Defense Satellite Communications System (DSCS) or the Military Communications Satellite (MILSTAR); and, at the heart of the Department of Defense information distribution system, a commercial satellite network publishing information wideband to recipients with a nine-inch receiver dish. In the next year or two, the technology will be in place to provide recipients with image quality on par with home video systems.

This process, called direct broadcast of information, utilizes commercial equipment and technology. The system anticipates user needs and customizes the requested data to fit its end function. One way to conceptualize the process is through comparison with television "channel surfing." A viewer may have an outdoor activity planned for the next day and will switch to the Weather Channel for an update, next turning to CNN for world news. Later, the viewer might alternate between a basketball game on ESPN and a movie on A&E. In much the same way, WarNet will provide field commanders the capability to "surf" among channels published by the CINC or the JTF commander, satisfying their particular information needs.

For example, a tank company commander in the desert of Saudi Arabia may use a channel published by the JTF commander to provide situational awareness through the tank's three-channel select display. Access may be limited by classification, echelon, or sphere of interest. Assuming a particular tank commander does not need to survey the entire battlefield, the computer is automatically limited to, perhaps, a thirty-five-kilometer range. This threshold would be set on the tank receiver by the theater commander, but it can be changed as the tank commander's sphere of interest on the battlefield expands. The classification may also be changed. For example, if friendly forces are able to operate within the decision-cycle of a enemy, information normally distributed on a limited scale may well be broadcast unclassified. Even if the enemy receives such information, they will not have the connectivity, the training, or the capability to react within a useful period of time. Free access to information enables friendly forces to maneuver more rapidly due to dramatic reduction of the query-response requirement. However, for such a system to operate efficiently, users must train and exercise with it on a daily basis.

Consider how a warfighter might employ this system. On one channel, comprehensive situational awareness might be displayed. On another, the corps commander's intent is elaborated, giving the tank commander the benefit of understanding the comprehensive corps plan. The system eliminates uncertainty by conveying a commander's intent directly to the person who will execute it. Other channels might carry weather information, logistics capability, AWACS pictures, and JSTARS. The system will thus be able to carry both classified and unclassified material. Depending upon situational needs, any matrix of information may be fed into the system and channeled directly to the appropriate recipient. The technology required to construct this system is already available and may even be introduced, on a limited basis, among the forces in Bosnia.

To utilize this mode of information architecture effectively, the warfighter must master a new set of tasks. First, information must be assessed to determine how it meets a warfighter's needs. Next, a warfighter must identify fusion points for the information flow. For example, three tactical fighter wings deployed to Saudi Arabia must be accompanied by communications, intelligence, and information equipment, as well as by analysts. The information fusion will then take place in Saudi Arabia. On the other hand, if eight F-15E fighters are deployed out of Seymour Johnson Air Force Base in North Carolina, the information fusion will be completed at Seymour Johnson. Providing the fused information picture to the warrior in-theater significantly diminishes deployment requirements. Another task for the warfighter is control of access and dissemination limits, facilitated by the broadcast system's reduction of query-response connectivity. One of the more difficult tasks is the management of system vulnerability. A commander cannot tolerate catastrophic failure and must have the capability to manage graceful degradation of the system. Information must be prioritized, edited, and filtered to facilitate its assimilation by war-riors. This is a critical issue; if warriors are bombarded with information out of context they will become distracted from the task at hand. Finally, the warfighter must have the ability to alter the information system as the mission changes, as the force changes, and as circumstances change.

The key to the success of this system is an understanding of knowledge relationships. Correlation, integration, and aggrega-tion add value to information. Most people comprehend this concept intuitively but, perhaps, have not applied it to infor-mation technologies. The necessity of referencing to a framework provides one example. Today's intelligence databases are not linked to a single reference system. To solve this problem, the Defense Science Board recommended shifting the mission of the Defense Mapping Agency away from publishing maps and toward the task of maintaining a single common geospatial data-base, temporally referenced. As a result, information flowing into the system is referenced to the same geospatial database. The information product becomes much more valuable because the new approach permits instantaneous correlation, integration, and aggregation. Visualization of such relationships and the abil-ity of technology to realize this potential will raise human understanding of complex issues to higher levels.

In the past, a warrior was compelled to integrate all manner of information without a foundation of knowledge or an under-standing of the potential information relationships. Once that correlation is automatic, the information presented to the war-rior is well integrated and complex issues can be handled more readily. The consequences of supplying a warrior with infor-mation that is not well integrated can be severe. For example, the principal responsibility of a tank company commander is to manage a battle by looking outside the tank. If a commander consults a computer display and becomes involved with managing its image and information, attention is diverted from the primary task. The appropriate system allows a warrior merely to click from one channel to another to access information that can be rapidly assimilated. If it is not that simple, it should not be available.

Today's method of warfighting, particularly such approaches as the sensor-to-shooter concept, makes WarNet indispensable. Precision weapons require precision target location. The distribution of strike information and target identification, allocation, and assignment to a large number of warriors using long-range precision weapons increases the complexity of the issue. Parallel or simultaneous operations will only increase with time. In short, full integration of sensors, WarNet, and shooters is critical.

This leads to the conclusion that the WarNet concept is missing a link. To direct information flows, some form of organizational responsibility, operational concept, or automated system for guidance must be developed. Most likely all three are required. To understand this, consider how it is possible to transmit the correct annotated target image and execution direction to a designated F-16 in flight from among one hundred airborne aircraft. Clearly, operational capability is developing before operational concepts. Application of the current "system of systems" plan is too complex for a single manager or process, and thus demands further study for effective employment.

WarNet and the Future of Warfighting

WarNet makes warriors as knowledgeable as the system by facilitating individual empowerment. In the traditional hierarchical system, the commander was the only one with full knowledge, and thus maintained a disciplined force because soldiers did not have the same level of understanding. The new system enables more dynamic tasking and information support simultaneously. Now, when a commander sends out a tasking order for a unit to strike a particular target, the unit simultaneously receives the imagery and intelligence assessment. Thus, the pace of activity is more rapid. Relying on more knowledgeable warriors, a commander can alter tasking quickly to take advantage of a changing situation. More importantly, if warriors understand their commander's intent and share the same situational awareness, they can exploit new developments, confident that their decisions are consistent with command objectives.

Under WarNet, warfare will change in a number of ways. The WarNet capability enables simultaneous or parallel operations. In the past, operations were sequential; only one action could be handled at a time. With shared situational awareness, everyone can work problems simultaneously. Furthermore, with advance mission planning and rehearsal, a higher level of mission success is probable. WarNet also significantly reduces decision time and enhances maneuver warfare. It allows for "control warfare," in which the dynamics of the situation permit commanders to apply power in isolated, highly vulnerable locations, rather than frontal ones. Finally, the heightened ability of commanders to bring power at various places simultaneously triggers a different enemy reaction. Consequently, ever smaller force applications will yield greater results. These changes in warfare will, in turn, produce organizational change. The military will become more flexible, flat, mobile, and joint. The creation of temporary joint task forces might become more common.

Of course, there are some concerns about the system on the part of commanders. Vulnerability of the system is the most obvious; confidence in the protection of combat information is difficult to achieve. Commanders also worry about political micromanagement. If everyone in the field has access to information, the number of opinions on how to fight a war will multiply. Finally, if the information structure significantly enhances performance, politicians might conclude that the current level of forces is unnecessary, engendering even further military downsizing.

Regardless of how the information revolution unfolds, warfighting is destined to change dramatically over the next decade. Real-time situational awareness has always been a goal, and now the expanding capability to aggregate information increases its value to the warfighter. Overall, the emerging information structure will permit new concepts of operation, promote organizational change, and have significant consequences for the conduct of conflict.

ENDNOTES

1. William A. Owens, "The Emerging System of Systems," *Proceedings* (May 1995).
2. Joint Surveillance Target Attack Radar System.
3. Craig I. Fields and James P. McCarthy, "Report of the Defense Science Board Task Force on Information Architecture for the Battlefield" (Washington D.C.: Office of the Under Secretary of Defense for Acquisition and Technology, 1994).
4. *C⁴I for the Warrior* (Washington, D.C.: Joint Chiefs of Staff, 12 June 1994).

chapter six

Tactical Situational Awareness: The Human Challenge

Frederic J. Brown

VISUALIZING COMPLEX ORGANIZATIONS is a formidable conceptual challenge. It demands attention to forms of warfare moving "… on timelines that are outside the human perception range across spatial dimensions that are global in nature."[1] The task is no less daunting as a practical challenge. Real combatants under stress must use information, not be used by it. Moreover, they must have situational awareness, the timely recognition of both enemy and friendly movements that enables warfighters to gain and sustain initiative while executing their command.

This chapter addresses the human aspects of visualizing complex operations that are likely to characterize conflict in the Information Age. The focus is on the challenges and potential solutions to enhancing the ability of humans to maintain situational awareness below the brigade level. There are several challenges; some are definitional, others require thoughtful development. The potential solutions cover a range of areas, from force design and support to doctrine and training.

Overcoming Hurdles in the Development of Tactical Situational Awareness

For a number of reasons, the greatest challenges to creating situational awareness arise below the brigade echelon. Leaders below the brigade level are generally less experienced, commanding smaller staffs with fewer trained officers. Higher-ranking officers possess both experience and specialized preparation, increasing their ability to interpret information in a timely, effective manner. Commanders at lower echelons are also more prone to personal distraction given their involvement in combat; this is particularly true in the case of mounted ground forces, where the commander is routinely located in an armored fighting vehicle (AFV). Though the AFV is often in a protected position, the fighter-commander is subject to the stress of immediate personal combat. At times of crisis, the commander is expected to lead by personal presence, employing information for immediate survival and unit mission accomplishment.

In lower echelons, the procedures designed to create or keep an advantage in situational awareness are frequently subject to disruption by enemy action, or misinterpretation by tired combatants under stress. Furthermore, in joint or combined operations, a brigade, regiment, or wing will face equally stressed counterparts probably less familiar with new doctrine, tactics, techniques, and procedures (TTP). Thus, disruption to the routine procedures established to support situational awareness becomes more likely.

To ensure effective situational awareness, three general command and control requirements must be addressed. First, the unit, and most particularly the commander, must practice competent battle command as described in Army doctrinal publications.[2] Second, they must master the tasks, conditions, and standards of control, including the enabling hardware and software of new Information Age battle tasks. Finally, it is necessary to create a high-performance organization that communicates effectively under stress, internally as well as externally. Solid translation of situational awareness into effective action is similar to building a three-legged stool based upon battle command, mastering the tasks of control, and creating a high-performance organization. All three legs must be sturdy and are critical to effective warfighting at all levels, from low- and mid-intensity conflicts to stability operations or operations other than war.

There are information implications for each of these three areas. In the first, competent battle command is often an art; it is the skill of knowing oneself, knowing the enemy, and then knowing what choices to make. The prospect of Information Age warfare promises nearly perfect awareness of the enemy. As observed in Operation Desert Hammer at the National Training Center in 1994, however, the ability to take maximum advantage of remarkable situational awareness is not simply a matter of instinct to stressed tactical commanders. To exploit nearly perfect knowledge, commanders need preparation, developed through effective planning in tactical decisionmaking – an issue rarely discussed in the literature of conflict or addressed in institutional training. The commander also needs both perspective and balance to respond when valuable enemy intelligence or friendly combat information is suddenly available or, conversely, when an information filter "plugs" and flows are obstructed.[3] There is a clear need to educate and train commanders to make optimum use of detailed, timely situational awareness – and to prepare them to respond and retain the initiative when they do not.

As regards mastering the tasks of control, the sheer complexity of focusing combat power in time and space is formidable. Effective deep attack or counterfire requires detailed, precise focusing of combat power in both time and space to hit fleeting targets. Synchronization can require action in minutes or even seconds when ten or twenty units may be involved in the information-processing cycle. Tactical decisionmaking in Korea approximates that situation with training to execute complex integrated operations, such as deep attack, across multiple joint and combined organizations.

To create high-performance organizations, commanders must create teams which communicate effectively under stress. This is a difficult task, since unit staff structures often reflect the different organizational structures and responsibilities among staff teams. It is even more complex at lower echelons, given the turnover of officers less experienced in tactical operations. Additionally, there is the turbulence created by the ever increasing number of combined operations, in which U.S. forces join with personnel from other nations and non-governmental organizations. The current command training guidance of V Corps in Europe incorporates as one of the major enabling tasks to the mission essential task list the ability to "rapidly tailor force packages as integrated, cohesive joint and combined task forces."[4] Under these circumstances, it is no small task to create a cohesive command and staff team that can rapidly and effectively translate situational awareness into timely battle action.

Issues of both quantity and quality apply across the three legs of the command and control stool and, in consequence, will become more critical in Information Age warfare. The quantity issue pertains to satisfaction of the objective task-loading requirement, such as how much information is required to enable successful mission completion. For typical missions, such as movement to contact or defense in sector for land forces, there is a clear need to determine exactly what tasks must be performed, at what time, to what standards, and under which conditions. It is necessary to determine the optimum and minimum acceptable flow of information required for successful execution of doctrine, tactics, techniques, or procedures. Next, the manner in which information is handled, either personally or in concert with others, must be clarified. The central concern must be mission task analysis, followed by training to enhance task execution under stress. Until this genuinely demanding though routinely neglected requirement is accomplished, effective situational awareness in combat will remain a chimerical goal.

The quality issue addresses the ability of the average soldier, officer, or leader to handle information. Information should be in a form that is useful to intended recipients, who must, in turn, be trained to take advantage of these new capabilities. Factors that may influence effective performance and use of information include levels of intelligence (AFQT-Mental Category), state of rest, competing signals, and the amount of experience in using and applying information. In concert or alone, these factors can nullify the impact of even the best situational awareness.

But even if conditions are optimum, high performance is not assured unless the individual and staff team have an opportunity to assimilate the new situational awareness. The battalion intelligence officer (known as the S-2) cannot utilize detailed broadcast intelligence and combat information unless and until he or she has mastered both the information hardware and software. The team must have the intelligence officer's analysis during the execution of a tactical mission, such as movement to contact or defense in sector. Lastly, all team members must understand how hardware, software, and routine mission tasks combine to generate new capability in order to improve task performance through increased situational awareness.

It is no trivial task to develop and sustain this proficiency. The automated fire support system (TACFIRE) for staff and non-commissioned officers in command posts required sixteen hours per week of training to sustain proficiency in fire planning. The level of training necessary might well increase substantially for battlefield commanders employing information sources on board an AFV. Among joint and combined task forces the problem is likely to be magnified even further. Ensuring training time for tactical unit leaders to exploit situational awareness may become one of the critical paths to unit readiness.

Force Structure and the Application of Situational Awareness

A by-product of the Information Age is the development of new training and education methods to prepare forces to make the most of improvements in situational awareness. Distributed tactical engagement simulation, consisting of variable combinations of live, virtual, and constructive simulation, now creates new capabilities for experiential immersion learning. As demonstrated in the 1994 Synthetic Theater of War–Europe (STOW-E) trials, it is now possible to create highly effective training to task, condition, and standard in stressful immersion-based experiential learning scenarios across simulation domains anywhere in the world. This capability is routinely demonstrated in combat training for several National Guard units (SIMITAR). Thus, while there are clearly new learning requirements, at the same time there is a prospect of dramatic improvement in the effectiveness and efficiency of learning.

The basic division of responsibilities between officers and noncommissioned officers is changing, reflecting the new Information Age realities:

The old blue-collar/white-collar distinction seems dated. I believe that this traditional distinction is inadequate today, post-AirLand Battle. It is more useful to think in terms of iron-, blue-, white-, and gold-collar personnel requirements. Iron-collar requirements are robotic, computer driven. Blue collar now includes disciplined execution of assigned individual and collective tasks by blue and iron collar. White collar refers to leading in the accomplishment of single BOS [battlefield operating system] missions (maneuver, fire support, air defense, or combat service support). Gold collar refers to the ability to integrate iron, blue, white, and other gold successfully, in a rapidly changing situation, under stress. More precisely, it is the ability to conceptualize and successfully execute the focusing of multiple BOS functions in time and space to achieve the intent of the higher chain of command.[5]

Officers above the grade of major now face gold-collar level warfighting responsibilities. Company-grade officers and senior noncommissioned officers are white collar. Senior noncommissioned officers are expected to be capable of commanding companies in combat. Junior sergeants are still blue collar. Nowhere is this change, still largely unique to U.S. forces, more in evidence than in U.S. Army Europe (USAREUR). Current USAREUR operations now include participation in "joint contact teams, bilateral exercises, partnership for peace, and other military to military exercises."[6] The demands on leader competence and time are significant. USAREUR training guidance continues: "Units must be capable of executing these events on short notice. When a company is committed, it must take with it a vertical slice of the chain of command representing battalion, brigade, and division."[7] Each echelon is drawn upon to train and to mentor multinational peers on the nature of the Army in a democracy.

The good news is that gold-collar officers are more likely to be trained and experienced in expanded situational awareness. The bad news is that their competence is being extended to new post-Cold War missions directly aimed at exploiting the excellence of gold-collar officers and white-collar noncommissioned officers in a new "Marshall Plan" to move democracy east. They will not necessarily be better prepared to use new Information Age capabilities in quick-response, mid-intensity conflicts, although proficiency in one should support the other.

Cross-cultural situational awareness, while elegant in concept, is exceedingly difficult to attain in practice. Even the concept of the noncommissioned officer, whether blue collar or white collar, is foreign to many military establishments. In fact, most countries with peasant traditions simply do not have noncommissioned officers, making it difficult to explain the sharing of responsibilities between officers and sergeants.

U.S. doctrine, tactics, techniques, and procedures are complex, and rely for their effect on synchronized cross-battlefield operating system interactions. They will become yet more complex in future concepts of full-dimensional operations.[8] The complexity of likely operations can be compared to the United States military moving from Buick to Cadillac, while some allies slip from Pontiac to Chevrolet; few other national military establishments are much beyond carts. These differences exist wholly apart from the complexity of matching the current spectrum of force projection commitments, ranging from peacekeeping to sudden mid-intensity combat. Each level of conflict has different information requirements.

The differences in information requirements and the ability to capitalize on situational awareness among militaries may become even more challenging with ad hoc functional commitments in force projection operations. Deployment of the balanced corps or division task force, composed of a judicious mix of combat and support units, is giving way to functionally weighted ad hoc organizations created "just in time." Each force mix has a unique combination of information requirements.

The explicit information requirement will be determined by the nature of a given conflict. The accelerated tempo of deep attack is obvious. Yet, stability operations and operations other than war (OOTW) are also affected. A hallmark of most OOTW is the need for force consistency and impartial response to the actions of all combatants. All such operations involve extensive coordination with governmental agencies, U.S. and foreign, as well as multi-national, non-governmental organizations. The situational awareness information cues must then expand to meet ever-increasing information requirements. The relative merits of the various cues must be assessed and prioritized, with precedence given to those cues that stimulate desired information flows. The practical problem is to vary the information filters in order to accommodate local prioritization of information flows.[9]

Information requirements for situational awareness will further change as new staff organizations are created. The trend is toward staff officers with multi-functional competence (S-1 through -4 combined), grouped in similarly composed teams operating together or separately. Questions arise as to the possibility of compensating for little individual experience or joint team background, or for turbulence within a staff team by the design of information flows. Clearly, there is a need for automated job assistance to compensate in periods when the human component of situational awareness weakens.

Finally, the fog of war (the friction of battle) may be compounded by the introduction of new systems – at least until the operational and training requirements associated with increased situational awareness are understood across units. As the tempo of warfighting increases, small errors become significant more rapidly. Complex operations are more subject to

108 |
     TECHNOLOGY & HUMAN UNDERSTANDING
     FOR WAR IN THE INFORMATION AGE

disruption. Tired staffs are less likely to recognize faulty information filters. Ad hoc joint and combined task forces may miss cues if not fully trained in current situational awareness filters.[10] Locally developed (albeit innovative) filters applied in new and unforeseen situations will only result in genuine confusion. Local operating procedures are a mark of innovation, but they can seriously degrade common situational awareness filters. Recognizing that the fog of war may well thicken, simplicity should prevail until forces have genuinely assimilated situational awareness. This will not take a generation but, perhaps, five to ten years of adjustment at the battalion level.[11]

THE TOUGH PROBLEM OF REQUIREMENTS DEFINITION

Detailed research is necessary to determine the amount and timing of information needed to increase actual combat situational awareness and combat effectiveness. The *Abrams* M1A2 tank offers an excellent example of the research and training challenges involved. The M1A2 vastly increases mounted unit situational awareness. It has all of the capabilities of earlier *Abrams* tank, as well as the Commander's Independent Thermal Viewer (CITV), a multi-sensor independent sight; much improved visibility and protection for the tank commander; and the Intervehicular Information System (IVIS), sharing data with other vehicles. Conservatively, the M1A2 can gather five to ten times more raw real-time battle information than the M1A1.

Yet, the question arises as to what information is truly needed during a particular combat mission. Today a battalion commander's tank has the same capabilities as a company commander, a platoon leader, or even a wingman. Can this level of information be effectively utilized by combatants when they are suddenly engaged from 4,000 meters – a distant speck on thermal imaging gunsights? Perhaps IVIS is merely a distraction to a unit crossing the line of departure in an attack, and should be disengaged. Tactics, techniques, and procedures of this nature need to be reflected in the tank combat tables or tank tactical tables used to train the force. Tactical engagement simulation training should be configured to ensure effective, sustained training. The task analysis needed to achieve this has not yet been completed.[12]

Once detailed mission task analysis is addressed it must include an assessment of how the flow requirements may vary as task loading changes, and how that information should be filtered in view of the average absorption capabilities of a soldier under stress.[13] Filtering implies reduction of information to levels required by leader and staff. Reduction can come from above and below, automatically or manually. One solution to reduction of information flow may be to aggregate as much to winnow; that is, to combine multiple reports of the same situation as well as to eliminate non-essential information. And if digital capability is degraded in information warfare, the requirements will not be to filter information but to supplement gaps. Artificial intelligence-based software may help fill in missing combat information or intelligence.

SOME SOLUTIONS TO HUMAN PERFORMANCE CHALLENGES
A key problem pervading battlefield information sharing and situational awareness is filtering under stress – while remaining sensitive to the battlefield flow of combat. Continuous assessment must be made of the amount of information necessary to win without overloading combatants, causing them to tune out if the default for information is not digital.[14] The tendency to remain digital should be strengthened, so that leaders and units do not revert to traditional analog communication means (voice radio or even arm and hand signals) at the first serious stress to digital capabilities. In reality, both voice and digital com-

munications are still essential. The elimination of voice communication, or its use only in an emergency, will only come
after the mounted force has fully assimilated digital technology, perhaps years from now. Clearly, the information need
varies by battlefield operating system and echelon, as well as a
combatant's level of proficiency in managing information.[15] All
of these considerations need to be incorporated into development. Fortunately, new forms of simulation now permit iterative
trials in case-based training vignettes, both to develop detailed
hardware and software requirements and to provide structured
training to standard.

Filter design is perhaps the toughest development challenge,
since the amount of filtering desired depends as much on the
user's ability to absorb information as it does on an accurate
reflection of actual tactical information needs. If improperly
developed, filters can become a new and unwelcome contributor to the fog of war. Thus, filter design should be guided by a
number of considerations.

First, prepackaged filter levels should be provided to combatants for use according to mission, enemy situation, and the
proficiency of friendly forces in exploiting situational awareness. It is advisable to have several information quantity
"presets." These reflect expert assessment of information needs
for typical units executing high-frequency missions – such as
movement to contact, deliberate attack, and defense in sector –
with a built-in ability to vary content locally. These presets
should be fixed to account for variations in needs as a battle
develops and commanders shift their focus from one level of
organization to another. For example, a company-level center of
mass information may suffice in movement to contact until contact is initiated. Then, platoon resolution may be required to
mass fires.[16] For force standardization, the default could revert
to the preset filter levels. The presets should be vertical as well

as horizontal, particularly addressing the preparation and execution phases in tactical decisionmaking. Two immediately apparent examples are all-source broadcast intelligence capability and the timely integration of close-air support with fire support, particularly for deep-attack missions.

Filter sets must be oriented to doctrine, tactics, techniques, and procedures for staff teams, designed to function even if one or more staff members are missing. The same flexibility will be necessary when and as staff team organizations are modified in Force XXI. Furthermore, rules for aggregating and disaggregating information should be specified. For example, one such rule might be: aggregate when multiple reports of events clog information channels; disaggregate to provide only immediate, tactically-relevant information to small units.

Structured training packages should be created, reflecting our "crawl, walk, run" expectations of user competence in applying filters to common tactical missions. The training could present doctrinely acceptable applications of the presets integrated into battle scenarios, demonstrating one way the information could be used successfully.[17] These scenarios could become the core of staff and small-unit training for successful situational awareness. A "sub-crawl" level training would be useful for liaison officers involved in combined operations with different nations. In such situations the various participants may possess varying levels of capability or competence in handling expanded situational awareness. Alternatively, such training would apply to situations involving high-low mixes of U.S. capability, as is often found in reserve units. Varying information filter levels are also required in combined operations, where different philosophies of battle command among and between armies influence information expectations.[18] Most important, filters need to be built into leader training and evaluation. Competency in use of filters should be expected of leaders, just as physical conditioning or weapons qualification are required today.

Harnessing the skills of Information Age military personnel. There is a pressing need to direct the education and training of white-collar noncommissioned officers and gold-collar officers toward developing tactics, techniques, and procedures associated with the expanded use of information. The first and perhaps most important step should be to simplify TTP. As the tempo accelerates, simplicity should prevail. Once the basics of enhanced situational awareness are mastered, higher levels of complexity may be introduced. At a minimum, tactical decisionmaking processes should focus on command and staff response to changes once orders have been issued.

A division of responsibility for tactical direction of small units among officers may be helpful. This could draw on the increased capabilities of both officers and sergeants to heighten application of improved situational awareness among combatants. One alternative to current policy might be to stipulate that white-collar noncommissioned officers prepare soldiers to fight and drill on basic tactical plays. Gold-collar officers would be expected to multiply the effectiveness of well-rehearsed tactical plays by focusing combat power in time and space, both vertically and horizontally. Training of gold-collar officers would emphasize developing the skills of visualization, somewhat akin to mastering the play of three-dimensional tic-tac-toe. Tactical warfighting examples for mounted forces might include:

- For horizontal, company echelon, white-collar forces: company maneuver right.
- For horizontal, battalion echelon, gold-collar forces: battalion hasty air assault or hasty breach of a complex obstacle.

- For vertical, fire-support BOS, white-collar forces: hasty suppression.
- For vertical, fire-support BOS, gold-collar forces: hasty counterfire, joint suppression of air defense (JSEAD).

This alternative division of tactical responsibility affects neither battle command nor the creation and sustainment of a high-performance organization. The overarching issue is training in the new tasks, conditions, and standards of control enabled by enhanced situational awareness on the tactical battlefield. New combatant capability will improve the probability of effective use of situational awareness under the direction of gold-collar officers and white-collar noncommissioned officers.

Training individuals and staff teams. Combatant competency in handling emerging capabilities can be increased two- to three-fold through effective and efficient training. Information Age warfare relies on leader abilities to acquire, assimilate, and use information under the stress of the battlefield. Given the direct command focus of information flows, sustaining high levels of personal proficiency now demands greater gold-collar involvement. Thus, tactical leaders must also be fully competent in the use of new technologies. For mounted forces, leaders must possess the skills to fight in an AFV; they must master hardware, software, and the tasks, conditions, standards of control for tactical command; they must also have a "know thyself, know thine enemy" approach to battle command. Both improved training and education are critical to attaining this level of competence, particularly in light of frequent software changes designed to take advantage of new doctrine, tactics, techniques, and procedures enabled by distributed information.

On the level of structured staff training, a few considerations are important. The development of information "ranges," which guide performance in tactical situations of varying difficulty, can foster proficiency in the application of information on the ground or in simulation. Fire coordination exercises, movement coordination exercises, and logistics coordination exercises were created to train command and staff to utilize the new capabilities of the *Abrams* and *Bradley* in the 1980s. Similar exercises are now needed to train the new tasks, conditions, and standards (TCS) of situational awareness and control in the 1990s.[19]

The purpose should be not merely to train but rather to over-train so the new capabilities are fully mastered and assimilation of skills is ensured, especially if the default under the stress of battle must remain digital. The creation of staff team "ranger lanes" to develop mastery in TCS of control enabled by new information filters is increasingly important. Similar "lanes" executed repetitively by small units in TES could become the basics of maneuver and fire support training, essentially using improved situational awareness to execute simple TTP much more rapidly.

In the formulation of structured education for commanders, the dominant role of the unit commander in Information Age warfighting must be the guide. As new information capabilities enable highly responsive, near real-time command direction, staff insulation may be reduced as the pace of combat intensifies. The trend is toward developing shared intent among and between commanders, both prior to and during tactical operations.[20] Second- and third-order issue teamwork should be developed among commanders through immersion-based experiential training in tactical scenarios. This is similar to current structured lane training of reserve units, used to prepare units en route to Haiti. This proven training could be modified to educate commanders. The training could be designed to fit a "crawl, walk, run" understanding of common TTP among and between commanders, both vertically and horizontally. The training should reflect likely information filters – both fully effective and degraded – to give commanders experience and practice in new tactical opportunities gained through improved situational awareness. This is education as well as training, since it develops the ability to understand the intent of senior command under which an individual commander operates.

The command challenge, and opportunity, is evident in these comments from the brigade commander in the Army's first "digitized" NTC rotation in 1994:

> ... there is a commander dimension of TTP here which has to do with familiarity of and confidence in equipment as well as [the soldier's] ability to use them. Without this certain knowledge, then one of the major benefits of enhanced situational awareness, namely a widely-shared common view of the battlefield, probably won't be advantaged by the commander.... Close in, short sword area, commander and staff must know that they have a certain common view of the battlefield up and down and sideways. Knowledge should be almost intuitive.[21]

There is another, less direct, benefit from the application of new training approaches to preparation of commanders. These same leaders are responsible for peacetime administration. Therefore, it is essential that new, more effective and efficient leader preparation be provided to preserve the traditional chain-of-command programs, despite the significant new education and training requirements placed on leadership.

Clearly, the human challenges of visualizing complex operations in an extended battlespace are formidable. The general trend of development to date has often been to encourage unrestrained technological development, implicitly assuming that combatants would be prepared to employ whatever became available. Users would rise to the challenge imposed by the need to maximize the advantages offered by new capabilities. The truth has more often been the degradation of new capability to the lowest common denominator of existing practice.

That need not be the case. Thoughtful development of information filters can ensure assimilation by the human combatant, provided battlefield responsibilities are varied to reflect both new tactical information demands and new personnel capabilities among gold- and white-collar combatants. Then, the capabilities generated by new technologies will be accompanied by a human ability to apply them to the fullest, even under stress in enlarged battle areas.

The task of creating and advantaging situational awareness is not impossible; most of the necessary tools are in place, although there are still many unknowns. Yet, a few conclusions seem certain:

- Combatants must be trained for "digital default" with both fully effective and degraded filters and networks.
- Experienced gold collar- and white-collar officers are essential to advantage potential.
- Frequent, highly focused and structured training is required for commanders, staffs, and small units.

Above all, it is imperative to recognize the extent to which change and adaptation are continuous and progressive. Today, the primary challenge, in addition to those listed above, is to extend capabilities to joint and combined operations. These challenges reflect new global realities and are indicative of the changing nature of warfare in the emerging Information Age.

ENDNOTES

1. Mark Herman, "Modeling the Revolution in Military Affairs" in Director, Net Assessment, Office of the Secretary of Defense, "Memo: Modeling and Simulation and the Revolution in Military Affairs," 5 September 1995, p.4.

2. U.S. Army, Field Manual 100-5, *Operations,* 14 June 1993. This keystone document gives the following definition of battle command: "The art of battle decisionmaking, leading, and motivating soldiers and their organizations into action to accomplish missions. Includes visualizing current state and future state, then formulating concepts of operations to get from one to the other at least cost...." Glossary p. 1.

3. One can only suspect how the unanticipated loss of Ultra, the intelligence source used to intercept and decode enemy ciphers, could have influenced operations at all echelons in World War II.

4. V Corps, "V Corps FY96 Annual Training Guidance," 10 September 1995, p. 3.

5. Frederic J. Brown, *Army in Transition II: Landpower in the Information Age* (McLean, Va.: Brassey's, 1993), p.110.

6. U.S. Army Europe (USAREUR), "Command Policy Letter 1: Command Training Guidance," 10 April 1995, p. 2.

7. Ibid., p. 2.

8. U.S. Army Training and Doctrine Command (TRADOC), Pamphlet 525-5, *Force XXI Operations: A Concept for the Evolution of Full-Dimensional Operations for the Strategic Army of the Early Twenty First Century* (1 August 1994). See particularly Chapter 3, "Force XXI Operations," pp. 3–3 to 3–16.

9. Combat Training Centers should help in defining requirements. Both the Combined Mechanized Training Center (MTC) and the Joint Readiness Training Center (JRTC) transition routinely from mid-intensity conflict to peacekeeping operations or peace enforcing operations. Observer Controller's observation and instrumentation systems documentation could be drawn upon to document changing filter requirements as missions vary.

10. Local command software innovation, however commendable, has greatly complicated the fielding of intelligence information systems (for example, All Source Assessment System).

11. Estimate based in part on division restructuring (DRS) to Division 86 with the *Abrams* tank and the *Bradley* armored fighting vehicle (AFV) in the 1980s.

12. This is not a trivial development problem. 3rd Squadron 8th Cavalry, 1st Cavalry Division is now receiving production M1A2s, and is learning about situational awareness. Appliques now come for TFXXI – an outstanding technological achievement presently unconstrained by human limitations.

13. This has been done for airframes. For the Army, this was the issue of one or two pilots for the *Comanche* helicopter. This work has not been done for armored field vehicles (*Abrams* tanks, *Bradley* infantry fighting vehicles, etc.).

14. The user must have absolute confidence that the battlefield rewards of passing digitized information are so great that system degradation will be "worked around" rather than ignored or turned off. Since commanders interface directly with screens, they must be at near-mastery levels of proficiency. For a good summary of issues from Desert Hammer VI, see Captain Ronald K. Kollhof, "Digitization Will Impact Many Areas of Training," *Armor,* (October 1995), pp. 41–43.

15. Comparable problems exist for fighter aircraft in a multi-ship dogfight. From discussion with General Merrill McPeak, Office of the Secretary of Defense, at Net Assessment Symposium, U.S. Naval Academy, 11 November 1991.

16. This insight was provided by Colonel Michael Deegan via electronic mail, "Comments on Info Age Conference Paper," 30 October 1995. Col. Deegan was the brigade commander in NTC Rotation 94-07 Desert Hammer.

17. The execution of tactical operations should be simplified as increased information becomes available. Perhaps development of simple "plays" executed at greatly increased tempos as commanders, staffs, and units become accustomed to improved situational awareness. Demonstrations in TES could provide useful training support.

18. For a useful discussion of national variations in battle command philosophy see David Alberts and Richard Hayes, *Command Arrangements for Peace Operations* (Washington, D.C.: Institute for National Security Studies, National Defense University, May 1995), particularly "Alternative Command Arrangement Systems," pp. 82ff.

19. New training development and support enabled by distributed tactical engagement simulation should present many more opportunities, both within the institutional training base and among units. Classroom XXI and distributed learning centers illustrate the path to new, case-based, interactive immersion learning that can be distributed among multiple participants.

20. For an excellent discussion of the concepts of mission command, particularly the importance of mutual understanding, trust, and teamwork, see Command and General Staff College (CGSC), Student Text 22-102: Command (Second Edition), January, 1995. See particularly Chapter 2, "The Foundations of Command."
21. Colonel Michael Deegan, "Comments On Info Age Conference Paper," e-mail, 30 October 1995.

chapter seven

Transition into the Information Age: Opportunities, Lessons Learned, and Challenges

John R. Wood

INFORMATION AGE TECHNOLOGIES ARE CHANGING the way the United States Army fights. Although the full impact of emerging information resources on weapons delivery remains unclear, one thing is certain: new technologies have not merely quickened the pace of the old business of warfighting. They add new dimensions, new requirements, and new challenges.

The 3rd Infantry Division (Mechanized) Artillery at Fort Stewart – the brigade-size artillery component of the 3rd Division – is one of the first units in the Army to be fully equipped with the weapons, communications systems, and support structure characteristic of the Information Age. From automated, digital fire-control systems to single-channel ground and airborne radio systems (SINCGARS) and *Paladin* howitzers, the hardware and software of the twenty-first century are in the hands of today's soldiers. The implications and required changes to doctrine, tactics, techniques, and procedures are just now becoming evident after four extended training exercises at the National Training Center, deployment to Kuwait and Egypt, and routine garrison training.

Revolutionary improvements in fire support present perplexing problems in the command and control of fires. Enthusiastic leaders and soldiers find few models and even less doctrine to guide their redesign of warfighting skills. Still, the excitement on the gunline and in the fire-support teams is high and infectious. The potential to leap forward in terms of lethality and mobility on the battlefield is glimpsed in every training exercise, and the skilled soldiers in today's Army sense that the future of fire support is very close at hand.

As division artillery soldiers employ new systems, discovering increased lethality and enhanced effectiveness, they find truth in the assessment of General Gordon R. Sullivan, former Army Chief of Staff, on the impact of Information Age technology on warfare: "What is new is the realization of the power we can gain by integrating those digital systems throughout the force. Integration allows us to execute with true precision to mass effects, not forces."[1] This integration of new systems across the 3rd Division Artillery is apparent in every operation undertaken. Examples of increased effectiveness, important new lessons learned, and difficult new challenges arise in every action. This chapter addresses the implications of new Information Age technology on soldiers, operations, and tactics. Clearly, this is not a complete catalog of effects across all battlefield operating systems; it relates only the experiences of field artillery soldiers within the 3rd Division Artillery. Additionally, this assessment is best characterized as a glimpse of the future battlefield, since not all the players or systems are in place.

Discussion of opportunities, lessons learned, and challenges in the integration and application of new technologies focuses on three areas: doctrine, training, and leader development. The observations presented here reflect how leaders and soldiers of the 3rd Division react to the new equipment and capabilities now in their hands. For many, the starting point is a Cold War mindset, reinforced by years of training on equipment designed to respond to strict hierarchical command and control. But if old operating procedures were static, the concepts they were built upon are not. Rather, today's soldiers are rapidly embracing new technologies, and accepting the changing concepts and doctrines that accompany such technologies.

A Catalog of New Systems

The most significant development in field artillery is the M109A6 *Paladin* howitzer. This new howitzer, which exemplifies the use of Information Age weaponry for fire support, arrives in a deceptively familiar package. The M109 howitzer was first fielded in the 1960s, and two generations of field artillery soldiers have spent careers learning to operate this system. But the M109A6 is no mere upgrade of an old friend.

The *Paladin* howitzer is equipped with communication, fire control, and other capabilities that enable it to operate independently, yet achieve massed fires. No longer is it necessary to mass weapons on a "line of metal." Instead, the effects of massed fires can be achieved from howitzers dispersed for survivability or other operational needs. The SINCGARS radios link each howitzer to digital fire orders that permit the calculation of platform-specific firing data by the onboard Automatic Fire Control System (AFCS). The AFCS automatically compensates for numerous variables that once occupied soldiers in fire direction centers and behind gun sights. Speed and accuracy of fire is dramatically improved. The *Paladin* can stop, lay, and shoot in well under seventy-five seconds. Further, it can displace after firing in under thirty seconds. No soldier exits the howitzer. The self-location and fire-control features on board assure true independence on the battlefield. The gun chief, who once fought from within a battery or platoon position, now operates within an armored system on a maneuver battlefield. The tempo of combat has accelerated because the *Paladin* is so seldom out of action. In fact, given the right information, support, and leadership, this howitzer can be continually mission ready.

Paired with the howitzer is the M992A1 Field Artillery Ammunition Support Vehicle (FAASV). This vehicle is also equipped with the SINCGARS radio, which permits decentralized operation. Its storage racks can hold the full range of ammunition currently in inventory or planned for production for the M109A6 howitzer. The capability of the *Paladin* to shoot the full family of present and future ammunition, as well as its inherent survivability, extended range, and immediate readiness to fire, will result in greatly increased ammunition consumption. The FAASV is critical to maintaining this flow.

Equally essential is the Palletized Load System (PLS) that is replacing the division artillery's older complement of ammunition-carrying vehicles. While similar to the High Mobility Medium Equipment Transport it replaced, this new truck transports cargo packaged aboard movable pallets that quickly download using the vehicle's own lift systems. Ammunition can now be easily moved and delivered at multiple locations by reduced ammunition teams. This capability is essential to *Paladin* operations, given its speed and mobility. Like all other newly fielded systems, the PLS truck comes equipped with a SINCGARS radio. A digital location and reporting system has been tested on these trucks and will permit the driver to self locate and interface with automated logistics tracking systems soon to be fielded.

The Initial Fire Support Automation System (IFSAS) replaces the TACFIRE system in the *Paladin* howitzer battery and throughout all other division artillery fire-control and fire-support elements. The heart of this system is the Lightweight Computer Unit (LCU), a 386K RAM, menu-oriented computer station. Easily reconfigured or updated and simple to use, this TACFIRE replacement frees the field artillery from heavy, slow automation that demanded robust mechanical and logistical support. Now, automation is virtually portable. The IFSAS nets with the *Paladin*'s Automatic Fire Control System – and equally important, with many of the newest intelligence collection and delivery systems now being fielded. This digital device opens the door to the horizontal integration of fire support with other battlefield operating systems on the Information Age battlefield.

Another digital device enabling horizontal integration is the Enhanced Position Location Reporting System (EPLRS). All command and control centers in the division artillery, as well as selected high value systems (such as Q37 *Firefinder* radars), are presently equipped with components of EPLRS. The location of all other subscribers in the division is immediately available to users. Battlefield awareness is significantly improved. Reporting channels are strengthened by EPLRS. The number of system transmitters in the division will soon double, and greater visibility of systems – down to the *Paladin* howitzer – is planned.

The routine use of one system by artillery soldiers – the AN/PSN-11 Precise Lightweight GPS Receiver (PLGR) – makes it easy to overlook. This global positioning satellite receiver is fielded down to the platoon level and its broad presence is already well accepted. Even so, the impact of this instrument on fire support is hard to overstate. At the touch of a button, location is determined within required tolerance for the delivery of indirect fire. The speed and tempo of fire support was long dependent on the extension of survey coordinates and direction in an arduous process. The *Paladin* howitzer equipped with the PLGR can now achieve what platoons of survey soldiers once spent days accomplishing. More than any other material upgrade, this device released fire support to fight on the new Information Age battlefield.

This brief catalog of the most significant additions to the capabilities of the 3rd Division Artillery focuses on the equipment presently in the hands of soldiers. Daily, such new systems as the All Source Analysis System (ASAS), *Guardrail* Common Sensor (GRCS), Ground Station Module (GSM), and Commander's Tactical Terminal (CTT) increase the flow of information reaching artillery shooters. Most if not all of this equipment arrives preceded by a new equipment team that teaches soldiers the technical aspects of the hardware and software. Yet, beyond on-site orientation, the insertion of new technologies must be supported by a foundation of integrated doctrine, training, and leader development.

CHANGING DOCTRINE

Doctrine lies at the professional heart of our Army. Changes in the nature of war and assessments of the means to fight it are continually evaluated through the lens of the central Army doctrinal publication, Field Manual (FM) 100-5: *Operations*. The fundamental tenets of Army doctrine – agility, synchronization, initiative, depth, and versatility – characterize successful operations. But as the strategic environment changes, doctrine cannot be perceived as merely prescriptive. Rather, it must be descriptive, illuminating the principles that should guide the thinking of adaptive leaders as they face the evolution of battlefield threats, missions, and warfighting capabilities. Doctrine is both the foundation and framework for thinking about the Army, and the driving force in thinking about how to change to meet future needs.

Changing tactics, techniques, and procedures, while remaining true to basic doctrine, stands as the most important challenge of our recent experience with Information Age technology and weapons. Fundamentally, doctrine describes how we fight. The "we" here refers to multiple battlefield operating systems, fighting on a joint and combined battlefield where each operating system is equipped with a variety of new and old equipment and, perhaps more importantly, a mix of new and old doctrine. As General Franks stated while commanding the U.S. Army's Training and Doctrine Command (TRADOC), "Synthesizing new developments is the real genius.... It is not the new technology which matters, but the synthesis of disparate parts – some old, some new – into a new concept for the battlefield."[2]

For the field artillery fighter of the 3rd Division, there are now added capabilities in weapons and equipment that must be integrated with other battlefield operating systems in order to achieve the desired increase in effectiveness and lethality. The doctrine that remains to be written is one that can describe the integration, both horizontal and vertical, of new fire-support capabilities with other evolving or fielded Information Age hardware and software. This task is most challenging within three areas referred to in Field Manual 100–5: battle command, battlespace, and deep and simultaneous attack.

Battle command for field artillery leaders – from colonel to sergeant – is now far less regimented and centralized, and much more dynamic. In the recent past, information available only at the division artillery and battalion level prescribed the actions of subordinate units. Assigned firing positions, target sets, fire plans, and organization dictated the fire-support operation. Troop leading procedures, such as operation plans and orders, were not stressed since actions were expected to proceed sequentially from one battle phase or firing position to the next in accordance with well-practiced movement techniques. The tempo of operations was set by periodic intelligence updates and the necessity to occupy battery or platoon positions, while establishing firing capability through a series of labor-intensive steps. Control was exercised by strict movement directives and the close supervision of all aspects of operations within a position area.

Today, there is far more information available to help the artillery commander visualize and direct action and, with the enhanced capabilities of the *Paladin* and battlefield intelligence systems, far more flexibility to achieve fire-support tasks. An individual howitzer, no matter where it sits on the battlefield, can mass fires with all other howitzers on a target. Tactics, techniques, and procedures now center on adapting to battlefield conditions, maintaining battlefield awareness, and exploiting opportunities. Control is exercised less by set movement procedures and more by publication of guidelines that free subordinates to adapt and alter procedures in order to achieve end goals. *Paladin* howitzers move along an axis, remain short of phase lines, or remain within or close to moving elements.

The central problem for the commander with all this enhanced capability and flexibility is how best to communicate decisions and assure compliance. Information Age technology has increased the number of moving parts within the fire-support system. It is now essential that leaders communicate the intent of maneuver operations and fire-support tasks to subordinates in a regular, clear manner to assure the accelerated tempo of operations now possible. Control, however, cannot be simply exercised by faith in the good efforts of subordinates. Reporting procedures, status checks, and performance measures must all feed information to the commander, who can then make sound tactical judgments. Communication networks must adapt to permit command from disparate locations on the battlefield. Given all the new systems, reporting channels, and tactics, this synthesis of increased information challenges even the best commanders.

As defined in Field Manual 100-5, battlespace is "a physical volume that expands or contracts in relation to the ability to acquire and engage an enemy."[3] Clearly, as Information Age technology increases field artillery's ability to find and kill the enemy, we must rethink our conventional concepts of battlespace. No longer can we think of battlespace as simply the area within the range of artillery. Information sources now offer intelligence that permits better visualization of a three-dimensional battlespace within which we must synchronize far more capable acquisition and weapon systems.

At the division artillery level, the task has always been to integrate fire-support systems and synchronize the attack of key targets to support the commander's intent. Now, better links to corps- and echelons above corps-level intelligence permit better deep and simultaneous attack of targets using lethal and non-lethal fire-support means. One challenge is to strengthen those links and develop procedures to shorten sensor-to-shooter timelines. Another challenge is to track and control the multiple systems within the division's battlespace in order to assure their security against enemy action or potential fratricide.

At the battalion level, battlespace has changed the most. The mobility and flexibility of the *Paladin* howitzer presents the commander with a number of challenges. Essentially, the battalion commander must integrate more moving parts into the brigade battlespace while ensuring continuity of fire support and security of forces. The good news is that the commander is less concerned about responding to a counterfire threat due to the ability of the *Paladin* to "shoot and scoot." Also, the *Paladin* can stop and shoot from virtually any location. The problem is that this movement, so essential to the survivability of the force, occurs most often without specific direction from a higher commander. Gun chiefs react to standing movement guidance or local intelligence. Fire-support positioning is a three-dimensional art. Not only must units be positioned on defensible ground, but they must also be able to range critical targets and meet certain trajectory requirements. The battalion commander, typically occupied with key fire-support coordination duties, must somehow direct positioning within the brigade battlespace that assures security and mission capability.

At the battery and platoon level, battlespace has expanded outside the old, familiar position area. In order to integrate moving *Paladin* pairs within the battlespace of surrounding maneuver units, more reconnaissance and coordination is necessary. Battlefield awareness must reach the gun-chief level. Obstacles, routes, coordination points and similar considerations must all be identified and plans must be disseminated to howitzer level. Formerly, movement techniques sufficed to move tightly controlled convoys sequentially along specified routes well behind maneuver units. Now, new maneuver techniques are necessary to integrate *Paladin* pairs into the battlespace of maneuver forces. The information requirements at the level of the howitzer chief have dramatically increased. The gun chief maneuvering a howitzer from position to position now works within a specific battlespace. There may be fewer systems to integrate, but a gun chief's success at effectively using this limited battlespace is no less important.

The goal of deep and simultaneous attack of targets is to stun and then rapidly defeat the enemy. The *Paladin*-equipped unit can sustain the attack of targets throughout an extended brigade battlespace due to the howitzer's increased range, agile fire control, flexible sustainment base, and ability to follow maneuver closely. Coupled with the increased number of Combat Observation Lasing Teams (COLTs) at the brigade level, improved command and control, and new electronic intelligence means, the *Paladin* battalion is able to respond more quickly and deeply against targets formerly thought to be in the division's deep battlespace. Artillery groups, air defense targets, high-payoff intelligence targets, and headquarters may all fall in range of direct-support artillery. The challenge is to synchronize the attack of targets within the total division battlespace using the organic sensors and shooters of the division, reinforced by those within the brigade. Where the capabilities of division sensors is inadequate to produce target-level intelligence for shooters, new links to corps or higher intelligence sources must be built. The doctrine must account for deep and simultaneous attack of targets without the false demarcations of battlespace that were designed to support old system capabilities. The ability to mass effects must not be fettered by doctrine that fails to acknowledge the versatility and adaptability of Information Age technology.

TRAINING TECHNIQUES FOR A NEW ERA OF COMBAT
The payoff of the Information Age is delivered by soldiers skilled in the use of Information Age technology to integrate systems and synchronize attack of high-payoff targets. The central training task facing division artillery is easy to state, but difficult and expensive to execute: Teach soldiers and their leaders to use information effectively, and to achieve lethal

decentralized fire support that increases effects against the enemy.

The individual and collective skills necessary to accomplish this task are diverse. Some have already been mastered, based on experiences with similar fire support, communication, or intelligence systems. Others are brand new, stemming from the enhanced capabilities of new equipment. Still others are simply old skills, used in new ways as a result of changing tactics, techniques, and procedures. Finally, some additional skills are generated by the increased responsibilities inherent in decentralized operations.

The most fundamental training task is the development and sustainment of the technical skills that permit the soldier to operate and maintain the new equipment. This is more problematic than it first appears. The new equipment training that precedes fielding accomplishes this task well. But, subsequent reassignment of trained soldiers rapidly degrades the status of training. New soldiers coming into units most often lack previous experience or training on new systems. Therefore, it is essential to develop a skills-assessment process and remedial training program at the unit level. Since Information Age technology will undoubtedly evolve at the speed of software development rather than just hardware replacement, the ability to train and retrain must reach beyond TRADOC to all levels.

While individual technical training is the most fundamental training task, it is not the most essential. The ability to use multiple sources of information, integrate systems, and synchronize the attack of targets demands more than merely proficient equipment operators. Collective training must be redesigned to stress repetitive, multi-echelon exercises that build the necessary integration and synchronization skills among both soldiers and leaders.

This does not simply mean more frequent training. It is a requirement to develop and execute more demanding multi-echelon training at division level and below. Synergy must be created in the training environment to illustrate to participants the success or failure of their efforts. Horizontal and vertical integration of information is both the most essential and the most difficult aspect of this new operational environment. Information that once only existed in intelligence, fire support, or maneuver channels is now available to a much broader set of battlefield users. Without comprehending the tactical demand for information, the supply of information is poorly understood and used. Given the number of new systems and improved capabilities, training must develop the skill of knowing the right question to ask, where and when to ask it, and how to use the answer.

An example of training conducted by the 3rd Infantry Division Artillery helps to illustrate the importance of integrated design. Realizing that the division's battlespace contained a range of new communication, intelligence, and weapons systems, the division artillery designed a training exercise that forced horizontal and vertical integration of information across multiple echelons in order to attack diverse targets. Called the Interdiction and Counterfire Exercise (ICE), this exercise brought together corps, division, and brigade systems to practice the "decide, detect, deliver, assess" methodology used to execute the division's deep attack. While this was the specific training objective, the broader operational objective was to stimulate new thinking by staffs and commanders on how to use information sources to attack more targets.

The exercise architecture brought numerous players together to fight iterative battles within the division's battlespace. Assets from the 18th Airborne Corps such as the *Guardrail* (common sensor) and the target-processing section from 18th Field

Artillery brigade were assembled with division intelligence elements and division artillery targeting and firing elements. Multiple intelligence channels – such as the Commander's Tactical Terminal and the Interim Ground Station Monitor – linked the division's Analysis Control Element and corps' sensors to the division artillery Tactical Operations Center (TOC). The aviation brigade TOC was also present to plan and execute aviation attacks against actual moving target sets. All actions were controlled with a master event list. Where possible, live artillery was used on targets in the impact area. To lessen communications challenges, all headquarters were co-located. Leaders and soldiers were forced to assimilate large amounts of conflicting, complementary, or redundant real-time information, culling only that which was relevant to current and future operations.

The result was predictable. Initially, information overwhelmed the system. The challenge of firing live rounds based on effective, efficient analysis of real-time intelligence proved more difficult than previous computer simulations suggested. But, because the exercise design permitted incremental, repetitive training, it was not long before new techniques and procedures evolved to use information more productively. Missions were repeated after pausing to assess and adjust procedures.

In this exercise, soldiers and leaders practiced new technical skills, cognitive tasks, and coordination functions. They began to understand the impact of better, more effectively processed information on the tempo of operations, battlefield calculus, and the focus of efforts. However, the example offered here need not be replicated exactly. The same effects can be achieved using other combinations of players, simulations, or scripted events to generate the stimulation, coordination, friction, and information flow that together can enable soldiers and leaders to build confidence in their ability to synthesize and use the streams of information now available. The addition of joint and combined information sources would only improve training. Ultimately, however, the ability to deliver effective fires is best tested with real soldiers firing against real targets. Linking the processing of information to the killing of targets is essential.

Integrated, multi-echelon training is equally valuable below the division level. The direct support field artillery battalions of the 3rd Division found that employment of multiple new systems within the brigade battlespace at the National Training Center tested their abilities to integrate and synchronize new information and weapon capabilities. Old tactics, techniques, and procedures failed to exploit the potential of both the systems or the soldiers manning those systems. A number of lessons surfaced based on these integrated, multi-echelon training experiences.

First, field artillery movement techniques designed to meet old requirements to mass weapons failed to provide the needed freedom to commanders, who were now concentrating on massing weapon effects. Given *Paladin*'s capabilities, the sequential movement of massed weapons is no longer necessary. New maneuver techniques were adopted to free howitzer section chiefs to employ the terrain better as they maneuvered in much closer proximity to tanks and infantry fighting vehicles.

Next, units discovered that information previously designed for battery commanders was now equally necessary at platoon and section levels. Information is power only if soldiers know what to do with it. Troop-leading procedures were quickly designed to permit low-level leaders to pursue their commander's intent with information that was readily available on computer screens.

Decentralized execution of intent, while desirable, created its own problems. Graphical control measures posted on maps to guide the actions of maneuver forces were not well understood by howitzer chiefs, operating as semi-autonomous firing units. Commanders above them had always guided their movement. New graphical control measures were developed to answer the specific demands of indirect fire systems on this far more integrated battlefield.

While the increased maneuver and firing capabilities of the *Paladin* assured better survivability and availability of fire support, it was apparent that the eyes of artillery – its observers – lacked similar enhancements to their capabilities. The information they could pass to shooters was still dependent on older, less-sophisticated equipment and somewhat outmoded target-processing channels. If the focus was to concentrate the effects of weapons, it was clear that the target itself, and its importance to the overall fight, were more important than what system killed it. Yet, boundaries, organization for combat, and communication procedures still dictated attack procedures. New procedures to focus killing fires on the targets most critical to division success await development, along with better procedures to direct information to key decisionmakers when such targets appear. Development of such procedures is best accomplished in integrated, multi-echelon training.

ENHANCED LEADERSHIP DEVELOPMENT

While closely tied to the training issue, leader development for the Information Age warrants some specific attention. After all, it is leaders who use information to make the most critical decisions. The whole design of Information Age systems is to improve delivery of critical information to leaders in order to facilitate decisionmaking. Yet, the development of leadership equipped to capitalize on emerging technologies still poses the greatest training challenge.

To understand this point, consider a platoon sergeant in a *Paladin* battery of division artillery. At this level, a noncommissioned officer (NCO) typically has seventeen years in service, most of which were spent on the M109A3 howitzer in various assignments in Europe and the United States. Advanced NCO training at Fort Sill would have trained the NCO to serve in a conventional howitzer battery, using tactics and techniques best suited for older equipment without Information Age technology. Most likely the platoon sergeant oversaw the fielding of multiple new systems over several months and witnessed the rapid introduction of new operational concepts. The NCO would have attended a two week *Paladin* course at Ft. Stewart but, now that the howitzers are fielded, would seldom directly supervise semi-independent gun sections operating from widely dispersed positions.

Or, consider the gun chief who now commands the *Paladin* howitzer. Technically skilled in the use of the new system, the gun chief has virtually no experience operating this weapon on an integrated maneuver battlefield. The basic NCO course would have prepared the gun chief to operate as part of a platoon that was led from position to position on the battlefield by platoon leadership. While map reading and troop leading procedures were important, the officer depended on higher-level leaders to meet these demands. Most likely, the battery and platoon leadership previously addressed all tactical needs as the gun chief operated the howitzer from within battery and platoon positions. Now, operating semi-independently, the gun chief must supervise a crew as they accomplish new tasks – such as nuclear, chemical, and biological operations, air defense, and position defense – formerly handled by special teams within the battery.

Finally, consider the *Paladin* platoon leader. This officer probably saw little Information Age technology in the basic course. Like other leaders in the division artillery, the *Paladin* leader would have attended a special leadership course. Yet, typically commanding from a static position adjacent to the platoon operations center, the *Paladin* platoon leader spends virtually no time operating inside the howitzer. The command vehicle possesses no digital interface with the howitzer or other digital information sources on the battlefield. Simply stated, the command and control capabilities and the experience of a *Paladin* platoon leader do not match the capabilities of the systems in the command.

Ironically, perhaps, the individual most at ease in this setting is the young enlisted soldier, familiar only with the *Paladin* system. Those above the enlisted soldier are in various stages of adjustment and re-education. By contrast, the enlisted soldier is learning to use and apply Information Age technology every day and is very comfortable with the equipment.

The varying levels of experience and training described here are natural, given the magnitude of change introduced in such a short period of time. They are not meant to imply inability or unwillingness among leaders to face these challenges. On the contrary, division artillery leaders are excited by the potential transition and its concomitant glimpses of dramatic improvements in warfighting capabilities. Nonetheless, it is important to understand the current state of affairs as leader development programs are designed.

The central task is to assess the leadership skills necessary to handle the new and, no doubt, expanded responsibilities of leaders at every level. This assessment is well underway in division artillery. Armed with more information and charged with the responsibility to operate as part of an integrated effort, officers and NCOs must learn to view the battlefield with broader scope and deeper perspective. Army doctrine captures the expanding vision of the battlefield in the term "battle command." This term describes a commander's battlefield ability to assimilate information and make timely decisions that lead a unit to victory. Battle command encompasses a commander's ability to pursue the fundamental tenets of Army doctrine and demonstrate the leadership qualities of flexibility, judgment, intuition, and empathy. Battle command is recognized as more art than science. It is based on experience, intuition, and knowledge.[4]

For the leaders of division artillery, now equipped with Information Age systems, battle command has fundamentally changed. Their past experiences and technical knowledge no longer suffice to meet evolving battle command requirements. While he was Army Chief of Staff, General Sullivan posed the leader development challenge clearly:

> Our leader development program will shift to accommodate the new conceptual, technical, and organizational skills required of Information Age officers and noncommissioned officers. Using more information, coming faster; making decisions at a faster rate; executing over increasing distances in decreasing time and under more diverse conditions; orchestrating the maneuver and fire systems of all services; and creating and maintaining cohesion among more dispersed units – all under the watchful eye of near-instantaneous media coverage, leaders of America's Information Age Army will "think differently" than those of the Industrial Age. At first, this difference will be only one of degree. As the Information Age matures, however, the difference will be one of kind.[5]

Programs are underway in division artillery to allow leaders to "think differently," to visualize current and future operations, to assimilate more information, and, ultimately, to exercise battle command. Redesign of the *Paladin* command course, integration of more diverse systems in multi-echelon training, and development of expanded troop leading procedures all are steps in this direction. Ongoing reviews of tactics and techniques as well as battle drills and standard operating procedures require leaders to rethink their roles and responsibilities and incorporate new approaches in operations. Maneuver exercises that require more detailed reconnaissance, different movement techniques, and better coordination with external elements develop leaders with better battlefield awareness. And, of course, reviews conducted after training exercises prompt learning and enhance leadership development.

There is no shortage of energy as leaders in division artillery revise the way they deliver fire support using Information Age technology. The added responsibilities are welcomed, and innovations occur daily. Training is no longer centered only on what to do; the more relevant question asked by leaders is who else to do it with. The art of battle command for leaders uses new tools, new partners, and new methods. Practice and experience in multi-echelon exercises promises to build the skills necessary to fight and win in the Information Age.

With new doctrine that recognizes the enhanced capabilities of Information Age forces, training that reinforces new technical skills and integration tasks, and leader development programs that develop the art of battle command, the promises of the Information Age will, no doubt, be realized. The 3rd Division Artillery is actively engaged in assessment, innovation, and execution. At present, there are more questions than answers. But increases in the ability to fire more deeply, accurately, and effectively – along with expanded tactical options and leadership opportunities – make this an exciting time for soldiers on the cutting edge of the Army's application of Information Age technologies.

ENDNOTES

1. General Gordon R. Sullivan, "A Vision for the Future," *Military Review* (May-June 1995), p. 10.

2. General Frederick M. Franks, Jr., "Army Doctrine and the New Strategic Environment," in Robert L. Pfaltzgraff, Jr., and Richard H. Shultz, Jr., eds., *Ethnic Conflict and Regional Stability: Implications for U.S. Policy and Army Roles and Missions* (Carlisle Barracks, PA: Strategic Studies Institute, U.S. Army War College, 1993), p. 277.

3. Headquarters, Department of the Army, Field Manual 100–5: *Operations* (June 1993), p. 6–12.

4. Field Manual 100–5, pp. 2–14, 15.

5. General Gordon R. Sullivan and Colonel James M. Dubik, *War in the Information Age* (Carlisle Barracks, PA: Strategic Studies Institute, U.S. Army War College, 6 June 1994), p. 61.

chapter eight

Exploiting Battlespace Transparency: Operating Inside an Opponent's Decision Cycle

John W. McDonald

THIS PAPER ADDRESSES DECISION-CYCLE THEORY, and the advantages that accrue from operating inside an opponent's decision cycle. It focuses on the application of the theory to the twenty-first century battlespace – where potential opponents may or may not have visualization capabilities – and methods for capitalizing on battlefield transparency in a variety of conflict settings. Accordingly, this essay will first elaborate decision-cycle theory, discussing advantages as well as challenges. The essay will then examine the implications of transparency for decision-cycle dominance and the means to exploit the decision-cycle advantage.

Decision-cycle theory has emerged within the past forty years to explain increased combat survivability through the application of combat experience to the education and training of forces. The theory centers on activities that occur within defined loops termed "observe-orient-decide-act" (OODA), and relates to the speed with which participants transition from each phase of the loop and reset for the next action. The critical element is time. The actor who completes the loop most quickly, operating "inside the opponent's decision cycle," generally wins. Within the loop, the final action depends upon collection and assessment of information at the start of the loop (observe) and preparations to act based on that information (orient). The observe function can occur either visually or as the result of information collected from multiple sensors. At the individual level, where study of the phenomenon began, the observe function results from methods of scanning and acquiring potential targets. At higher levels, to which the theory has been extrapolated, all source analysis becomes essential to "visualizing" the battlespace. To orient implies the ability

FIGURE 1: *Oberve-Orient-Decide-Act*

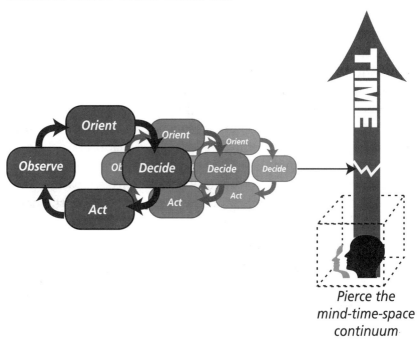

Pierce the
mind-time-space
continuum

quickly to focus effort – or forces – on potential targets, and to set the conditions for success. The decide function implies a "man-in-the-loop," although more recent studies indicate an increasing requirement to make decisions autonomously in order to react to extraordinarily short response threats, such as the critical mobile target problem. These decisions would then be executed on the basis of observing defined parameters, alerting systems or forces automatically, comparing observations with established criteria, and deciding and acting based on that match. As each cycle or loop is carried to completion, a new loop begins. In some cases, the individual or unit may reconstitute; in others, particularly at lower levels, they may immediately restart the cycle.

In theory, success within the loop depends on maintaining a variety of responses that can be applied rapidly. This demands harmonization of activities. At the individual level, it calls for user-friendly systems and a level of training and experience that allow both physical and intuitive response to perceptions of threat. At unit levels, it necessitates organization, procedures, and systems that allow multiple individuals to see the same picture, alert commands, provide recommendations for decision, and execute a wide range of both prepared and ad hoc responses flexibly. To win, forces must exploit initiative. Friendly forces cannot remain passive and succeed. Even if the enemy acts first, speed in moving through the decision cycle will theoretically permit friendly forces to respond inside an opponent's decision cycle.

While the importance of speed is implicitly understood in the act phase, the amount of time expended in each segment of the loop is critical to completing one loop and rapidly starting another. For example, if during the observe phase, the quantity and accuracy of information is challenged, time spent confirming that information, without accomplishing parallel actions to alert the force, may slow reaction time and allow the opponent a decision-cycle advantage. Similarly, forces unprepared to react in the orient stage may lose time between the observe and decide phases, and thus may not achieve dominance.

A critical factor in decision-cycle theory lies in the contention that learning occurs within each loop, improving the decision process and accelerating responses over time. This explains the high survival rate of individuals who have successfully completed a number of combat missions. For aviators, survival generally increases logarithmically, topping 95 percent after ten missions. Consequently, learning in peacetime is critical to success in war. Enhanced survivability following a small number of combat missions has driven the development of training exercises, while greatly increasing the Army's emphasis on combat training centers and simulators to replicate initial battle contact.

TRANSFORMATION OF DECISION-CYCLE THEORY:
FROM THE ANCIENTS TO MODERN WARFARE

Decision-cycle theory has evolved principally from John Boyd's work focusing on "transient" maneuver and the advantages that accrue when an opponent can be outpaced in the decision cycle. Boyd, an Air Force fighter pilot in the Korean War, observed that U.S. pilots flying the F-86 were disadvantaged in speed and climb rate over their North Korean and Soviet counterparts, but used the greater maneuverability of the F-86 to defeat their opponents routinely. This maneuverability advantage provided pilots the opportunity to engage targets selectively, either by forcing opponents to overshoot or turning inside a foe's radius. Importantly, it provided a range of responses to the U.S. pilot which inhibited an enemy's ability to predict or anticipate maneuvers. Boyd asserted that the capability of U.S. pilots to act quicker than the enemy created ambiguity about U.S. reactions to enemy attack. The array of alternative responses to enemy attack precluded ready identification of U.S. patterns of response. It confused an opponent trained only to use certain maneuvers and approaches. The enemy became disoriented when U.S. pilots failed to react in the expected manner, and thus lost the ability to focus on new stimuli. Finally, Boyd claimed that, given the ambiguity of the U.S. response, and enemy confusion, rapid transient maneuvers forced opponents to make mistakes upon which U.S. forces could capitalize to create opportunity.

The objective of decision-cycle dominance under these conditions was to disrupt the enemy's thought process. While considerations of time, space, and speed had an important impact on success and failure, the moral and psychological dimensions played a dominant role. Boyd developed the OODA loop to describe this psychological phenomenon, and advocated both for shaping the training and education of pilots and emphasizing the acquisition of systems to exploit the decision-cycle process. The early focus applied decision loops to unitary actors and exploited asymmetric strengths, primarily in the air-to-air combat domain. Later analysis and experimentation led to the application of decision-cycle theory to larger, more complex formations to determine whether similar phenomena could be derived and applied to warfare in general.

Figure 2 demonstrates the use of decision-cycle theory to explain Genghis Khan's campaign of 1219–1220 in central Asia. The Mongols possessed numerous advantages over their opponents, whose cities lay astride the trade caravan routes between China and Europe. As a nomadic culture based on the horse, the Mongols had great mobility. They had no infantry, lived off the wealth of conquered peoples, and were not tied to fixed sites for command and control or logistics. They had a sophisticated system of communications, relying on couriers operating

FIGURE 2: *Genghis Khan Campaign of 1219-1220*

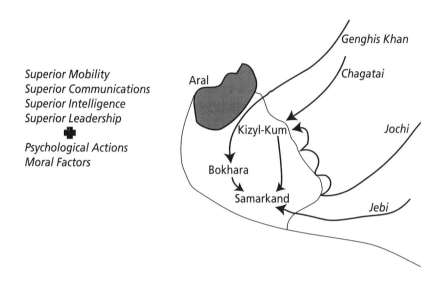

in relays between headquarters and forces spread throughout the empire. They recruited spies throughout the Eurasian landmass, exploiting the growing East-West trade to gather information covertly. Finally, they exercised superior leadership over both their own and conquered peoples, in order to retain control without diverting forces to occupation duties. Operating on accurate intelligence over widely dispersed axes (even by modern standards) the Mongols employed small bands of forces moving rapidly to achieve surprise and destroy enemy forces piecemeal. They used baited retreats and wide envelopments to confuse, deceive, and exploit vulnerabilities. They avoided enemy strengths and used propaganda and terror to amplify enemy fears, undermine their resolve, and destroy their will to resist. The Mongols operated inside the enemy's decision cycle. They appeared out of nowhere, yet seemed to be everywhere, creating the impression of terrifying strength – despite being greatly outnumbered.

Similar instances of the application of decision-cycle theory can be found in other historical battles or campaigns. The German blitzkrieg in World War II demonstrates many of the components of decision-cycle theory. Importantly, it reflects the bottom-up approach to warfare implied in decision-cycle theory. German use of directive control in which "…the subordinate commander is free to modify the task set him without referring back, if he is satisfied that further pursuit of that aim would not represent the best use of his resources in furtherance of his superior's intention" allowed units to function as unitary actors and exploit the opportunity inherent in moving through the cycle faster than the opponent.[1] The focus on achievement of operational goals fostered the loose control of these organizations.

DECISION-CYCLE DOMINANCE IN THE EXTENDED BATTLESPACE OF THE TWENTY-FIRST CENTURY

Decision-cycle dominance confers numerous advantages on the holder. It allows the dominant force to shape the battle, and helps set the conditions for success by denying an enemy the ability to perceive the attack and gain initiative. The intentions of friendly forces may be masked by presenting the enemy such an extensive array of apparent options and alternatives that defense of any one would create unacceptable vulnerabilities in other areas. By operating at a higher tempo, friendly forces can deceive the enemy regarding the principal point of attack, achieving either moral or material surprise. Moral surprise occurs when the enemy is unaware of the attack or its location, leading to total collapse. Material surprise is achieved when the enemy knows an attack will occur, but cannot affect the operation.[2]

The key is to achieve not only physical superiority but to generate the fear, anxiety, and uncertainty that degrades morale and destroys the will to fight. In this sense, operating inside the enemy's decision cycle has cumulative effects that surpass the linear impact of simple destruction of forces. Alvin Toffler explained that when a system is not in equilibrium, small inputs can have large, non-linear effects. These effects can lead to collapse of the system.[3] Turning inside the enemy's decision cycle produces the disequilibrium that could lead to collapse. It fosters confusion and disorder in the enemy's plans by introducing new factors and problems that lengthen the decision time needed to respond. Consequently, the enemy's ability to adapt to changing situations is reduced. In Clausewitz's terms, operating inside the enemy's decision cycle creates increased friction for the enemy, as plans and procedures for reacting to attack fail to accommodate reality.

Decision-cycle dominance enables friendly forces to attain decisive results by producing consistent and cumulative physical successes on the battlefield, while progressively eroding an opponent's capability to continue. The number of friendly casualties can also be reduced by denying the enemy the ability to plan, execute, and target forces effectively, or to reconstitute and reset for future battles. Finally, decision-cycle dominance is self-reinforcing; once attained, it allows quicker reconstitution of friendly capabilities through continuous orientation to enemy activities, thus accelerating movement from observation to decision and action.

Despite these apparent advantages, which may not always accrue concurrently, challenges do exist in applying decision-cycle theory. The bottom-up approach to warfare implied in decision-cycle theory, in which small units operate as unitary actors to exploit speed, opposes more traditional approaches. In the conventional top-down mode, intelligence flows upward, decisions are made, and orders are then passed down. Bottom-up warfare may require new relationships between command and control in which control is indirect, in the form of operational concepts with clear objectives and allocation of resources.[4]

To achieve decision-cycle dominance, layers of command must compress their decision cycles to exploit enemy vulnerabilities. Though timeframes vary at each echelon of command – according to the mission and battlefield perspective – decision cycles must be sufficiently synchronized to exploit both sequential and cumulative opportunity. These opportunities become apparent both at higher levels of command, with their broader view of the battlespace, and in the much shorter cycles at tactical levels. However, once decisions to act are delegated to tactical levels, higher levels may lose some ability to adapt future operations to emerging information without jeopardizing current operations. Indeed, delegation of authority and responsibility to lower levels within the more transparent battlespace of the future may create essential horizontal synchronization through a synoptic view, while degrading vertical synchronization. New concepts will be required that generate the ability to synchronize supporting capabilities to reinforce success.

Given the nature and volume of information collection now possible, higher echelons will need to expend more effort just to keep pace with the data gathered. Understanding the implications of data and sustaining situational knowledge demands faster processing, improved visualization, and a flexible, comparative basis upon which to assess information. Raw data alone cannot yield the patterns needed to predict and anticipate enemy operations. In the diverse global security environment, operations against unfamiliar enemies for which extensive knowledge does not already exist may create serious challenges. As such, leader development becomes more critical. Future leaders must possess the ability to define minimum critical information requirements (CIR) necessary for decisionmaking, otherwise the system will be unable to sort through the massive volume of information available. In some past exercises to define CIR, lists have been compiled that totaled over ninety requirements, an unmanageable load. At progressively higher levels, information cannot simply be compiled, but must be formatted to present a synthetic view of the battlespace, adapted to the decision needs of the commander. Additionally, in order to dominate decision cycles, leaders will need intuitive filtering and synthesizing skills, based on a strong knowledge base and experience.

Synchronization of sensors and collectors in the observe function will remain important to success within the OODA loop. Despite the presumed dominance of U.S. capabilities in data collection, they cannot focus everywhere all the time. Even with relatively unfamiliar enemies, it is critical to project enemy operations, target them with sensors, and direct forces against them. Herein lies the challenge of global awareness versus targeted knowledge. The fog of war cannot be eliminated, but can be pierced by focusing appropriate assets sharply within defined time periods.

Finally, continuous operations undertaken to exploit the momentum achieved by means of decision-cycle dominance may conflict with the notion that fewer forces can achieve greater effects as information capabilities improve. The need to reconstitute while maintaining continuous operations may demand larger numbers of smaller units, as the discrete performance capabilities of forces steadily grow.

Past efforts to apply decision-cycle theory to the twenty-first century battlespace have typically focused on the technological challenge in the observe stage of harnessing and disseminating sensor data for all levels and for reporting battlefield information. In some respects, this stems from threats to U.S. and allied forces and populations in the Gulf War, namely the *Scud* or theater ballistic missile (TBM) threat, and its growing importance in a world of arms proliferation. The incredibly short response timelines have driven programs to close the OODA loop, directly linking the observe phase with the act phase. By maintaining forces in a general orientation or alert posture in the face of any TBM threat, and by developing appropriate parameters for automated decisionmaking, the possibility increases of destroying a TBM launcher before it returns to a sheltered position. The imposition of dynamic control through command negation could add precious seconds to the decision process, although even then it would shorten current timelines for response. The challenge lies in fully understanding the circumstances surrounding the missile launch in order to respond properly. While the threat of weapons of mass destruction (WMD) represents a unique case in which all measures of response may be appropriate, conventionally armed missiles launched from sites adjacent to media-sensitive sites, like hospitals and schools, could make responses politically difficult. The depth of appreciation for the terrain required to execute automatic responses appears daunting in such circumstances.

In such cases, and in a range of others, it is not immediately clear whether information is solving or creating the problem. In the past, large staffs could handle what was then considered a heavy volume of information. Progressively larger staffs at each level processed information from the bottom up, constrained by the capability of systems and operators. However, efforts to promulgate information through broadcast to progressively lower levels and to achieve a common view of the battlespace at progressively higher levels, may create a surfeit of information at all levels. Accordingly, processes and systems are adapting to accommodate this burgeoning volume. If unsuccessful, the excess of information could itself contribute to the fog of war among friendly electronic capabilities, slowing the decision process by generating so many perspectives and options that it paralyzes the ability to decide. Similarly, commanders and staff might delay action by waiting for the last piece of data to create the "perfect" information picture. The issue of how much information is enough at each command level begs solution – whether in the development and acquisition of systems, concepts, and doctrine for employment of information-based capabilities, or in the context of training and education.

The synoptic view of the battlespace – the what, where, and when of warfare – that helps shorten decision cycles for platforms and small units may also cause commands to focus on data and ignore the "why" of the enemy situation. At higher levels, this could create vulnerability, decreasing friendly ability to anticipate, predict, and orient forces for forthcoming operations, while allowing the enemy to develop deceptive situations. At the platform and even small-unit level, the "why" is implicitly understood. For larger formations, the "why" becomes more complex and crucial to deciding what and where to observe, how to orient, and how to define decision criteria. To shorten the time required to implement each cycle, platforms and small units may operate as unitary systems, particularly since speed becomes the most important factor to success. As units become more complex, they no longer function as unitary systems. Speed thus remains important, but may not be as critical as accuracy and understanding.

Additionally, computers may not provide the right means to communicate information at all levels. They are not yet as fast as voice and, at critical moments, may be too slow. It is often difficult to see small screen displays in certain environmental conditions – and focusing on the screen may divert a commander's attention from the immediate observe-orient challenge on the ground. These challenges of developing optimal man-machine interfaces are critical to exploiting speed of decision. These systems also remain sensitive and vulnerable to environmental and operational conditions; and, as yet, there are no update or back-up systems at the individual and small unit level.

Environmental considerations also pose some considerable challenges. Many systems that provide the visualization of the battlespace depend on digitized terrain data. However, less than 40 percent of the world's terrain is presently digitized. While radar mapping systems are in development to speed digitization of unmapped regions, it will take time to fly the missions necessary to map areas, convert the data, and then insert it into appropriate digitized systems. In other cases, weather and terrain limit the abilities of certain sensors to provide information critical to transparency. The locations of potential conflicts may also preclude full coverage, particularly with national sensor systems.

IMPLICATIONS OF TRANSPARENCY
FOR DECISION-CYCLE DOMINANCE
The battlespace of the twenty-first century will be characterized by a number of factors critical to the discussion of decision-cycle dominance. At the theater level, the multitude of netted national, theater, and tactical sensors will provide some limited, continuous, theater-wide visualization of the enemy and operational situation. This will help increase detail and accuracy

at lower levels, creating near-perfect knowledge of narrow targets. Data on friendly forces will be available in real time, and accessible at virtually all levels. However, the volume of information available to friendly forces by the year 2000 will be so high that reporting on units, platforms, and sensors may sometimes saturate tactical communications that are dependent on frequency of reporting. On the other hand, the speed of information dissemination on enemy forces may take thirty minutes or more for correlation of enemy data from all-source analysis centers and transmission to tactical units.

The power of computers will double in speed and volume every eighteen months, making processing algorithms and the selection of critical information requirements the prime obstacle, rather than advancing technology. The pace of this change will be driven by the commercial sector, challenging the military with a continuous need to integrate new capabilities, systems, and technologies, while creating potential vulnerabilities to enemy assessment and development of countermeasures from open-market acquisition.

The battlespace transparency projected for the twenty-first century will have direct impact on individuals and units at all levels, on battle management, and on precision attack of forces and systems. Changing concepts will most likely challenge both joint and service doctrine and their associated tactics, techniques, and procedures, thus allowing quicker, decentralized operations. Rigid maintenance of traditional boundaries and other control measures may impair the increasing potential for operational flexibility and agility.

At every echelon, transparency of the battlespace will permit faster decision-cycle times. The tremendous growth in coverage, resolution, and responsiveness of sensors at the national, theater, and tactical levels, together with the ability to share data, fuse information, and alert forces of impending enemy actions, will decrease time spent in the observe phase. At the same time, enhanced dissemination will produce common views of the battlespace, allowing rapid orientation of forces at each level. The broadcast of critical targeting information related to short-duration mobile targets will greatly decrease decision cycles for the employment of long-range systems.

The greater range of options and alternatives resulting from transparency – the ability to bypass, to attack by fire or other means, or to attack directly – may present an enemy with an overwhelming number of possibilities, thus decreasing the potential effectiveness of any one response. For friendly forces, the increased range of options demands more complex command and control processes that must be balanced with the need for speed. Given this conflict, leader development to provide greater understanding of operations, together with experiential learning to increase the intuitive nature of the commander, will be essential to the success of operations with faster tempos and rhythms.

Importantly, forces will have the ability to execute cumulative operations at lower levels. Cumulative operations comprise multiple independent attacks against targets at all echelons, throughout the depth of the military and civilian sectors. They are an alternative to sequential operations, in which interdependent actions occur within an established sequence for the attainment of specified objectives. For example, in campaign planning, each phase is essential to full execution of the following phase, such as attaining air superiority prior to initiating the ground phase. Transparency offers the opportunity to undertake cumulative activities against an enemy with full knowledge of their impact on capability, morale, and the will to fight. As an enemy loses equilibrium, small inputs may have the potential to cause total collapse. Special operations forces and capabilities may make significant contributions to conventional war, as small but disproportionately important factors in cumulative operations.

Transparency and the ability to conduct non-linear, sequential, or cumulative operations argue for forces which are more self-contained, but highly tailorable to meet changing operational demands. Simple units that can function as unitary actors may present the best solution. The difficulty lies in defining core units and rapidly tailoring modules for mission-specific requirements. The structure, grades, and skills required may differ significantly from current organization. The impact on functional areas – for example, logistics, communications, command and control, and fire support – may require reconsideration of current structure and doctrine. Development and fielding of equipment for greater self-sufficiency and sustainment is critical to exploiting decision-cycle dominance. Transparency will likely have logistics implications, reducing munitions demands at all echelons from the depot to the unit, while increasing fuel demands.

The improved ability to anticipate enemy activities provided through battlespace transparency will shorten the observe, orient, and decide phases of the cycle, allowing friendly forces to operate consistently inside the enemy's decision cycle. This will support an improved allocation of forces to each discrete action. By applying only those forces or systems required to accomplish objectives against a well-defined threat, greater effectiveness and efficiency will be attained. Forces will thus become available for commitment to other important targets in the battlespace. The increased real-time knowledge of both friendly and enemy actions will also allow greater consideration of tactics and techniques in which forces attack and withdraw in rapid sequence, searching for weaknesses to exploit in the enemy plan or disposition. Through greater transparency, commanders will have the ability to exploit

opportunities or disengage before the enemy can bring sufficient combat power to bear. Furthermore, commanders will be
able to discern enemy patterns of operation, and adapt force
dispositions and allocations, in order to attack critical points
in the enemy decision cycle. The commander with visibility
can strike before the enemy reaches the decide-act phases, when
forces are better prepared to defend or attack.

Integrated management of sensors could improve with greater
visibility of the enemy situation. Assets would be allocated and
integrated from the bottom up to meet tactical requirements,
and from the top down to achieve a global view of the battlespace. The crucial factor in exploiting decision-cycle dominance
will be achieving adequate responsiveness and detail from available sensors at the lower levels, rather than focusing collection
priorities at higher echelons.

Commanders will face serious battle-management challenges
in integrating the operations of modernized and non-modern-
ized forces. This will occur whenever operations require a
linkage between active forces, trained to employ fielded systems using new concepts, and forces of reserve or coalition
components that are not as well equipped. Solutions will be
found in time and spatial separation of forces similarly equipped
through vertical echelons, and perhaps with greater use of liaison teams to coordinate operations horizontally between
echelons with unequal capabilities. From the vertical perspective, new forms of warfare are unlikely to emerge until echelons
– from corps through company – are similarly equipped and
can develop visualization, competence, and confidence in new
operational concepts.

In the area of precision attack, transparency will compress
sensor-to-shooter timelines, particularly if both positive and
dynamic control of assets is ceded to automated responses. At
theater and operational levels, discrete fires will require response

times measured in seconds or minutes. Only by drastically reducing time expended in the orient and decide phases can these extremely short timelines be achieved. On the other hand, massed fires at the theater and operational level, if required in the future environment, will take minutes or hours, allowing movement through the entire cycle and, hence, dynamic control. The potential challenge to precision attack with autonomous control, as well as to the ability to exploit the decision-cycle advantage fully, lies in political constraints on the employment of fires and the willingness to accept risk in specific situations (such as, for example, an enemy's threatened use of WMD). Such constraints will depend on the nature of the war, the situation on the ground, and the regional relationships between coalition partners, the host nation, and U.S. forces.

At tactical levels, massed fires against discrete targets will also be required in seconds or minutes. Attaining this capability is possible given smaller, self-contained units operating in lower-level decision cycles with common views of the battlespace and the consequent ability to orient on targets without explicit guidance. The increased range of future fire-support systems, the ability to call for longer-range joint fires, and successful fielding of future automated fire-support systems will enable mass fires and delivery of precision fires at any point in the battlespace. The ability to clear fires in seconds – the decide phase – through real-time knowledge of friendly force locations will greatly facilitate this process.

APPLICATION OF DECISION-CYCLE DOMINANCE
TO A RANGE OF OPPONENTS AND ENVIRONMENTS
The implications of gaining decision-cycle dominance against enemies with similar visual capabilities and those without are summarized in figure 3.

	VISUAL-VISUAL	VISUAL-BLIND
COMMAND	Highly Educated Experienced Intuitive	Less educated Experienced Understands
CONTROL	Highly decentralized Bottom-up	More centralized Top-down
OPERATIONS	Non-linear Cumulative Create friction Focus on attack of C^2 and protect C^2 Emphasis on moral / psychological	Traditional sequential Or non-linear Focus on attack of forces Protect against asymmetric response
SIGNATURES	Limit, change Update enemy Need for databases	Less important
SYSTEMS	Continuity of ops Ability to regenerate Ability to update	Less risk Manual update and regeneration feasible

FIGURE 3: *Summary of Implications of Force Pairings*

Decision-cycle dominance in a "visual-visual" confrontation. Decision-cycle dominance in a visual-visual pairing of forces — that is, an engagement between forces with roughly equal capabilities to see the battlespace using modern sensors and information systems — can be analyzed in five areas: command, control, operations, signatures and systems. For command, decision-cycle dominance against similarly armed opponents will require enhanced leader capabilities in order to understand and manage information sources and data processing, and to derive intelligence. It requires an ability to correlate information capabilities with enemy intent, and the skill to limit information requirements needed to move through the decision cycle. This will depend on a commander's ability to deal with uncertainty, gaps in information, and conflicting information. The capacity to identify and limit information requirements will allow a commander to act more quickly than the enemy and, thus, overload the enemy system. While knowledge will assist in selecting information requirements, experience in battle will improve the commander's combat intuition and skill in addressing uncertainty. Without intuitive insight, commanders might spend inordinate amounts of time in the observe and decide phases, ceding advantage to the visually equipped opponent. Excessive control in a visual-visual conflict will most likely elicit patterns of action that provide an opponent potential decision-cycle advantages.

Consequently, decentralized or bottom-up operations orchestrated at higher levels may provide a means to avoid development of discernible patterns. In particular, the sequential nature of current operational concepts plays strongly to the opponent with visual abilities comparable to those of the United States. Cumulative operations better exploit the loose control possible with transparency and decision-cycle dominance, avoid pattern definition, and strike at weaknesses in enemy capabilities that derive from less-educated and trained forces. Cumulative operations should not be perceived, however, as random events in the battlespace, but as movement toward established objectives by manipulation and exploitation of a wide range of unit actions, seemingly disconnected in space and time.

In operations, decision-cycle dominance relies on exploiting asymmetric force capabilities to achieve decisive effects. In a visual-visual pairing, advantageous asymmetry exists for U.S. forces in leadership, training, longer-range precision fires, integration of joint capabilities, and special operations capabilities. These asymmetries can be leveraged to produce non-linear operations and effects, creating friction within the enemy. The enemy can be outsmarted and demoralized through attack on diverse military and civil institutions. Asymmetries in enemy organization, structure, doctrine, and training will also become more apparent through transparency.

To dominate the decision process, U.S. forces must conduct both physical attacks on enemy visual capabilities – to slow an opponent's cycle and create opportunity – and non-overt attacks through electronic or other means to destroy, manipulate, deceive, or shut down information capabilities. While physical attack can be planned and executed in wartime, non-overt attack may require extensive peacetime planning, development, and intrusion. Because the enemy has the visual means to assess attacks to their own capability, selective use of force highlights the rapidity and cumulative nature of friendly attacks, and thus presents opportunities to achieve moral and psychological victory well before physical defeat.

The visual capabilities of future opponents will increasingly cause concern for the signatures of U.S. forces and systems. In the visual-visual pairing, the enemy has greater opportunity to deceive, confuse, and overload friendly systems than in other match-ups. Operations must address the potential for deceptive measures and develop plans and countermeasures to deal with the problem. Specific signatures on the battlefield will provide an enemy with the information needed to target forces, actions, and plans. Means to decrease and manage friendly signatures include: changing the physical attributes of the signatures; changing the electronic attributes of systems, such as the nature, frequency, source, and density of emissions; and using deception to define the footprint of organizations arrayed on the battlefield.

The enemy signature problem also demands consideration. Peacetime development of databases on potential visual threats can provide an analytic baseline for exploitation of data collected. Without such a database the time required to perform detailed collection and analysis on the battlefield will slow the decision cycle greatly, and concede advantage to the enemy. Additionally, since enemies may develop the capability to manage signatures, U.S. forces must have the ability to update databases during the observe phase to cue sensors and warheads dependent on pre-loaded signature data.

In the visual-visual conflict, reasonable assumptions about enemy capability to target and attack U.S. systems require addressing the issue of continuity of operations in the event automated systems crash, are destroyed, or are manipulated by the enemy. Further, given the pace of operations with decision-cycle dominance, forces must possess the ability to update databases continually with friendly and enemy information, whether static or on the move.

Decision-cycle dominance in "visual-blind" confrontation. The visual-blind pairing of forces – which assumes an engagement between forces in which the enemy lacks the ability to see through the battlespace – differs from visual-visual conflict in a number of ways. In a visual-blind confrontation, the same degree of commander development, while beneficial, is not critical to the success or failure of an operation. During early fielding of U.S. forces with visual capabilities, attention to differentiation in the personal capabilities and the training and education programs for commanders may yield tangible performance gains. Consequently, criteria for the selection of forces for conflict with visual or blind forces may include the state of development of commanders who can effectively exploit the fielded information capabilities.

In the area of control, an opponent's inability to exploit transparency relieves some of the importance of avoiding patterns and top-down operations, even though these patterns can still be discerned over time if commanders are not sufficiently cautious. However, the time lag in the enemy decision cycle will be relatively long, allowing frequent adaptation of U.S. force plans and actions. With visually blind enemies, more traditional sequential operations can be planned, allowing improved interoperability with allies. The visual-blind disequilibrium offers an opportunity to increase the tempo of friendly operations to achieve early, decisive results. Attack of enemy command and control becomes less critical in these cases, while protection of friendly command and control becomes even more important, since the visual capability represents a principal source of asymmetric advantage. A significant challenge will reside in responding to unanticipated asymmetric responses to U.S. force activities in the conflict. Few blind opponents will opt for direct battle with U.S. forces, but may attempt indirect approaches.

Signature management becomes less relevant to the outcome of operations when facing a blind opponent. Furthermore, blind opponents are less able to influence or destroy the visual capabilities of friendly forces, creating less risk in the event systems crash or are destroyed. Longer enemy decision cycles following such events may even allow manual regeneration.

Confronting low-technology forces. In many cases, low-technology forces will be blind when matched against the United States. Hence, certain sensors, particularly those focused exclusively on military capabilities and activities, may be inappropriate for gathering the information needed to fight lower-intensity conflicts. Low-technology foes, lacking sophisticated weapons systems, organizations, and infrastructure, usually present a diminished signature. This may initially slow the observe phase of the OODA loop, until sensors adapt to the new conditions. Adversaries whose organizational structure centers on family, ethnic, or tribal ties will also slow collection and analysis. In these instances, human intelligence, rather than data from electro-optical sensors, may prove most critical.

Similarly, in densely populated areas and close terrain, sensors lack the range, resolution, and collection capabilities they have in more open spaces. Low-technology forces will most likely view dense areas and close terrain as potential force multipliers. The difficulty of collecting detailed information in such areas may preclude precision attack, producing less-decisive results from engagements or increasing the risk of extensive destruction to civilian infrastructure.

Low-technology opponents may also operate defensively, refusing engagement except on overwhelmingly favorable terms. The collection and processing systems essential to speedy observation and decision phases may then be hindered by the difficulty of identifying patterns of activity, and triggering appropriate and timely responses. Moreover, unfamiliar values and norms may complicate the ability to focus sensors and identify patterns of activity relevant to the war being fought. Finally, even if sensors can focus on specific enemy activities and accelerate the decision cycle, winning the battle may not ultimately be the most important factor for success in such engagements.

In operations other than war, transparency may have great utility, especially in instances where the situation is relatively benign or only low levels of conflict persist. In that event, transparency and speed of action within the decision cycle may allow greatly decreased density of forces in operations. This will preserve flexibility for major conflict, lower the commitment of forces to extended overseas operations, and decrease the funding expended for such operations.

ORGANIZATIONS AND PROCEDURES: THE KEY TO SUCCESS

Arguments continue about the need, utility, and future of complex technology solutions to current challenges. In reality, there must be continued development of both technology and the concepts to exploit it. The pace of technological change, dominated by a "more is better" attitude, drives current programs. However, this fervor for cutting-edge technology must be adapted to military problems, and harnessed to doctrine and concepts to generate success within decision cycles.

The technology challenge lies in building filters at all levels to sort massive amounts of data by type, time, and spatial orientation to meet the critical information requirements of the commander. Only by limiting information requirements can commanders approach becoming a unitary actor at lower levels and fully exploit the advantages of faster decision cycles. A corollary to the filter issue is the need to control data in order to prevent overloading of systems and decisionmakers. Without tight controls, the risk of falling prey to the "flash message" syndrome increases; when the system becomes clogged, users continually upgrade the precedence of messages to insure they arrive. In the end, few messages of any precedence move through the system.

To exploit decision cycles, in terms of organization, structure, and concepts, simplicity is best. Decision-cycle dominance relies on maximizing asymmetries to provide a range of options and alternatives to quickly evolving situations. The ability to select some asymmetric capabilities for development, while deferring others until later years or more mature technologies exist, may have useful payoffs. Furthermore, focusing on self-contained units may help accelerate movement through the phases of the OODA loop.

At the core of the decision cycle is the ability to decide rapidly, while coping with the uncertainty that can arise from conflicting data or, simply, the absence of sufficient information. These organizational issues, inherent in the application of new technology and doctrines, have important implications for leader development and training. Leadership development for the new operating environment demands a broadened knowledge base and greater operational experience, even at lower echelons. Enhanced skills at all levels are essential to exploiting decision-cycle advantages, determining critical information levels, and controlling the tasking, collection, and processing of information. Training to build pre-conflict experience that enhances initial survivability will provide the intuitive edge needed to speed the decisionmaking process and achieve critical decision-cycle dominance.

ENDNOTES

1. Richard Simpkin, *Race to the Swift* (Washington, D.C.: Brassey's Defense Publishers, 1985), p. 232.
2. Simpkin, *Race to the Swift*, p. 182.
3. Alvin Toffler, "Making Sense of our Chaotic World," *The Washington Post,* 19 October 1986.
4. Jeffrey Cooper, briefing entitled "Joint Coherent Operations," 21 September 1995; cited from United States Marine Corps, Fleet Marine Field Manual: *Command and Control.*

SECTION
III

The Operational Issues

The
Operational
Issues

IN THE PREVIOUS TWO SECTIONS OF THIS VOLUME, authors have described the broad ramifications of the information-based revolution in military affairs on the emerging security environment and the implications of integrating information systems and enhanced weapons platforms into the armed forces. The authors in Section III examine the impact of the RMA on operational issues and how U.S. military doctrine may have to change to account for the new capabilities that advanced weapons and command and control systems of the RMA will bring.

William W. Hartzog and Susan Canedy offer a framework for analyzing the effects of the Information Age on the Army's conduct of war. They identify precision as the defining characteristic of the new capabilities. They define precision not just as surgical strike, aerial strike, deep fires, or satellite technology; rather, it is "part of every operational pattern" of the Army. According to Hartzog and Canedy, increased precision

– of munitions, intelligence, and sensor capability, among others – will impact each of six key mission categories: projecting the force, protecting the force, information dominance, shaping the battlespace, conducting decisive operations, and sustaining and transitioning operations. Like the authors in Section II, however, Hartzog and Canedy point out that the human element will still be crucial for warfare. The increased operations tempo created by precision technologies will demand ever more human endurance, unit cohesion, and intelligent decisionmaking.

Richard P. O'Neill argues that the emerging RMA is a challenge that will require an entirely new approach to operations. In fact, he views the impact of information technologies as not only a revolution in military affairs, but as a revolution in security affairs and a military-technical revolution. That is, the RMA has expanded the concept of national power; now, it is not only physical strength, but information dominance that must be accounted for. Thus, O'Neill explains, conducting warfare in the Information Age will require a synergy of offensive and defensive capabilities, with robust command and control. Offensive information warfare will require strong intelligence operations and analysis to understand foreign cultures, language, and leadership decisionmaking. Also, we will need intelligence on information systems and how they may be used by potential adversaries. Defensive information warfare, on the other hand, will require a risk management strategy – such as blue team/red team exercises – for finding, assessing, and limiting vulnerabilities in our own information systems. According to O'Neill, defense can be achieved through "soft" elements, such as policy initiatives and organizational reforms, and "hard" elements, such as firewalls between elements of systems and intrusion detection software. He stresses the need for the United States to develop "cumulative strategies" at a national level that integrate economic warfare, political warfare, psychological warfare, and covert operations using the means made possible by the information revolution.

In his essay, Huba Wass de Czege also describes how the information revolution will change the conduct of war, focusing on the art of maneuver. According to Wass de Czege, "combat power" remains the key to success on the battlefield. However its primary elements – the synergy of firepower, protection, maneuver, and skillful battle command skills – will be transformed by Information Age technologies. Firepower will increase, protection of friendly forces will improve, and command structures will become more effective but less hierarchical. Maneuver – the ability to achieve a "position of advantage relative to the enemy" – will improve with enhanced "anticipatory planning." Information Age technologies will enable U.S. forces to see what the enemy is doing, predict an opponent's options for action, and then successfully counter enemy moves. With these advances, Wass de Czege argues, maneuver warfare will enter the temporal or psychological realm in addition to the spatial arena. Nevertheless, the principles of surprise, concentration of effects, audacious offensive, and rapid tempo will remain critical to success.

In an essay on the modernization plan of the U.S. Army, John P. Rose illustrates that the Information Age will change the way in which war is conducted as well as the tools for combat. In creating what has been labeled "Force XXI," he explains, the Army has focused on six modernization goals: owning the night, that is, dominating periods of limited visibility; improving combat identification to avoid fratricide; extending the depth of precision fires by employing greater numbers of smart and brilliant munitions; controlling information war with enhanced command and control (C^2) capabilities; protecting the force with tiered defenses against weapons of mass destruction; and digitizing the battlefield through use of information-enhanced platforms. This modernization, in turn, will support five broader goals for the Army, similar to those discussed by Hartzog and Canedy: projecting and sustaining the force; protecting the force; conducting precision strike; and dominating maneuver. Crucial to the success of Army modernization is the concept of horizontal technology integration (HTI) which allows for common technology to be used in different platforms. Rose calls it the "linchpin" of the Army program because it allows for less expensive procurement, standardized components, simplified maintenance, and more efficient use of manpower.

chapter nine

Operations in the Information Age

William W. Hartzog
Susan Canedy

SOME 2,000 YEARS AGO, Sun Tzu advised that success in war was determined by information. His maxim, "Know the enemy and know yourself; in a hundred battles you will never be in peril,"[1] remains true today. Without information we can neither gauge our enemy, nor prepare ourselves. This chapter explores the effect of information on war in the future, addressing U.S. Army integration of information technologies. The emerging Information Age is the doorway to a new era of combat. To draw an analogy from airborne warfare, the Army, recognizing the need for change during the Gulf War, and in Somalia and Haiti, is now hooked up, standing in the door, and ready to jump. Where the descent might take us is unclear; the future is murky, and the full dimensions of this Information Age are as yet unknown.

The Army of the twenty-first century will be required to deploy globally and perform across the operational continuum in situations that may be vastly different from traditional concepts of war. Today, instead of shaping our posture in response to a specific threat, we posture against capability. The Army must organize, equip, and train to face a myriad of capabilities – from the standing armies of foreign powers to the irregular forces of ethnic militias, terrorist groups, or criminal organizations. Combat may be waged throughout an expanded five-tiered battlespace of air, land, sea, space, and electronic dimensions, calling for fewer soldiers and simultaneous operations. However, even with the changes engendered by the information explosion, war will remain a human endeavor. Battles will still be subject to strong emotion. Land warfare will become ever more lethal, tough, and unforgiving, and will demand, as always, high-quality soldiers and exceptional leaders. Clausewitz characterized war as a test of will and faith. Technology cannot substitute for the skills and virtues of the warrior needed to meet that test.

A Perspective of Change

Change is not new to the Army. With the transition into the modern age, warfare was dramatically altered. The entire force – from weaponry to force structure, doctrine, and training – was affected by innovations such as the telegraph, wireless radio, television, computer, and satellite. The new technologies fostered increased range, accuracy, and lethality in weapons systems. Radio communications, along with mechanization, brought mobility and control to battlefields. Air power extended the battlefield to civilian society. In the modern age, "total war" emerged as a dramatically real prospect; even the fundamental concept of the war of attrition took on new meaning.

For the United States, modern warfare was pioneered in the Civil War. That conflict was characterized by large armies, several separate theaters of operation, modern technologies, and participation, to some degree, by almost the entire population. Many new technologies were introduced during the war. For example, the telegraph, invented in 1837, was first used tactically in June 1861 to direct the fires of Fort Wool against Confederate positions at Sewell's Point opposite Fort Monroe. As a result, Fort Monroe remained a Union stronghold for the duration of the war.

Yet, information transfer and intelligence gathering on those Civil War battlefields were still primitive. Communication was often difficult. Order was maintained by messenger, rider, or signal flag, resulting in tight formations and close battles. At the end of every engagement, activity stopped temporarily to restore order and reestablish communication lines. With time, the ability to communicate over long distances improved. By the time American soldiers were sitting in trenches during World War I, battle lines were drawn around the capabilities of the wireless radio and the flying machine. These two innovations brought communications and information flow to a new level. Communication was now longer-range, and both more reliable and more accurate. Information moved faster and farther than ever before.

By the Second World War, dramatic expansion was seen in the reliability of communications pathways, transmission distances, and the amount of information available. Although still primitive by today's standards, communication was established between platforms, allowing man to talk to machine. The man-to-machine interface, evidenced by the Enigma coding machine and the code-breaking Ultra, were innovations of such significance that the Allies gained information superiority and, concomitantly, strategic choice. That advantage facilitated the end of World War II.

During the Cold War, the United States, its allies, and its enemies continued to develop weaponry, fine tune organizations, and hone both warfighting and leadership skills. In the summer of 1945, work was completed on the ENIAC computer, the first electronic computing machine. In 1951, the commercial exploitation of computer technology began with the marketing of the universal automatic computer, UNIVAC. By 1963, some five thousand computers could be found in the United States. By the end of the Vietnam war, technological advances facilitated nearly instantaneous and regular televised coverage, low-level precision bombing, and the beginnings of small computerized systems, such as the digital navigation and tracking system.

Today, Information Age technology is fostering dramatic changes in the conduct of land warfare. Networked systems of databases allow access to a broad range of information in seconds. This potentially overwhelming amount of information will affect the structure of the battlefield. Order on the battlefield is key to effectively synchronizing all parts of the warfighting organization. In the past, order was achieved by drawing boundaries and phase lines, and by physically placing units shoulder-to-shoulder to concentrate their effects. These tactics may no longer be necessary. The future may bring less reliance on the physical order of formations. Commanders will be free to move as the command post is redefined to harness technologically enhanced communication, real-time intelligence, and shared situational awareness.

Indeed, technology has already compressed time and events. Soldiers make decisions on the ground even as assessments are made at the highest levels. While this may not be new, communications now make both the soldier and the diplomat visible. Each decision cycle can affect the other. A seemingly tactical decision can have operational or strategic implications because information is widely available. As was apparent in

Haiti, time and technology have compressed the decision cycle and thereby compressed the action cycle.

THE PATH TO THE FUTURE: FORCE XXI

The Army of the twenty-first century will be in large measure a power-projection force. It must be capable of rapid deployment to accomplish a wide range of contingency missions to which it will be specifically tailored. Battle command will be enhanced through improvements in organization and facility as well as the application of common situational awareness. It must be capable of continuous operations; planning, preparation, execution, and recovery must be seamless. It must be capable of quick and decisive victory with minimum casualties and maximum efficiency.

The program for Army modernization and change is referred to as Force XXI. The twenty-first century Army that will emerge from this process is called Army XXI. Ever mindful of the six imperatives for an effective, lethal force – doctrine, training, modern equipment, leader development, force mix, and quality people – the Army has mapped a development strategy that emphasizes balance and targets information capabilities. This is a new approach to both war and operations other than war (OOTW). It ties together many elements, including Army information systems, enemy information systems, command and control warfare, and the global information environment.[2] The technological revolution provides unprecedented tactical and operational capability, which must be harnessed and applied to meet ever-increasing mission needs. The challenge is not so much to put bombs on targets or men and matériel in landing zones, but rather to identify strategically relevant targets and landing zones using information technologies to enhance precision.

Toward that end, Army XXI is designed to carry out six patterns of simultaneous operations: project the force, protect the force, gain information dominance, shape the battlespace, conduct decisive operations, and sustain (and transition to) future operations. Precision is the underlying theme, enabling greater battlefield efficiency in personnel, consumption of matériel, and application of force. Precision improves accuracy, increases lethality, enhances clarity, and facilitates information superiority to assure tactical, operational, and strategic choice.

The American predilection for precision operations is not new. During World War II, the Royal Air Force destroyed such cities as Hamburg and Dresden in wholesale bombing raids conducted at night to protect their bomber crews. The American Air Force, on the other hand, suffered high casualties in precision daylight bombing. American tactics were dictated by a desire for both the destruction of enemy capabilities and the avoidance of mass civilian damage. Today, the imperative remains not only to neutralize enemy targets while avoiding civilian casualties and collateral damage, but to do it with minimal loss of American life. Information technology helps facilitate that goal.

Precision is much more than surgical strike, aerial strike, deep fires, and satellite or "death-ray" technology. According to the Army definition, precision will be part of every operational pattern, from electricity supply in Port-au-Prince and port construction in Mogadishu to warfighting in Kuwait. It is the application of definitive technology to the way the Army does business.

Current reality suggests that much of the Army of the twenty-first century will be based in the continental United States. In responding to regional contingencies, force projection will be the first pattern of operation. Precision information and weapons will play key roles from the outset. By their nature, early entry forces are not generally equipped to over-come emplaced enemy threats. Real-time precise intelligence will minimize the problem by enabling force projection to air-fields or coastal locations with light enemy presence. The ability to strengthen this initial stage of force projection through the use of precision munitions strengthens the operation overall. Early entry operations are not only assured a greater likelihood of success, the transition to main force operations is eased once the catastrophic number of casualties that often accompanies early entry is avoided.

Gaining information dominance will be as critical in the next war as gaining air superiority was in the Gulf War. We must be able to detect exactly where an enemy's information capa-bilities and communications nodes are located. Once detected, a commander may decide whether there is greater advantage in the destruction of an enemy's information nodes or in allow-ing enemy communication to flow uninterrupted. With the knowledge offered by precise technology, communication, and intelligence comes the power of choice. If the choice is to destroy the enemy's communication source, the task is expe-dited by precision capabilities. Information systems are often small, discreet targets, located in areas where collateral dam-age would be unacceptable, such as a microwave tower in a small village or a communications node in a major city. The ability to eradicate such tiny targets – without causing serious damage to surrounding structures, people, or culture – offers immense advantages.

The concept of precision is central to the pattern of shape the battlefield. The days of mass destruction are over. Oppo-nents can no longer be bombed "back into the stone age," for both logical and ethical considerations. Army XXI is too small to conduct such destructive warfare; moreover, high levels of civilian damage are now simply unacceptable. The application of precision technologies meets current warfighting needs by dramatically increasing the probability of hitting a target. Exact targeting affects not only the "kills per hit" or "hits per fire" ratio; it allows entry into an enemy's battlespace, both physically and intellectually, while exiting unscathed. An enemy can be fired upon from a great distance, with extreme accuracy, minimal collateral damage, and limited human force. In addition, precision hastens enemy demoralization, as enemy forces witness the lethality of these munitions. The environmental implications are also significant. The ability to strike the enemy means just that – to strike the enemy – not the land, the vegetation, the physical infrastructure, or the environmental balance.

Maneuver is also critical. Precision maneuver allows us to make attacks against limited objectives, as well as to attack or seize key terrain from which to launch decisive operations. Combining these tactics with a heightened understanding of enemy calculations, facilitated by information dominance, commanders can choose deceptive operations and feints or direct engagement of the enemy. In short, the effective application of technology fosters a greater range of choice.

Three paths lead to precision in decisive operations and the attainment of maneuver dominance. The first avenue is through munitions, including the laser-guided *Hellfire* or the wire-guided TOW missile. The second is through systems such as the *Paladin, Apache,* or *Comanche.* In both cases, direct links between advanced sensors and the systems vastly increase weapon accuracy. The third avenue is maneuver. With accurate and real-time intelligence preparation of the battlefield, commanders can pinpoint exactly where an enemy is located. It will no longer be necessary to concentrate units, men, or matériel in order to explore or exploit. Men and units will have the freedom to conduct whatever mission has been assigned, from taking a village to opening a road. Importantly, precision maneuver will affect the enemy without the use of mass force. The need to concentrate huge armies with vast war stocks shoulder-to-shoulder and hub-to-hub is eliminated, as is the accompanying carnage and the wholesale destruction of territory.

One of the main goals in decisive operations is the ability to operate within the enemy's decision cycle, disrupting the path of decisionmaking – scan, focus, act, and evaluate. In fact, with precision information, Army XXI will be able to operate faster than an enemy can focus. Multiple missions can be achieved using the same force that today requires multiple units. With detailed information provided by digital technology, orders and intelligence estimates will be available on the move. A synergy will build in which enemy forces will be destroyed more quickly, while fewer friendly forces are exposed. As the force moves from objective to objective, enemy capabilities will be eliminated along with their opportunity for effective action. The tempo will further accelerate, with the reduction or elimination of halts for reorganization and redirection of operations. A seamless combination of joint effects – Army, Air Force, Navy, and Marine – will be woven together to achieve optimal results.

Throughout the conduct of operations, precision will enable unprecedented protection of the force. Accurate knowledge of both enemy and friendly locations and activities goes a long way toward splitting the Gordian knot of fratricide. This is especially important given changes in the way battles will be fought. Unlike the present paradigm of deep, close, and rear battle, future operations will probably be conducted in a more multi-dimensional, multi-directional battlespace. A graphic representation of future battlespace may be better represented by a bull's eye, rather than the more familiar series of lines and arrows. The outer rings of the bull's eye represent enemy capabilities targeted for destruction, in order to maximize the effect of a strike against the enemy's center of gravity. Decisive action against that center of gravity is the key to success.

Aggressive actions are much more likely to be conducted simultaneously than sequentially. In the past, forces were arranged in a linear fashion, to shield them from deliberate enemy attack and inadvertent friendly strikes. Weapons can now seek an enemy target as well as avoid friendly units. The approach heeds the old saying: the best defense is a good offense. In terms of force protection, accurate targeting and destruction of key enemy weapons capabilities and short-circuiting of the enemy's decision cycle are essential to protecting the force. By preventing the enemy's ability to focus on attacking units, they are shielded from destruction – what an enemy can't see, can't be hit.

The high operational tempo accompanying precision maneuver can only be sustained by effective logistics. If, as in the past, operations must halt to refit, the concomitant breather allows the enemy's decision cycle to keep pace. By creating a digital environment in which the status of resources can be identified at a glance by logisticians at all levels, units can be sustained in a fashion similar to "just-in-time" manufacturing. Total asset visibility, the procedure of electronically tracking equipment, provides the needed knowledge. Rather than waiting for unit assessment of requirements to enter into requisitioning and distribution systems, logisticians will be able to anticipate exact requirements throughout the conduct of operations, and efficiently forward materiél and other resources.

This has strategic implications as well. While peacetime stockpiling of materiél is unavoidable, the propensity to flood combat theaters with spare parts can be averted by tailoring resources to meet needs. Split-based operations will expedite the movement of supplies to any theater. While no digital system can eliminate the requirement for humans to rest and units to pause in order to integrate replacements and restore cohesion, Army XXI units will be able to avoid the suspension of operations for logistical shortcomings.

The information era holds many challenges. Success in information-driven conflicts demands careful determination of how to organize forces for the next century. A cooperative approach is critical among the sister services, as well as in partnerships with other nations – an increasingly common arrangement. One thing is certain: Army XXI will not consist of cyber-warriors launching precision munitions from the safety of air-conditioned armored command posts. If anything, the increased tempo of operations enabled by precise operational and logistical information will magnify the importance of human endurance and unit cohesion. The stress induced by not knowing will be replaced by the pressure of knowing and having to choose. To make the right choices, confidence in capabilities and forces is imperative. The current plan for change, combined with the commitment and high quality of today's soldier, insures that level of confidence will remain.

ENDNOTES
1. Sun Tzu, *The Art of War*, fourth century B.C..
2. The U.S. Army's concept of warfighting in the future is published in TRADOC Pamphlet 525-5, *Force XXI Operations* (1 August 1994).

chapter ten

Integrating Offensive and Defensive Information Warfare

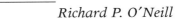

Richard P. O'Neill

THE SYNERGY BETWEEN DEFENSIVE AND OFFENSIVE information warfare is an essential element of information warfare
strategy. However, with so many independent definitions of
information warfare currently under discussion, clarification
of what constitutes information warfare in both the military
and the civilian spheres must precede all else.

The starting point for a discussion of information warfare rests
with an understanding of the emerging security environment.
National security is not upheld merely on the battlefield. Defense
of the sanctuary of the United States includes protection of information-intensive economic institutions, logistics, and
transportation infrastructures. These interconnected global information systems present high-value targets to antagonistic state
militaries, terrorists, or criminals. The U.S. military relies on commercial information systems and networks to command and
control its forces in-theater and to provide logistics from the sup-

port base for military operations in the United States. Disruption or denial of service can pose serious problems for military operations. The same is true for domestic commercial and government services, many of which underpin society and are the basis of citizen trust and confidence in their institutions.

Conflict in the Information Age takes on wholly new dimensions. The range of potential confrontations now includes everything from information-based terrorism to strategic engagement, possibly redefining the role of the military and the use of the term warfare. The proliferation of technology and the resulting interconnectivity of government and commercial systems, both global and domestic, also create a new series of questions about national security. The Information Age and the technologies which shape it have given rise to new systems, processes, and procedures in the conduct of international relations. The same hardware and software innovations that enrich daily life and work are also cornerstones of commercial and industrial well-being. National well-being may be described in one sense as the guaranteed functioning of economic and social institutions and of energy, transportation, and communications utilities. As systems become more complex, information technologies help simplify them for daily use; as markets become global, they are connected by supporting databases. The world is becoming digital.

The more traditionally defined areas of national security, those of foreign relations and national defense, also face new dynamics from improvements in technology. At a recent conference on the media's impact on statecraft, a former ambassador recalled a favorite anecdote from the Jefferson administration. When informed that there had been no news from his ambassador to France for nearly two years, Jefferson instructed his secretary of state to wait another six months and then send a letter asking for the ambassador's impressions. Today, global interconnectivity relays messages in seconds among leaders, governing bodies, economic and political elites, and commercial markets. Embassy representatives often hear news of events in their assigned countries after the world has seen television footage and formed opinions.

Consider how events have been shaped and managed since the advent of the ubiquitous camcorder and CNN broadcasting. Traditional military operations have been enhanced by new information technologies to achieve stunning results through precision-guided weapons and synoptic battlefield intelligence. In the Gulf War, allied forces rendered the Iraqi air defenses ineffective, guaranteeing allied air supremacy from the first moments. CNN carried live and continuous broadcast of precision attacks on Iraqi targets. Iraqi leadership acknowledged that they received much of their information from CNN, which functioned as a clear conduit between the United States and Iraq.

Today's concept of national security extends beyond military protection of our borders, and is based on connectedness. Disruption, denial, or destruction of government, commercial, utility, or social-service infrastructures is unthinkable; even the temporary loss of service due to a natural disaster can have effects that ripple throughout society. The use of information technologies to simplify, enhance, or speed operations has led to massive dependence and, consequently, critical vulnerability.

RESPONDING TO THE IMPERATIVES
OF INFORMATION AGE WARFARE

To determine the impact of this connectedness on the military dimensions of conflict, the Department of Defense (DOD) is now focused on the information battlefield. Attention centers on more capable precision weaponry, improved intelligence for threat warning and targeting, and reliable command and control to orchestrate the myriad elements of warfare. The need for improved, interoperable systems to support execution of a commander's plan has resulted in a variety of new architectures which take advantage of the latest technologies. With the rapid replacement curve for both hardware and software, DOD no longer expends limited and decreasing funds on long lead-time systems. This is particularly true now that industry has underwritten large investments in research and development (R&D) and replaced government as the leader in R&D of electronics and communications. New products and standards quickly overtake systems that have imposed a legacy of high costs. Most of these products or components are available to any buyer in the commercial marketplace.

In such an environment, it is necessary to consider how to ensure information investments and protect our forces. Heavy use of information processors clearly causes total dependence in some vital areas. Market realities yield a policy encouraging purchase of commercial off-the-shelf (COTS) equipment for military procurement. Much equipment available under COTS procurement is developed by overseas manufacturers, or by domestic companies relying to a degree on off-shore subcontracting. New systems purchased by DOD offer a challenge in detecting and correcting potential vulnerabilities.

Further complicating this picture is the reliance of the military on the civilian public switched network (PSN) for almost 95 percent of its communications. There are few military-dedicated systems. The PSN is the same network that makes it possible for the Internet to link millions of people around the world, for funds to flow, for financial transactions to take place, for air traffic safety to be monitored, for health and credit databases to be maintained. There is significant DOD reliance on these systems, though no DOD responsibility for its protection. The overlapping information infrastructures create sizable problems for public policy as well as military strategies. The continuum from peace to war in an Information Age offers a new security conundrum. Antagonists' actions may be transparent and untraceable. The ability to detect an attack and draw a distinction between war and crime may be limited at best. The attendant questions of who responds and in what manner may create gaps that allow greater opportunity to attackers.

Taking a purely theater-based military view of conflict in an Information Age makes the problem somewhat more manageable. The elements include protection of information assets and all the actions necessary to gain information superiority over an adversary. Both a defensive and offensive strategy are needed. But there is a third essential portion: a robust command, control, communications, computer, intelligence, and information system (C^4I^2), vital to winning any war. It begins in requirements statements and leads through effective systems architecture, procurement, fielding, training, and employment. With a robust and secure system in place, the synergy between protection and offensive information operations can be realized, increasing overall command effectiveness. This is the approach taken by the Joint Chiefs of Staff (JCS) in the cooperative information-warfare arrangement between the J-3 (Operations Directorate) and the J-6 (C^4I Directorate) created by the Joint Requirements Oversight Council.

The JCS coordinates a Joint Warfighting Capability Assessment (JWCA) which balances offensive and defensive information warfare concerns with systems requirements in the overall requirements process. The JWCA cuts across every warfighting area to compare requirements and to make possible synergy, interoperability, and efficiency. This process was designed to ensure creation of the systems necessary to meet future contingencies and gain distinct force advantage. It is one essential method of providing offensive and defensive synergy through system requirements, procurement, and attendant doctrine development. On an operational level, however, the JCS problem is complicated by the likelihood of operating in a coalition setting. Frequently changing combinations of allies bring vastly different C^4I systems with which to interconnect a joint force. Accordingly, improved, secure interoperability is an area both DOD and its potential allies are currently addressing.

THE SHAPE OF FUTURE CONFLICT

Clearly, information warfare will not replace traditional forms of warfare, but it may enhance or change warfighting. In addition, it affects assessments of what systems to employ and how they may be managed and protected. To keep pace, a simple taxonomy is necessary to distinguish the range of national security implications inherent in the information revolution. One useful structure delineates three distinct forms of potential conflict resulting from the information revolution: the military-technical revolution, the revolution in military affairs, and the revolution in security affairs.[1]

In the military-technical revolution, new technologies affect the tools used in combat and enhance available systems and processes, capitalizing on current knowledge. Some observers contend that this first category describes U.S. military operations in the Gulf War. The second category, the revolution in military affairs, is a true revolution that can be compared to the development of the blitzkrieg in World War II. Change is profound, and affects the conduct of war with new organizations executing new operational concepts. Information warfare concepts are still in the developmental stages, and progress from the military-technical revolution to the revolution in military affairs has yet to be realized. The third category, the revolution in security affairs, may be thought of as a return to strategic war. In this revolution, information and information technology serve as new sources of national power. They affect the very nature, scope, and intensity of war, and certainly help to define new objectives and targets.

With the global diffusion of information technology and its assimilation throughout governments, societies, and economies, the range of interconnected actors creates a strange brew of potential threats. State and non-state actors possessing information technology – or employing astute information mercenaries – can conduct theft, data corruption, or denial of service against an opponent's infrastructure, intelligence collection, or military support operations. Skeptics of this view, who believe the information infrastructure too robust to be "taken down," miss the point. Taking down a financial network may not be possible, but it also may not be necessary. Causing disruptions that raise a threshold of pain or cause the electorate to lose confidence in its elected leadership may be a sufficient goal. Even competitors with asymmetric capabilities in relation to the United States are able to use information media to obtain their objectives. The manipulation of media or the use of the Internet to convey a message are powerful tools for information for countries or groups with a technology disadvantage. These varied threats foster a DOD integrating strategy that allows for development of both offensive and defensive concepts. A useful definition of information warfare might thus be: Actions to achieve information superiority by affecting an adversary's information-based systems, while defending one's own.

As in the examination of our defensive concerns and requirements, it is also essential to develop new ways of employing information technologies, systems, and processes for offensive purposes. Future combat will not always be a "shooting gallery" affair, as was the Iraqi campaign. Conflict may involve peer competitors with robust information-based fighting capabilities, capable of damaging U.S. forces and national infrastructures. The range of low-intensity operations, operations other than war, or engagements with non-governmental organizations may expand. While warfare will likely continue to be bloody and brutish, offensive or defensive information warfare will be essential to new forms of battle, as well as to non-traditional information-based strategic or terrorist conflicts.

Of major import is the challenge facing the intelligence community. Gathering and analyzing information in new ways and from new sources is critical to a solid offensive and defensive strategy. In the technical world, where military C^4I^2 or national information infrastructures are powered by data networks, knowledge of new product capabilities, proliferation, and probable use is essential. Anticipating potential attacks, their point of origin, and possible impact on the United States and its allies creates many questions that are not clarified by information currently available to defense planners. As most militaries become consumers of information technologies provided by a robust international industry, greater use of open-source information, and the availability of analysts who understand information technology, is pivotal. To anticipate the choices of foreign leadership and detect their psychological operations, improved understanding of foreign cultures, language, and leadership is essential. In realizing the advantage necessary for victory, and the synergy possible in the execution of offensive and defensive information warfare, intelligence is a critical element.

DEVELOPING STRATEGIES THAT WORK

The range of potential threats and vulnerabilities demands a strategy that incorporates an understanding of the new security environment in a risk management context. The emerging DOD defensive IW strategy is illustrated in figure 1.

FIGURE 1: *IW Defensive Strategy*

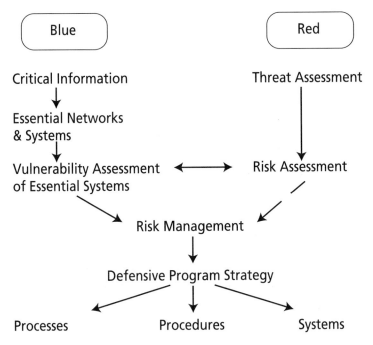

U.S. information and systems requirements work in parallel with an intelligence estimate that covers an adversary's threat. For example, on the U.S. side (represented by the blue team in figure 1), a decisionmaker begins with a statement of critical information needs, fully recognizing that they shift with the stage of execution. Next, the model calls for tracing the essential networks and systems along which critical information rides. A vulnerability assessment is then accomplished on those essential networks. This is a difficult undertaking; identifying the systems in-theater that support operations on the battlefield, as well as the "reachback" information systems to the PSN in the United States, is a dynamic problem. The need for system and network knowledge along with an advanced modeling and simulation capability will be most important.

Additionally, DOD is pursuing "advanced concept technology developments" to support the red-teaming of U.S. systems. This concept builds on knowledge gained from analysis of the technologies and functionalities of DOD-purchased systems, attaching them to new state-of-the-art tools available through the most accomplished hardware, software, and network engineers. On a parallel track, DOD is conducting intelligence estimates and risk assessment of possible threats. The result is a risk-management methodology able to compare the findings of risk/vulnerability assessments. A set of priorities then emerges on how to allocate resources for identification of processes, procedures, and systems.

A similar process is applied to crafting an offensive strategy, the next step in achieving offensive and defensive information-warfare synergies. Once elaborated, DOD envisions an iterative loop, illustrated in figure 2.

FIGURE 2: *Offense/Defense Synergies*

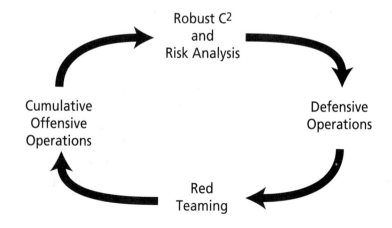

International competition in information technologies demands commercial off-the-shelf procurement for U.S. forces and its allies as well as for its adversaries. All forces are in the same marketplace, often sharing the same communications path. Analysis of their commonalities teaches a great deal about vulnerabilities on all sides. In modeling, simulation, and war gaming, cumulative offensive operations can be conducted to derive tools, techniques, and tactics for red-teaming of U.S. systems. Completing the first cycle are defensive operations based on conclusions from the red team attacks. With technology constantly improving, new players entering the fray, and offense always running ahead of defense's capacity to protect itself, the adjustment process is continuous across U.S. forces.

With the added sensitivity of information on vulnerabilities as well as on attack methods and tools, an orange team is established to deconflict and coordinate the process. The tools necessary to defend successfully against any type of information-based attack include both "soft" and "hard" elements. First and foremost, awareness and knowledge must travel from senior leadership down to system users. This demands vigorous training and education, emphasizing continuous learning from personnel accession points through professional training. Critical points may require new forms of in-depth factory training and security clearance for system and network administrators, the key people in operations. Effective policies that are enforceable and make sense must be written into every organization. New organizations need to be established, nurtured, and accepted, from the red teams at one end to emergency response teams at the other.

On the hard side, architectures must be built that not only minimize routine accidents but identify anomalies. Simple protection like firewalls and automated audit trails should be standard features of any system. One promising tool under development is intrusion detection. While there are simple forms currently available, work is underway on pattern-recognition software, based on biological principles, which not only detects a different user than the one authorized, but also detects codes which do not match the system's own "genetic" code. Through learning algorithms the computer will, upon detection, notify the system manager and generate its own genetic code antibodies to fight the malicious code inserted in its system, much like antibodies released in the human immune system are dispatched to combat disease.

The pressure for rapid development and procurement of such tools, procedures, and training increases with time. In less than four years the number of attacks or intrusions on DOD systems has doubled. The Defense Information Security Agency estimates that only one in five hundred incidents is reported. While these incidents are relatively low level, and are largely against unclassified, unprotected systems, the numbers are similar for civilian systems. Civilian systems are atomized; no large management structure governs them to ensure common architectures or protective measures. They include telephones, banking, utilities, transportation, and private credit history databases. Most attacks are not recognized, as they are either too sophisticated or are below the noise threshold for response. The vulnerability of these networks is worrisome. They can become prey, not only to cyber-criminals, but to adversaries seeking to avoid confrontation with military forces on the battlefield.

The emergence and assimilation of new technologies have frequently brought about significant changes in military organization, doctrine, and warfighting strategy. The speed, power, and miniaturization of information-processing components have brought greater lethality and precision; increased stand-off distance of command, forces, and firing platforms; and improved knowledge of the battlespace from intelligence, surveillance, and reconnaissance. As seen in the Gulf War, this capability can be used to blind and deafen an opponent, while enabling friendly air forces to deliver massive destruction of defenses, ensuring ground forces meet little or no resistance. Military analysts from many countries mark the lessons of the Gulf War. Most adversaries will not want to engage the United States in such a conflict in the future. How they might choose to attack U.S. information centers is a more pressing question. The important issues to be wrestled with now are how the emerging technologies have made new types of conflict possible, and how they can be best utilized, even as other countries and non-state actors are learning and adapting.

PAST LESSONS AS A STARTING POINT FOR FUTURE INNOVATION

There is truth in the bromide, "if you want a new idea, read an old book." New concepts do not so much require an original idea as the encouragement to think in a new way. In his seminal 1924 study *The Great Pacific War*,[2] Hector Bywater, a British naval correspondent for the *Baltimore Sun* and the *New York Times*, looked at changing technologies and the strategies made possible by them. He predicted the Japanese surprise attack on the Pacific fleet, battles of aircraft carriers, *kamikaze* raids, and a new type of amphibious warfare supporting a major U.S. counterattack. This work, little known today, stirred significant debate in military thinking around the world in its day. An immediate result of his writing was a series of changes incorporated into war plans by U.S. naval strategists. Of considerable irony is that one of Bywater's avid readers and correspondents, Admiral Yamamoto, based some of his war planning on Bywater's work. This new operational level of thinking and use of technology spurred the Japanese military to leapfrog in their planning.

Another forgotten author, who may be essential to understanding conflict in the Information Age, is Rear Admiral J. C. Wylie. In 1952, Wylie wrote a theory of power control, focusing on the use of sequential and cumulative strategies. Sequential strategies are a series of discrete steps that serially compose the entire sequence of a war. In cumulative strategies, the entire pattern is made up of a collection of lesser actions, but these individual actions are not necessarily sequential. They might include elements of economic or psychological warfare. Wylie stressed the power of cumulative strategies, in particular, their magnifying force when used with a larger-scale sequential plan. Twenty years later, in 1972, he reassessed his earlier writings, coming to the conclusion that "cumulative strategies are probably more important... and the information management revolution has probably made cumulative strategies more readily subject to analysis in planning before the events...."[3] His recommendation to capitalize on less-obvious cumulative strategies, such as economic or psychological warfare, offered effective options in an era of emerging information technologies. It has even more relevance today.

In a world of increasing regional instability, declining budgets, and smaller force levels, maintaining economy of force, proportionality, and discrimination become paramount. Previously, advantage was achieved through massive use of force. Capturing or destroying physical objectives might have been the first or only choice. In many future cases, neither attrition nor annihilation may be acceptable. Strategic objectives must now be achieved without exposing troops. With a broader reading of new capabilities and concerns, potential targets will change. Military acupressure and control may substitute for massive force. Some of the tools are already available to realize sooner and more efficiently the same or greater gains. If major breakthroughs in operationalizing information advantages are indeed imminent, the extra time invested in debate and war gaming is well spent. We have already made advances in the means, the tactical side of war. The dialogue within DOD, and between government and industry, spurs understanding of strategic information crime or conflict in which the interdependent nature of telecommunications and institutions creates lucrative targets. To be sure, the probability remains slim that entire networks, whether telephone or energy, can be completely disabled. However, today's adversaries can still cause considerable damage. These threats demand the protection of national information assets, and the organizational and fiscal requirements to bring such a strategy to fruition. The landscape of conflict in the future may be a mix of what is now known and what has yet to be envisioned. Employing an integrated strategy of information warfare – one that applies targeting and weaponry to information warfare over a wide range of opponents and circumstances – can empower U.S. forces and offer far greater security than previously imagined.

ENDNOTES

1. Jeff Cooper, "The Revolution in Security Affairs" (Unpublished paper).
2. Hector Bywater, *The Great Pacific War* (New York: St. Martin's Press, 1991).
3. J.C. Wylie, *Military Strategy: A General Theory of Power Control* (Annapolis, MD: U.S. Naval Institute, 1989).

chapter eleven

Maneuver in the Information Age

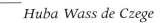

Huba Wass de Czege

BY DEFINITION, maneuver in warfare centers on achieving positions of relative advantage from which to strike an enemy more effectively. However, with the insertion of new information technologies and the accompanying enhancement of situational awareness, one might ask, "If both sides can see one another, how can maneuver occur?" As in chess, where both players can see each other clearly, maneuver in the Information Age is not only possible, it is vital to defeating an opponent expeditiously and decisively.

Tactics is the art of transforming combat capability into the power to influence battlefield outcomes. Emerging technologies enable a remarkable transformation in tactics. Their application facilitates the simultaneous employment of large quantities of precision munitions and sensors, secure and reliable digital communications, and advanced information technologies for planning, decisionmaking, and information sharing. Information technologies enable a quantum increase in the combat potential of military forces, creating a synergy of firepower, maneuver, and protection effects. This chapter will illustrate Information Age division-level tactics for attack and defense which incorporate maneuver, firepower, and protection effects directed by information technology-enhanced battle command.

THE ART OF MANEUVER AND THE GAME OF CHESS

Those who use the chess analogy to understand warfare in the Information Age speculate about a condition in which opponents can see each other's moves, and possess equal strike and mobility capabilities. They tend to conclude that maneuver is not possible under such conditions. Yet one could argue that even in chess, where mobility is evenly matched and both sides see all, maneuver is critical. A player like Anatoly Karpov wins because he thinks several moves ahead, and moves to achieve a position of relative advantage later in the game. He understands his opponent's options at any point in the game, and explores ways to counter or preempt them. Chess masters win because they understand patterns of play and anticipate future moves. This is the essence of maneuver in the Information Age.

However, war in the Information Age will not unfold like an orderly game of chess. In chess, each player has an equal number of pieces. Players take turns moving one piece at a time, inhibiting maneuver. By contrast, warfare is chaotic. In the deadly game of war, the size of the board and the number and variety of pieces are multiplied. In war, both players can move at any time, governed only by the laws of logistics. The two sides are not symmetrically matched in numbers and types of pieces. One player may see more clearly than the other. Relative strengths and weakness are not balanced and may not be readily apparent. As disorder increases, the scope for surprise and maneuver rises.

Warfare can be a direct "slugfest" or an exchange of indirect, though bloody, blows. In a direct confrontation, the player able to inflict the greatest attrition will win, and is usually the one who is technologically and numerically superior. But a player like Karpov will win quickly and decisively even against a slugger of equal or greater capabilities. He triumphs by maneuvering his opponent into a position of disadvantage, then striking a quick and fatal blow. Maneuver is the only way for the technologically or numerically inferior player to offset an opponent's strengths. The superior player maneuvers to minimize losses and to achieve decisions more quickly.

Maneuvering to achieve relative advantage when both parties can "see" one another depends upon the number and quality of decisions made by opposing leaders within short time frames. Preparation to exercise multiple options is key. The decentralization of decisionmaking to prepared and informed subordinates is also critical. The quality of leaders and soldiers has always been a major determinant of successful maneuver, but as warfare grows in complexity, the preparedness of leaders and soldiers takes on increasing importance. U.S. forces cannot rely on technological superiority alone for success in future operations. Even numerical parity will be difficult to attain. Achieving decisive results rapidly will only come about from superior maneuver.

VISIONS FOR THE POTENTIAL FORCE OF THE TWENTY-FIRST CENTURY

The current vision of the potential fighting force of the early twenty-first century can offer only the outlines of what is yet to come. But the image builds upon already proven technologies that could be fielded within the next two decades if decisions are made now to acquire them. While the individual capabilities of new systems is too lengthy a topic to address here, some conclusions may be drawn regarding the combined effects of emerging precision systems, intelligence and targeting sensors, digital communications, and information technologies.

The capability to launch high-quality precision munitions against an enemy simultaneously or in very close succession will define tactics. Precision munitions are not new, but they have been employed with a great deal of care against high-value targets. All of the eight hundred fighting vehicles and over 2,200 support vehicles in the average division of any potential opponent of the next twenty to thirty years can be attacked and defeated in a ten minute engagement by weapons organic to or in support of a brigade of the potential force. The proliferation of large numbers of high-quality sensors — from space-based systems to hand-emplaced acoustic sensors — enables observation of an opponent from the moment enemy forces leave their barracks until they have been engaged and defeated. Unmanned aerial vehicles (UAVs) with sophisticated sensor packages are also becoming more reliable, stealthy, and available. The capability to sort, process, and analyze the vast quantities of data these will produce is growing rapidly.

Digital communications are becoming capable of linking sensors to databases, analysts, planners, decisionmakers, and shooters. Information technologies will make it possible to explore maneuver options earlier and to prepare plans with many branches and sequels. Information-processing technologies will allow valuable information to be continuously updated, heightening the availability of information critical to decision-making in fast-paced operations. Of great value will be the ability to accomplish anticipatory planning, especially evaluation of an enemy's options and possible friendly counters and preemptions. This will lead to preparations for timely and appropriate action.

If skillfully employed, the enhanced capabilities of the twenty-first century force will generate enormous increases in combat power – the optimization of firepower, maneuver, and protection capabilities to achieve combat superiority. Improvements in battle command systems will magnify the ability of leaders to apply new capabilities skillfully to a wide variety of battlefield situations.

Firepower. Firepower effects will multiply as targeting is enhanced, systems become more flexible, delivery ranges are extended, the lethality of individual munitions is increased, and precision is improved. The key to these enhancements is the widespread application of information technologies and operations to massing firepower effects at the right time and place on the battlefield.

The number of targets that can be engaged precisely and simultaneously will increase exponentially. It will soon be possible to launch deliberate attacks on large formations with precise, violent, and devastating concentrated effects from extended ranges. The artillery systems of a division-sized element alone will launch over seven thousand precision projectiles within ten minutes. The bulk of these can reach up to forty-five kilometers, but there is also the capability to launch three hundred precision projectiles well over two hundred kilometers. During the same ten-minute time frame, attack helicopter battalions can launch over three hundred precision-guided missiles, capable of destroying the most modern tank at a distance of seven kilometers after penetrating over one hundred kilometers into enemy territory. They can also defend against air defense systems at ranges up to two hundred kilometers, and against other helicopters up to ten kilometers away.

At the same time, heavy and light ground brigades will be able to launch a considerable number of precision mortars and non-line-of-sight precision missiles, in addition to longer-range and more-precise versions of current direct-fire systems. The flexibility of systems is increased by the mobility of cannon and rocket systems and the digital interconnectivity of fire control systems. This permits fast-paced operations and concentration of effects from widely dispersed locations.

Maneuver. Maneuver effects are enhanced as mobility and speed are improved, navigation is eased, and anticipatory planning is streamlined. Maneuver effects derive from attaining a position of relative advantage, thus enabling the most lethal application of fires and inflicting the greatest psychological shock upon an enemy. Information technologies, rather than mobility technologies, will be most critical to the enhancement of maneuver effects. Of these, anticipatory planning is the most significant. Though mobility technologies are not anticipated to advance dramatically, formations will move more quickly as even the slowest vehicles are upgraded with chassis capable of keeping pace with the M1/M2 family of vehicles. The reliability of vehicles and automatic monitoring of vehicle performance will reduce breakdowns. More importantly, as a result of these improvements, the larger tactical organizations – battalions, brigades, and divisions – will be able to maintain a much faster tempo of operations.

While the speed of Army heliborne mobility has not greatly increased since the 1980s, the impact of heliborne mobility will magnify by early next century as a result of better intelligence, improved navigation, and enhanced passive and active counter air-defense measures. Not only can attack helicopter and air cavalry formations now penetrate faster and more securely, but air assault potential has grown. Reconnaissance and infantry combat troops can be inserted more securely, and in greater numbers. Precision indirect-fire systems can be repositioned securely, far behind enemy lines, to extend the reach of massed precision fires. Better navigation and route planning capability, already evidenced in the satellite positioning systems used by most American soldiers during the Gulf War, will permit more rapid arrival to a position. Better navigation will also insure that more units and systems engage the enemy from intended positions of relative advantage.

Surprise is more readily achieved with greater situational awareness and more effective operational security. The ability to track an enemy's movements during maneuver facilitates adjustments to optimize relative positioning for surprise and weapons effects. Many enhancements contribute to denying the enemy knowledge about friendly positions, movements, and intentions. Enhanced obscurants, protected electronic emissions, rapid movement, and many other features of the twenty-first century force, ensure surprise and effective maneuver.

Protection. Protection effects are strengthened through the increased survivability of individual systems, and also because of enhancements in dispersion, active deception, security operations, speed and agility, and the ability to exploit limited visibility. So, too, recent innovations have made for improved nuclear-, biological-, and chemical-defense operations, multidimensional air defense, and increased situational awareness. These combined active and passive measures create ambiguity for the enemy and enhance the security of the force many times over present capabilities. The greatest contribution to protection derives from the pervasive effect of embedded information technologies and information operations.

Speed and agility in operations are facilitated by information technologies that promote situational awareness and refined planning and coordination. Increased awareness of friendly and enemy situations and superior battle command systems will enable the potential force to disperse. This degrades enemy intelligence operations, targeting, and lethality. Future deception operations are also empowered by decoys and false signatures, enabling a division to give a false impression of its concentrations.

Enhanced security operations increase the survivability of the force. Division security benefits from accurate, updated intelligence, coupled with near real-time situational awareness. Commanders can optimize employment of their security elements more easily, as they are reinforced with air and ground sensors linked to rapid-response fires and dynamic obstacles. Screens will generally incorporate sensors and weapons aimed at interdicting enemy ground and air reconnaissance elements, UAVs, and air reconnaissance flights.

In addition to operating within the context of potent joint counter-air operations, protection from air attack is improved. Active employment of air defense assets becomes more effective because they are better positioned with sensors capable of locating enemy aircraft and by quick fire-shooter linkages to sensors. Passive air defense is enabled through better early warning and reduced signatures resulting from dispersion.

Battle Command. Battle command effects will intensify with the application of new information technologies that amplify knowledge, resulting in faster and better-informed decisions and planning. What differentiates future battle command from traditional challenges is the scope, intensity, and tempo of operations created by the lethality, precision, and range of modern weapons, coupled with the timeliness and accuracy of information provided by Information Age systems and sensors. The ability to make and communicate decisions faster than the enemy is key to establishing a tempo of operations to which the enemy cannot react.

Although battlefield decisionmaking and control of units will become more scientific, leading soldiers and units to success will remain an art. Marginal differences in the quality of soldiers and leaders will be magnified in a future conflict between technological equals. The tempo of operations will introduce new stresses on soldiers and leaders. Victory and defeat will still turn on the determination of leaders to venture into a high stakes arena and the willingness of soldiers to follow.

Through a combination of technological applications, automated processes, and command and staff procedures, the Army of the next century will enjoy significantly improved battlefield awareness. Leaders will be able to react faster to unforeseen circumstances and enemy initiative. However, even when complete information about present circumstances is available, leaders must make judgments about the shape of future engagements. They must plan the tactical actions of large formations based on informed assumptions about future dispositions and conditions. To the extent that they can do this, they retain initiative by planning ahead and setting the tempo and conditions of battle.

The increased tempo of decisionmaking places a premium on intelligent delegation of authority, rather than on centralization. With so much information now available, the challenge is to transform data consistently into sound and timely decisions. Simulation exercises indicate that potent capabilities are underutilized when commanders and staff have too many decisions to make. Often, they do not have time to think of creative ways to use capabilities. Even though a commander may have all the information necessary to make decisions for subordinate levels, a leader may refrain from doing so because the time spent deciding would reduce the tempo of operations. This encourages the horizontal and vertical distribution of the relevant information, facilitating the "mission orders" style of command advocated by current U.S. Army doctrine.

Battle command nodes and processes will enable battle command from anywhere in the battlespace. Headquarters will be echeloned for mobility and flexibility. Seamless communications will allow some support staffs to remain in secure enclaves, or at a home station. Digitized systems will rapidly transmit directives and orders vertically to subordinate levels, while transmitting other essential information horizontally across the organization to present a common relevant picture of battlefield conditions and information critical to upcoming decisions at all levels of command.

The combination of effective firepower, maneuver, protection, and leadership will have dramatic impact on tactical methods. If properly led, educated, and trained, future Army elements can be an extremely powerful fighting force. In offensive operations against the most technologically advanced opponent, the future division will be capable of attacking and defeating an enemy of corps size. In defensive operations, such as the defense of a lodgment area, it will be able to defeat more than two simultaneously attacking corps.

As in other eras of technological advancement, the basic principles of defensive and offensive operations will not change in the Information Age, but the methods of applying them will. Similarly, the principle of integrating varied arms and systems to achieve enhanced synergistic effects will remain, but the methods of combining arms at tactical and even technical levels may be transformed considerably. In some cases, previous methods are merely upgraded. In others, new methods must be designed to optimize emerging capabilities and to take advantage of the potential synergies between systems. The following discussion illustrates the changes in methods that will result from applying new capabilities.

OFFENSIVE CONCEPTS AND
METHODS IN THE INFORMATION AGE

The purpose of offensive operations is to compel enemy compliance when non-military means are ineffective. The immediate objective of attacks are to disrupt enemy synchronization, destroy unit cohesion, and shatter the enemy's willingness to fight. Traditionally, commanders have chosen to attack when seizure of terrain or enemy demoralization is vital to achieving higher aims.

The potential force may also fight to recover territory seized by aggression or to destroy the military capability of an enemy regime. In either case, offensive operations of the future will maintain a force, rather than terrain, orientation.

The fundamental principles that have shaped force structure and operations until now remain a sure guide to future offensive methods. Taking, maintaining, and exploiting initiative is the key to dominating an enemy. Future offensive operations will continue to be characterized by surprise, concentration, tempo, ambiguity, and audacity. As events unfold, the enemy will be forced continually to account for, and react to, several possible threats. From the moment that an offensive force commits itself, the enemy will have very little time to identify the focus of the blow. With shared situational awareness of friendly and enemy dispositions and movements, the division will achieve dispersion without loss of control. Decoy movements and false concentrations will also be more manageable and effective because the force will not depend on predictable formations; thus, the enemy will have greater difficulty templating its operations. The lethal systems of the offensive force division will be brought within striking distance of their targets "just in time" to deliver precision fires, and will then be rapidly repositioned. The decisive phase of the battle will be brief but violent, and exploitation will be swift and decisive.

The Army will concentrate effects rather than forces when it attacks. Concentration has previously been thought of primarily in terms of space, or frontage. It should now be thought of as a concentration of temporal effects against a particular formation or capability of the enemy – a focused pulse of high relative combat power. It will not be necessary to bring units together to achieve the massing or concentration of their effects. The extended ranges of weapons systems will allow physical dispersion without giving up the effects of concentration. Much smaller fixing elements will be required. It will also be unnecessary to face a concentration of the enemy in order to concentrate effects. The precision attack capability of the division can be targeted against a particular formation even though it may be widely dispersed. For instance, the object of the attack could be a large marching formation stretched over one hundred kilometers. Or the object of a preparatory attack could be the entire artillery organization of the enemy capable of ranging the point of penetration.

This form of simultaneous attack against the most vital functions of the enemy resembles a classical ambush in which an opponent is suddenly rendered helpless and vulnerable to exploitation. The potential force will be able to discern and track large numbers of targets anywhere in the battlespace that may be vital to an opposing force. With sufficient planning and preparation, the force division will be able to track, target, and engage an enemy corps rapidly. It will attack with fires or maneuver against targets up to 250 kilometers from its center, while striking multiple capabilities simultaneously. The enemy will encounter attacks from all sides that will break the ability to decide and dissolve the will to fight. As always, boldness will be rewarded with magnified success. To realize the capabilities of the twenty-first century force fully, prudent risks must be taken. The main killing systems of the deliberate attack may be stand-off precision systems, but the effects of these weapons must be exploited by close combat. As in the past, the audacity of an attack plan and the soldier's execution of it will determine the success of close combat.

The methods of the future Army will adhere to the logic of traditional warfighting principles, but will differ in form. In the past, hostilities often began with tactical units conducting movements to contact, using formations optimized for security and flexibility. Contact with the enemy was followed by a series of hasty attacks to further develop the situation and to gain initiative. This method was appropriate in conflicts where detailed tactical information was scarce. Deliberate attacks usually followed when information was sufficient. Exploitation followed deliberate attacks to insure results. Pursuit usually completed the defeat of a beaten foe.

In the twenty-first century, movement to contact as we know it will change. An offensive action will unfold according to deliberate and focused layering of sophisticated surveillance systems linked to air and ground reconnaissance units. Down-linked overhead platforms from high echelons will cue reconnaissance and surveillance by subordinate elements. Air and ground scouts, whose mission is to refine information on the enemy and the terrain, will be cued by UAVs and down-linked broadcast radar and signals intelligence. The information thus generated will permit the force to attack earlier, under the most advantageous conditions, and usually with enough information to launch deliberate rather than hasty attacks. Hasty attack will also be transformed as totally unplanned and unexpected engagements become less likely. Yet, an enemy may still react in unexpected ways, creating a continuing need for some form of hasty attack, although it will be better informed and more decisive. They will usually take the form of fixing attacks by nearby ground and air maneuver units, followed by the rapid, deliberate, and decisive massed effects of precision indirect fires.

The potential force should have sufficient information to execute decisive attacks early in a campaign. Deliberate attack will be conducted when enough information about the enemy allows a focused application of combat power. All application of combined arms will be optimized for defeat of a specific enemy element or seizure of a specific piece of terrain. Twenty-first century deliberate attacks will require a 70 percent ground truth solution (actual location and disposition of the enemy) for planning, and a 90 to 95 percent solution for execution. At the outset of a major regional conflict, a great deal of detailed tactical information will be down-linked for planning purposes. The unpredictability inherent in planning will be compensated by a greater capability to analyze enemy courses of action and create sufficient options to account for variations in the opponent's dispositions at the time of attack. This greater capability to observe, track, and analyze the enemy's activities after the receipt of the initial planning information will enable the 90 to 95 percent solution by the time it is required for execution and exploitation.

The principles of ambush provide the foundation for the methods of deliberate attack. The ability to identify, monitor, and track an enemy undetected enables a commander to decide when the enemy formation to be attacked is optimally positioned for ambush. Multiple, adjustable engagement areas can be planned within the precision firepower "footprint" of the potential force. The ambush "kill zone" may be a wide area, limited only by the reach of precision weapons, the ability to concentrate sufficient firepower effects, and the capacity to place sufficient precision "shooters" within reach of potential targets. The availability of large numbers of precision indirect firing systems – from precision-capable mortars to long-range missiles – combined with accurate target information provided by reconnaissance systems will make indirect systems the most attractive option for deliberate attack. Maneuver units can fight to position the precision-capable firing units for optimal employment effects. Maneuver units may then protect and reposition them. They can also exploit the effects of the deliberate attack.

Exploitation will immediately follow deliberate attack to ensure a decisive result. Usually, the conditions under which exploitations can occur are difficult to predict. In eighteenth- and nineteenth-century warfare, exploitation was the role of the heavy cavalry held in reserve. Now, highly mobile maneuver units will take the lead, while the most flexible indirect-fire systems provide immediate support. Each deliberate attack engagement area is assessed and exploited by the local commander, overseeing close-combat exploitation following deliberate attack engagements by precision-capable systems. Division commanders will also exploit the success of brigade-level attack. Commanders at higher echelons will exploit the success of division-level deliberate attacks. Sometimes they will turn to air power supported by long-range artillery only. At other times, corps or higher-level exploitation will entail the rapid continuation of the attack by other forces while the division is recovered and reconstituted for the next action.

TWENTY-FIRST CENTURY DEFENSIVE PRINCIPLES AND METHODS

Preparation, security, disruption, flexibility, and mass and concentration will continue to be fundamental. Yet, as in offensive operations, the methods for achieving these goals will change. Traditionally, commanders have chosen to defend when they needed to achieve specific goals: to buy time, to hold a piece of key terrain, to facilitate other operations, to preoccupy the enemy in one area so friendly forces can attack in another, or to erode enemy resources at a rapid rate while reinforcing friendly operations. Higher commanders will still use forces for many of these same purposes. For instance, the twenty-first century division will be ideally suited to seize and defend a lodgment for follow-on forces. It can establish a wide security zone, and hold off the enemy until the force as a whole is ready to undertake offensive missions. In a situation of active aggression, it may act as a counterattack force under a corps, or function independently under the land component commander of a joint task force. It may also be assigned a sector within an allied defensive campaign once hostilities ensue.

Thorough preparation is critical to successful defense. In principle, a defender will arrive first, establish security to prevent surprise, prepare the ground, position forces to maximum advantage, prepare detailed fire plans, and rehearse movements and counterattacks. Information technologies will allow the force to make the most of preparation time. Currently, much valuable time is lost to preparation of plans and dissemination of information. The potential force will disseminate precise information rapidly; digitized map systems and associated terrain analysis and war-gaming tools will produce plans quickly, permitting soldiers to focus their efforts speedily.

The reconnaissance, surveillance, and target acquisition (RSTA) and security-forces capability of the potential force enhance the rapid establishment of a deep and comprehensive security zone to prevent surprise. The ability to link a multi-layered and seamless reconnaissance and surveillance web to the long-range lethal precision systems and mobile exploitation forces of the potential force provides a great defensive advantage. The division will be able to track the enemy at great depth without violating frontiers or making contact. Under some circumstances it can project force forward to shape the enemy's attack options before close combat ensues. The depth of defense is augmented by this ability to project RSTA and combat power forward. The width of sectors are also enlarged because fewer avenues of approach need to be physically occupied at any one time. As the enemy approach is studied, approach options narrow, as do positioning and engagement-area priorities. Lateral repositioning by potential force division elements can take place earlier, leaving more time for preparations to engage an enemy in the new positions.

Ground preparation is enhanced in several ways. The potential force will have better analytical tools for determining what preparations are most advantageous in the time available. For example, it will be easier to determine the optimal positioning of weapon system emplacements when line-of-sight and fire distribution studies can be accomplished quickly and accurately, using digitized terrain models and global positioning systems. New technologies also contribute to more effective systems for the construction of obstacles and protected positions and their improved utilization due to greater situational awareness. Many fighting systems will better utilize natural terrain protection because their longer ranges allow greater stand-off. This will reduce the need for prepared fighting positions and permit more flexibility in the plan of fires.

Movements and counterattacks will become more effective as they are more easily rehearsed. The key to successful counterattack has always been rehearsal to achieve proper timing and relative positioning of forces. But since rehearsals are time consuming, they are often overlooked. The simulation rehearsals made possible by emerging information technologies may help overcome some of these time constraints. Precise navigation under all conditions is also essential to successful counterattack. The space-based navigation systems of the potential force will ensure that movements in relation to the enemy are economical and achieve the required relative position of advantage.

The ability to disrupt an attacker's main effort increases with the application of new technologies. In principle, a defender disrupts the tempo of the attack, causes the attack to culminate before its objectives are achieved, and maintains a posture that enables the defender to seize the initiative. The defender identifies the main effort and disrupts the attacker's combined arms cooperation and synchronization. The battle is "shaped" by the use of fixing forces and terrain-enhancing obstacles. The tempo of the attacker's follow-on forces and reserves is disrupted. The potential force can also shape the battle by more effectively denying maneuver options to the attacker through a combination of attack aviation, precision rocket artillery, and rocket- and air-delivered "intelligent" minefields. This is done more subtly in the potential force without giving away the intended focus of main effort within the defense. Disruption of an attacker's main effort need no longer be a sequential effort; the potential force will be able to achieve a simultaneity of effects that magnifies the result. The combination of enhanced information operations, long-range precision systems, long-range deliverable "intelligent" minefields, and other new capabilities will permit the potential force to disrupt the enemy attack more economically, preserving a larger force for exploitation by counterattack.

In principle, as an enemy's attack culminates, the defender must be capable of massing overwhelming combat power at decisive moments. In the potential force, the range and mobility of precision systems, as well as the benefits of superior battle command systems, will trigger quantum improvements in the capability to mass effects for this purpose. Enhanced situational awareness will allow early, more accurate recognition of where the decisive point will be. With the ability to develop varied branch plans, the massing of effects can be synchronized to a much higher degree as the enemy approaches the security zone of the potential force. The enhanced flexibility generated by these capabilities is critical. The defender must anticipate and react quickly to overcome the attacker's advantage. This requires flexible planning and agile execution. Plans must anticipate multiple enemy options and must be well coordinated and rehearsed. Flexibility is also undergirded by a logistics system that replaces a "just in case" mentality with a "just in time" orientation. Less bulk is prepositioned forward and there is greater visibility of assets that can be rapidly moved to support the main effort as it shifts.

Two primary forms of defensive operations have traditionally been mobile and area defense. These have applied to both the tactical and operational levels of war. Mobile defenses focus on the destruction of the attacking force by permitting the enemy to advance into a position that enables counterattack by a powerful mobile reserve. Area defenses orient on retention of terrain by absorbing the enemy in an interlocking series of positions and destroying the opponent largely by fires. A commander may elect either form of defense if the mission requires retention of terrain. If the retention of terrain is dictated by a lack of available maneuver room in depth, then an area defense is usually required.

These two types of defense combine static and dynamic elements of defense in different patterns. The static elements of the defense – terrain-oriented engagement areas defined by natural and man-made obstacles and covered by units in prepared positions – have predominated in area defenses. The dynamic elements of the defense – spoiling attacks and counterattacks over rehearsed terrain – predominate in mobile defenses. Static elements delay, channel, and ultimately halt the attacker; dynamic elements exploit these effects to achieve decisive results. In mobile defenses, static elements support the main effort of the mobile striking force by controlling the depth and breadth of enemy penetrations and ensuring retention of ground from which to launch decisive counterattacks. In area defenses, static elements comprise the main effort, and dynamic elements — such as patrols and counterattacking reserve forces — support by maintaining the integrity of the defensive system of interrelated engagement areas. The character of these static and dynamic elements will change as new technologies are employed. The static elements of the defense will become more flexible and more economical of close-combat forces. The dynamic elements of defense will be more potent and more decisive.

While engagement areas will still be defined by terrain and man-made obstacles, both hand-emplaced and artillery-fired minefields will provide far greater flexibility for the use of resources. The potency of the overwatching close-combat force is enhanced with more lethal direct-fire systems capable of higher rates of accurate fire under all conditions. Potency is further multiplied by the availability of two kinds of indirect precision fires in large numbers. Those with seekers built into the warheads automatically seek out vehicular targets. Others can be remotely directed to discriminate among vehicular targets to seek out command vehicles and air-defense weapons or other high-value targets. The two can achieve complementary effects when employed together. Since a smaller close-combat force can cover each engagement area, a far greater number of engagement areas can be prepared than will eventually be required as the battle unfolds. Enhanced situational awareness allows the defense to track and orient on specific elements of the attacking force. This means activation of only those areas which coincide with the movements of the enemy force and the overall plan of defeating it. The effects combine to create ambush conditions that can be more easily exploited by the dynamic elements of the defense.

CONCLUSION

Warfare in the Information Age will not revolutionize principles, but it will revolutionize methods. In the Information Age, the time available to consider information and select options will be limited, even when plans have anticipated events. The pace of combat, and thus the pace of decisions, will demand prudent delegation of decisionmaking authority and responsibility. Ambush tactics, stealthy preparations, "just in time" positioning, concentrated employment of precision munitions, and rapid exploitation of effects will become the defining characteristics of twenty-first century combat.

The tactics of the Information Age can be likened to "man to man" rather than "zone" basketball. Missions will focus on a particular enemy force or capability rather than geography. Tracking and battle-damage assessment for a particular enemy element will be assigned to the unit charged with defeating it. There will be less restrictive, terrain-oriented control. The operational defeat mechanism will be the cascading effects of simultaneous and sequential tactical engagements. A rapid sequence of deliberate and concentrated precision strikes, followed by quick maneuver, will maintain tactical initiative, lead to operational initiative, and culminate in speedy strategic successes.

Even if both sides possess advanced information capabilities on the twenty-first century battlefield, an enemy's use of information is little cause for concern if friendly forces can stay one or two steps ahead. Clearly, information does not win a battle unless it empowers combat actions. Information technologies make possible better plans, rich with options for early and effective decisionmaking. This makes initiative possible; and it is initiative that enables the crucial element of maneuver in Information Age warfare.

chapter twelve

Force XXI: U.S. Army Requirements, Priorities, and Challenges in the Information Age

John P. Rose
Robert M. Evans
Mark J. Eschelman
Jack Gerber
Jo-Ann C. Webber

The information explosion, coupled with the revolutionary pace of technological development, poses considerable challenges for both the civilian sector and the Department of Defense. Within the U.S. Army, much attention has been focused on the conduct of warfare in the political and technological environment of the twenty-first century. The result is a program for change that gives close consideration to the way Information Age technologies reshape visions of the Army in the next century, referred to as "Force XXI."[1]

The Army that will emerge from the Force XXI program will be capabilities-based, designed to achieve competitive advantage through the effective use of information. The Force XXI process integrates and leverages information technologies, building upon a versatile concept of information-based battle command. It is not designed to produce an overmatch in individual weapons systems, but rather to synchronize all elements of combat power before an adversary can react. This capabilities-based Army will still be characterized by the basic tenets of Army operations — initiative, agility, depth, synchronization, and versatility. Yet, it must also be rapidly tailorable, expandable, strategically deployable, and effectively employable as part of a joint and sometimes multinational team. While keeping the evolution and integration of information technologies in mind, the primary mission of the U.S. Army should not be forgotten. The Army's mandate is to confront and destroy enemy forces. One key to fulfilling this mandate has traditionally been the maintenance of greater situational awareness over opposing forces. As such, the requirement for information is not new, although techniques for handling information have radically changed. Today, control and domination of the flow of information is essential for success in an uncertain and unstable global security environment.

The central purpose of Force XXI can be expressed in a simple analogy to today's personal computer systems. The computer has evolved dramatically over the past twenty years. Not long ago, computing meant batch processing, with its decks of key-punch cards and reams of computer printouts. Next came the transition to time sharing, featuring shared access to a mainframe computer and the ability to conduct some analyses on line. Significant advances followed the leap to the personal computer (PC) in desktop and laptop form. In this new environment, computer enthusiasts could work at their own pace within a localized database. Changes and upgrades to hardware and software now occur so regularly that there is an unending race to keep pace with technology.

In the late 1980s, the 60286 Intel microprocessor, the heart of any 286 PC, offered unprecedented computing speeds and capabilities. But in the few short years since, continued growth of computer capabilities to the Pentium standard and beyond have made even the 486 PC of two years ago seem obsolete. Many 286

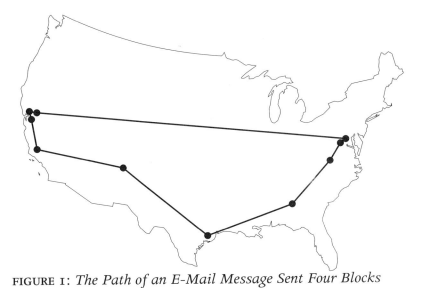

FIGURE I: *The Path of an E-Mail Message Sent Four Blocks*

owners can no longer find software that will work on their machines. As decision cycles and processing speeds are reduced to milli- and microsecond increments, software that does work on older machines operates at speeds that may delay decisions and extend response times to noncompetitive levels. Finally, the most recent advances in real-time Internet capabilities further complicate the problem of keeping pace.

A recently published article in the *Washington Post* entitled "The Medium is the Mess," described an e-mail message that was encoded to trace its route from the *Post* building on L Street to the White House, about four blocks away. Transferring its way through Internet linkages, the message went through twenty different links – covering a coast to coast route of over six thousand miles in only sixty milliseconds.

The ability to exploit these data-transfer rates and capabilities is crucial to deciding future conflicts. In short, the adversary must be kept at a 286 operating speed, while the Army must operate at Pentium efficiency.

THE PACE OF CHANGE

Technological advances have changed the way wars are fought throughout history. In agrarian societies, war pitted large armies against each other. With the advent of the Industrial Age, technology led to greater lethality and mobility. Entire societies mobilized to produce professional armies that could capitalize on technological advances, often allowing a small force to defeat a larger one.[2] Application of Information Age technologies will most likely lead to yet another order-of-magnitude change in the way warfare is conducted. Anticipation of this paradigm shift calls for new methods of organization, mobilization, training, and projection of forces.

This escalating pace of change also means potential adversaries can more quickly make widespread use of new capabilities. With available financial resources, any nation, group, or individual can leapfrog into the Information Age by purchasing off-the-shelf technology. In Somalia, Agrarian Age technologies existed beside the latest advances: warlords communicated with cellular phones, Somali soldiers used rocket-propelled grenades to shoot down helicopters, and paramilitary elements used cow bells as early warning devices in the street battles of Mogadishu.[3]

As such, the "key piece of terrain" to hold in the twenty-first century will be information. A reconceptualized and redesigned force will integrate and leverage information technologies to provide greater performance at all echelons. Information technology will enable simultaneous operations across the continuum of military operations, from peacekeeping to land combat. Leveraging information and information technology facilitates the creation of joint forces, through the exploitation of digital connectivity both vertically and horizontally. It fosters a common view of the battlefield, not just among Army units, but with air and maritime forces as well.

The result will be a competitive advantage if information systems can be guarded and protected while used to defeat an adversary.

As the Army continues to focus on readiness for war, the capability to conduct a wide range of other operations must be maintained. Information connectivity, provided by such techniques as digitization, is critical to functioning effectively in varied environments. Digitization is "the application of information technologies to acquire, exchange, and employ digital information throughout the battlespace, tailored to the needs of commanders, shooters, and supporters – allowing each to maintain a clear/accurate vision of [the] battlespace necessary to support planning and execution."[4] Digitization allows synchronization of combat power across all battlefield operating systems and on both strategic and tactical levels.[5] The result is enhanced lethality, survivability, and operating tempo of forces. Although the concept of digitization is not new, earlier systems could not "talk" to each other. Now, a multitude of systems can become interoperable.

Not long ago, one of the more difficult tasks of a battalion operations center was accurately tracking forces and posting maps with friendly and enemy locations. Maps at various battlefield operations levels were frequently different. Digital connectivity provides commanders with the same map, generated by sensors identifying both enemy and friendly locations, that is electronically updated in real time. Not only will the map show topography, derived from satellite and reconnaissance imagery, commanders will have immediate access to the status of logistics as well. This technology will have a tremendous impact on the ability to synchronize combat operations, concentrate the effects of forces, and prevent fratricide. Furthermore, it will act as a combat multiplier, substantially improving situational awareness.

• WAR IN THE INFORMATION AGE •

Situational awareness and its impact on the commander's decision cycle – observe, orient, decide, and act – has evolved significantly since the Agrarian Age. During the American Revolution, General Washington's observations were limited to what he could see through a telescope. He oriented his battle plan in weeks, decided over the course of months, and acted through the large part of a season. In the Civil War, General Grant was able to gather important situational information through the telegraph, subsequently orienting plans and forces in days, deciding on a course of action in weeks, and acting within a month. During World War II, General Patton could observe through radio and wire and thus orient in hours, decide in days, and act within a week. In the Gulf War, General Schwarzkopf had the capability to observe in near-real time, through intelligence systems like JSTARS. He was able to orient forces in minutes, decide in hours and act within a day.[6] The key to success in the Gulf War was leveraging myriad information technologies, such as the Global Positioning System and tactical satellite communications. The early years of the twenty-first century will bring the ability of real-time observation, allowing forces to orient, decide, and act simultaneously. For the first time, it may truly be possible to see multiple dimensions of the battlefield at one time. In this environment, the commander dominating battlefield awareness holds the key to triumph.

Attainment of information dominance is central to modernization of the Army's command and control systems and its intelligence systems. Information dominance is achieved by maximizing the ability to transmit and process critical, relevant information. It is maintained by guarding those capabilities while degrading an adversary's ability to use and protect information.[7] Gaining information dominance requires a long-range view of Army roles and missions, an operational synergy among evolving resources, and a doctrinal framework that supports high-technology capabilities.

The development of information sometimes requires inputs from a variety of critical reporting networks. The goal of the digitized battlefield system is instantaneous communication with numerous sites across the battlefield, in order to receive data and provide timely, useful feedback. Information must be easily understood, meaningful to the military commander, and displayed in a manner that provides clear options for action. Most often this is achieved through pictoral displays of information. Understanding the difference between the effective transmittal of data and information is critical. A commander can easily be inundated with data. The goal is to frame this data and present it in a way that provides critical, relevant information. The end result must be maximum situational awareness and improved fratricide avoidance. To reduce an adversary's ability to upset information processing, the systems used must incorporate a mix of security procedures and protection systems that prevent compromise and minimize disruption. These include features to support brief independent operations, and to provide backup through redundancy.

In the transition to a new strategic and operational construct, a well developed triad of assured communications systems, reliable intelligence, and command and control protection (C^2P) techniques is imperative. Linkage of this triad to a highly accurate set of lethal combat systems is critical to power projection and split-based operations. The ability to see the battlefield, relay data instantaneously, verify, and cross-check, should prevent many communications breakdowns. The result: quick, decisive victory with minimal loss of life.

THE PLAN OF CHANGE

To meet Force XXI goals, the Army has established five modernization objectives: project and sustain; protect the force; win the information war; conduct precision strike; and dominate maneuver.[8] The Army's plan is to achieve increased lethality, survivability, deployability, and sustainability. This transition affects all the functional domains of doctrine, training, leader development, organizational structure, matériél modernization, and soldiers.

Although winning the information war has been identified as a modernization objective unto itself, it is essential to all aspects of modernization. Intelligence that is now gathered in near-real time must be elevated to real time. Tactical commanders must have assured access to intelligence through national systems. Command and control platforms must have continuous all-weather, digital capability and wide-band terrestrial communications systems to support increased transmission. Finally, current stovepipes in existing data communications that hamper interoperability must be overcome. The Army Battle Command System (ABCS) is a multi-faceted program that addresses these issues. The specific azimuth for Army modernization includes the following:

- *Owning the Night.* Dominate periods of limited visibility.
- *Improved Combat Identification.* Facilitate target identification and fratricide avoidance.
- *Extending the Depth of Precision Fires.* Apply smart and brilliant munitions.
- *Controlling the Information War.* Enhance command and control while degrading the enemy's capabilities.
- *Protecting the Force.* Focus on tiered defense and countering weapons of mass destruction.
- *Digitizing the Battlefield.* Full use of digitized platforms.

In each of these, information is the key to achieving a dominant advantage. Information is also key in each of the other modernization objective areas.

To meet the objective to project and sustain, the Army will acquire capabilities for rapid, global force projection. The modernization plan calls for continued support for sister service programs, such as the Air Force C-17 and the Navy roll-on/roll-off ship programs. The plan calls for improved logistics using Information Age technologies, such as in-transit visibility and total asset visibility, to track supplies and requisitions. The plan also requires improving the power-projection capabilities of U.S. installations by upgrading rail heads and air bases, as well as by upgrading the information infrastructure to allow for split-based operations.

To protect the force, the Army must address the proliferation of nuclear, chemical, and biological weapons and delivery systems. These weapons pose one of the greatest threats to ground forces, especially during early-entry operations. For this reason, current emphasis on theater missile defense programs, such as Theater High Altitude Area Defense (THAAD) and Corps Surface-to-Air Missile (Corps SAM), is well founded. Extended range intelligence systems will provide early warning and targeting against enemy weapons systems. In addition, such initiatives as telemedicine could provide medical emergency assistance to soldiers in remote locations.

In order to conduct precision strike, seizing and controlling territory will continue to be the mission of the land component commander in the twenty-first century. Commanders must have an organic capability to conduct precision strikes. Programs such as JSTARS enable commanders to locate high-payoff targets at extended ranges. Advanced munitions, such as GPS-fused artillery rounds, enable increased precision, lethality, and effectiveness of fires and will reduce civilian casualties and collateral damage.

The ability to dominate maneuver allows for rapid, decisive victory, the essence of land force dominance. Future modifications to existing systems, and the development and introduction of new platforms, can provide forces with overmatching capabilities to defeat any threat. The *Abrams* tank, *Comanche, Apache Longbow,* and other systems offer improvements in a number of areas: increased weapons ranges, better night and all-weather fighting capabilities, the ability to conduct command and control on the move in a combined arms environment, automated threat location data, enhanced situational awareness via digital map displays, and the ability to disperse forces rapidly, while massing the effects of fires.

The "linchpin of [the Army's] modernization strategy for the future"[9] is a process called horizontal technology integration (HTI). The approach identifies common enabling technologies and platforms to be integrated across the force to improve warfighting capability. HTI breaks away from traditional vertical technology integration based on stovepiped requirements and matériel acquisition processes. Past programs often produced systems with mission-specific capabilities for combat and support with little regard for other systems or purposes. HTI incorporates dissimilar platforms with common technology through new acquisition, pre-planned product improvements (P^{3}I), and system component upgrades. The use of common subsystems reduces operational and support costs by allowing standardization of components, simplified maintenance, and more efficient use of manpower.

Fiscal constraints, acquisition reforms, and the rate of technological and manufacturing advances affect the Army's joint warfighting capabilities, particularly the information-based operations of Force XXI. To maximize commonality where matériél solutions are required, the Army is pursuing innovative processes such as appliqués, the integration of common hardware/software across a variety of systems and platforms. The common use of off-the-shelf GPS receivers during the Gulf War is one example of such innovations. Other examples of major HTI efforts currently underway include:[10]

- *Second Generation Forward Looking Infrared Radar.* Designed to provide a wider field of view, greater range, and improved infrared sights from the first generation forward looking infrared radar.
- *Battlefield Combat Identification System.* A fratricide reduction system, designed to permit the warfighter to distinguish between friend or foe throughout the target engagement process.
- *Suite for Survivability of Enhancement Systems.* Capitalizes on technologies that are designed to enhance the "don't be hit" area of integrated survivability.
- *Digitization.* Designed to apply information technologies across the force to provide communications and processing capability to impose control over the battlespace dimensions of speed, space, and time.[11]

THE COST OF CHANGE

Army modernization is a continuous process facing formidable challenges in today's austere fiscal environment. In fiscal year 1989, the research, development, and acquisition (RDA) portion of the Army's budget was approximately $22.5 billion or 24 percent of the Army budget. In the budget for fiscal year 1996, the Army portion was reduced to $59.5 billion, down from $96.7 billion in 1989, and the Army's RDA was reduced to $7.7 billion, or 13 percent of the Army budget. The cut in the Army's RDA allocation is the largest among the armed forces,[12] creating a situation in which Army modernization is seriously under-funded.

Traditional methods of developing and procuring matériel and upgrading weapons systems have become less cost effective and more inefficient. HTI provides an approach to modernization that aggressively exploits leading-edge technologies in this austere fiscal environment. The "across-the-force" development of requirements and supporting acquisition strategies permits the Army to optimize scarce modernization funds.

The Army also considers thorough risk assessment of internal vulnerabilities a critical component of future developmental decisions. Risk management models help evaluate acceptable trade-offs, an important tool in cases where budget constraints

FIGURE 2: *The C²-Protection Road Map*

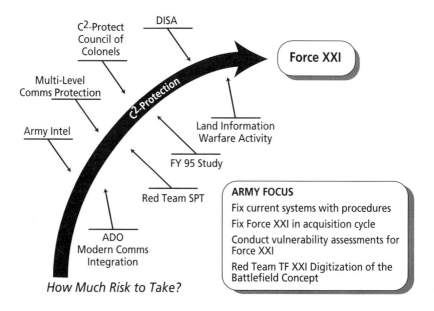

C²-Protect Council of Colonels

DISA

Force XXI

Multi-Level Comms Protection

C²-Protection

Army Intel

Land Information Warfare Activity

FY 95 Study

Red Team SPT

ADO Modern Comms Integration

How Much Risk to Take?

ARMY FOCUS
Fix current systems with procedures
Fix Force XXI in acquisition cycle
Conduct vulnerability assessments for Force XXI
Red Team TF XXI Digitization of the Battlefield Concept

necessitate acceptance of known vulnerabilities. Red Team training efforts against developmental components of Force XXI will yield key insights into the types of vulnerabilities acquired through commercial off-the-shelf technologies (COTS) or through new, reduced organizations. Fixing these vulnerabilities or making critical decisions based on risk analysis involves many key players for the Army in command and control protection (C^2-P), as shown in figure 2.

THE DIRECTION OF CHANGE

Information dominance is more than just technology and matériel. Countless historical examples of battles won and lost lead to useful observations about the control and handling of information:

- Problems in information create confusion when the initial plan changes.
- Delayed instructions affect all phases of the battle.
- Delays in reporting enemy actions and reactions inhibit initiative.
- Good planning is essential to battle but the battle is primarily the execution of changes to the plan.
- Communication is the key to transmitting changes.
- More eyes and better means are needed on the battlefield to get observations reported quickly to all levels of command.

As the old adage warns, the failure to learn from mistakes increases the risk of repeating them. As such, attention must always be focused on new trends and their effects on warfighting doctrines. In today's information-intensive environment, threats range from known hostile nations to economic competitors, terrorist groups, narcotics traffickers, and computer hackers. To maintain the edge on future battlefields, unique approaches to the requirements process are necessary. The dependence on long lead times to generate required capabilities for insertion into an eight-to-fifteen year developmental cycle must be broken. The pace of change in information technology is now measured in days, weeks, and months, not years. Fielding of programs must keep pace.

The technologies available to conduct war in the Information Age will provide the next paradigm shift in warfare – comparing favorably to the dramatic changes seen when gunpowder, cavalry, armor, or the atom bomb were brought to the battlefield. To assure victory on the future battlefield, numerous steps must be taken now. They center on a focused long-range plan that keeps pace with information technology; a capability-based methodology that maximizes the skills of the computer literate soldier; cost-effective commercial solutions found in off-the-shelf technologies and upgrades of existing systems; and implementation of HTI initiatives to maximize the use of like components across the force.

Meeting these demands requires not only the application and integration of new technologies but proper training of officers and soldiers. Quality soldiers, trained in the dynamics of Information Age warfare and "knowledge-able" of its complexities and challenges, lie at the heart of a modern, responsive force. For the Army is, first and foremost, the product of its men and women – and their immutable values of courage, valor, and commitment.

ENDNOTES

1. The Force XXI discussion illustrates a new way of thinking about future Army operations. For a full discussion of Force XXI see the Department of the Army publication, *Army Focus '94: Force XXI* (Washington, D.C.: HQDA, The Pentagon, DACS-CAD [3D636] September 1994).

2. In their book *War and Anti-War*, Alvin and Heidi Toffler describe three waves of development: the Agrarian, Industrial, and Information Ages. See Alvin and Heidi Toffler, *War and Anti-War* (New York: Warner Books, Inc., 1993).

3. General Gordon R. Sullivan and Colonel James M. Dubik, *War in the Information Age* (Strategic Studies Institute, U.S. Army War College, June 6, 1994), pp. 12–13.

4. Army Digitization Office, Army Digitization Master Plan, 30 January 1995, pp. 1–2.

5. The seven battlefield operating systems are: maneuver, fire support, command and control, intelligence, air defense, logistics, mobility, countermobility, and survivability.

6. Sullivan and Dubik, *War in the Information Age*, p. 5.

7. The Army has articulated its belief that information is becoming a major influence on combat power in a capstone manual, FM 100-6, *Information Operations* (Draft), 2 October 1995. See manual for a fuller discussion of the fundamental principles of information operations and a commander's ability to use, protect, integrate, and manage information, as well as exploit and deny the adversary's use of information.

8. United States Army, *1996 Modernization Plan* (Washington, D.C.: Department of the Army, 22 December 1995), pp.iii–vi.

9. General Ronald H. Griffith, "Army Modernization Forecast," *Army RD&A Magazine* (September/October 1995), p. 3.

10. The United States Army, *1996 Modernization Plan*, pp. 14–15.

11. Army Digitization Office, "Army Digitization Master Plan," pp. 1–2. This paper's discussion of the digitization of the battlefield is but a small part of the entire Army Digitization Office Campaign Plan to coordinate the integration of Army battlefield digitization activities.

12. The Army Budget Office, *1996–1997 Green Book: President's Budget* (April 1995), Program Balance, p. 5.

The Information Age & Nontraditional Military Issues

The Information Age and Nontraditional Military Issues

The final section of this volume contains chapters describing ramifications of the Information Age for U.S. strategy in non-traditional areas. While previous chapters have looked at the effects of information technologies on specific aspects of warfighting and how they will change, the authors in this section examine how the Information Age may create unique opportunities, such as the exploitation of technology for PSYOP, the use of the Internet in conflicts, and various applications of information resources for operations other than war (OOTW). Overall, the chapters in this section reinforce the commonly cited concern that war in the Information Age will require developing strategies across the spectrum of U.S. capabilities, within the military services themselves and within various sectors of civilian society.

Christopher Jon Lamb addresses the use of information technologies for the wide range of missions included under the rubric operations other than war. Although he cautions that low-technology adversaries may use indirect strategies to offset U.S. advantages, Lamb writes that, overall, force projection and information management will become easier due to the exploitation of advanced technologies. He identifies five specific missions where technology can make a substantial contribution. First, technologies such as robotics, lasers, non-nuclear electromagnetic pulses, non-lethal weapons, ultra-lightweight body armor, and unmanned aerial vehicles (UAVs), will be crucial to ensuring protection of U.S. forces. Second, precision technologies designed to pinpoint and neutralize targets will address the requirement to avoid collateral deaths and damage – a requirement that, in OOTW, is not merely important for mission success but is, in fact, a prerequisite for it. Third, advanced information technologies will make intelligence collection, evaluation, and distribution to warfighters easier, which is particularly significant in the rapidly changing OOTW threat environment, and in situations where military operations are exposed to intense media coverage. Fourth, psychological operations (PSYOP) for OOTW will be enhanced by communications technologies that not only enable precise targeting of audiences but also give a wider range of media for achieving goals. Finally, command and control will be enhanced through information technologies that can achieve a maximum unity of effort from all the actors in a complex political-military operation, one in which small units operating in disparate locations will play a key role.

Charles Swett describes how the most important new medium of the Information Age – the Internet – could be used by the armed forces. Swett argues that the role of the Internet is greatly expanding as governments, political parties, non-governmental organizations, and individuals use it to communicate with each other, spread propaganda, and garner support for their positions. Many groups, ranging from the Zapatista rebels in Mexico to organizations within the Office of the Secretary of Defense, use the Internet as a source of information for, and feedback from, the public. Fringe groups, such as American neo-Nazi organizations, use electronic mail and electronic bulletin boards on the Internet to communicate surreptitiously with their compatriots in Germany, while radical groups often spread false information about U.S. government actions and policies. At the same time, computer networks have been crucial to allowing people in conflict situations – such as the Tiananmen Square demonstration, Moscow during the 1991 anti-Gorbachev coup, and besieged Sarajevo – to communicate with the outside world. Swett urges, therefore, that the Internet's capabilities be exploited by the U.S. military in diverse ways: for intelligence collection; as a means to communicate with non-governmental experts on subjects being explored in the Pentagon; to disseminate timely and accurate information about U.S. military operations in a counter-propaganda role; and to gather information on erupting crises or conflicts.

Carnes Lord examines the future of PSYOP in the Information Age. He argues that, although PSYOP deals with information – the core of the new revolution in military affairs – it remains no more than a marginal concern of today's computer-armed information warriors. This is a grave mistake, Lord states, since the "psychological-political dimension of conflict" is greater today than during the Cold War as a result of the impact of global, real-time television reporting and an increase in the importance of nontraditional political factors, such as ethnic and cultural sensitivities, human rights, and environmental issues. In this setting, he suggests, PSYOP has a role as "strategic information" if considered in the context of broad psychological-political capabilities and activities. The key to developing a strategic information capability is combining PSYOP with other elements, such as public diplomacy, public affairs, covert warfare, and combat operations, to create psychological-political effects within the enemy. For this purpose, Lord urges that PSYOP be coupled with high-level policy through a "strategic information staff" in the office of the Under Secretary of Defense for Policy to plan and coordinate military PSYOP and defense-related public diplomacy.

Finally, Douglas Waller, while acknowledging Lord's point about the key role of the psychological-political dimension of warfare, disagrees strongly with the notion that strategic information warfare will be desirable or even possible in the future. The trend in the media, he concludes, is toward the increasing independence of journalists, as a result of technologies such as cellular phones, portable computers, and worldwide electronic link-ups. Media outlets already have their own aircraft and communications satellites, and may in the future possess their own imagery satellites. Combined with the skepticism of journalists toward military sources, this independence would prevent any attempt by the Pentagon to control the information flow. The Pentagon would, in essence, be in competition with multiple media outlets. Most importantly, Waller stresses, a strategic information campaign would be dangerous in a free society because it might subject the American public to disinformation or embarrass the Pentagon if exposed. In general, Waller argues, there are likely to be more and more conflicts between the military and the media in the Information Age. The military-media relationship, therefore, needs to be improved through increased mutual understanding.

chapter thirteen

The Impact of Information Age Technologies on Operations Other Than War

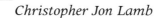

Christopher Jon Lamb

> Since the [First] World War there has been a flood of literature dealing with the old principles illustrated and the new technique developed in that war: but there always have been and ever will be other wars of an altogether different kind, undertaken in very different theaters of operations and requiring entirely different methods from those of the World War.
> *Small Wars Manual*, chapter 1, p. 8.[1]

THE EXTENT TO WHICH WE ARE WITNESSING an emerging revolution in military affairs – based primarily on the aggressive exploitation of real-time intelligence, precision targeting, and advanced delivery systems – is now a common concern of defense and national security analysts. Most of the attention paid to this subject focuses on large-scale conventional military engagements.[2] However, the impact of Information Age technology on what is currently referred to as operations other than war is also a subject of concern to Pentagon planners.[3]

Operations other than war (OOTW) – a diverse collection of military operations ranging from the highly specialized world of small-unit counterterrorism missions to division-sized interventions such as the NATO presence in Bosnia – continue to capture post-Cold War headlines, a nagging reminder that they have always been a more frequent if not more important challenge than war. This trend is unlikely to change. In fact, increasing the U.S. advantage in warfighting capabilities may also increase the likelihood of operations other than war, as adversaries undertake indirect or unconventional strategies to compensate for their lack of conventional military capabilities.[4] In recognition of the continuing importance of operations other than war, a recent Pentagon study project, mandated by the Office of the Secretary of Defense to explore the revolution in military affairs, included a task force on low-intensity conflict (LIC). The task force came up with an intriguing set of recommendations for exploiting micro-sensor networks, non-lethal weapons, hovering unmanned aerial vehicles, counter-sniper systems, and multimedia psychological operations, to name a few.[5] The real value of the task force's work, however, was not the identification of important emerging technologies, but rather the innovative application of those technologies to operational problems particularly relevant to operations other than war. This article will summarize some of the findings of this task force and place them in a broader setting in order to identify the prospects and limitations of exploiting emerging technologies in the environment short of war.[6]

~

How Important is Technology in OOTW?

...certain points which are peculiar to small war operations should
be emphasized. In particular decision must be made as to...the
requisition and distribution of special weapons and equipment
which are not included in the normal organization but which are
considered necessary.
Small Wars Manual, chapter 2, p. 1.

The casual observer of past and recent operations short of war
will note the salient roles played by both sophisticated and
rudimentary technologies. In Algeria and Vietnam, both helicopters and relatively primitive booby traps and landmines
were critical to the conduct of operations. During the war in
Afghanistan, both pack mules and portable surface-to-air missiles were considered indispensable to the success of the
resistance movement. In Somalia, U.S. Rangers employing the
latest technology available for long-range surveillance were
challenged by militia using human runners for early warning.
In Bosnia, the world's most advanced attack helicopters and
the most elemental means of military communication have
proven equally valuable in influencing the behavior of adversaries intent on challenging each other or NATO forces. This
cursory survey of technology and operations other than war
suggests that new technologies can play an important role in
this arena of conflict, but they may not be the most important
determinant of success.

Specialists in low-intensity conflict add other notes of caution
about the value of advanced technology. Traditionally leery of
reliance on technological solutions to their problems, they argue
that patience and restraint are the foundation for successful
policies and strategies in operations other than war.[7] The need
for patience and restraint condition the operational requirements for success in ways that previously have constrained the
overall importance of new technologies. For example, adversaries can choose indirect methods of aggression in part to offset

U.S. technological advantages. By attacking non-military targets and hiding among civilians, terrorists, insurgents, and irregular forces broaden their target range and narrow ours, largely negating our advantages in sophisticated targeting systems and firepower.

The multinational nature of operations other than war also limits the relevance of advanced technology. Operations other than war often require a multinational effort, either because the United States finds it convenient to work its objectives through third parties, or because the operation requires the sanction or combined efforts of the international community. Yet many U.S. allies cannot effectively utilize cutting-edge technology because it is too expensive, too maintenance-intensive, or too sensitive to be shared. In such circumstances more value is placed on reliability, simplicity, and exportability of applicable military systems than on cutting-edge technology.

Finally, and more generally, the political complexity and intensity of most sub-national conflicts and the extensive impact of humanitarian disasters on diverse parts of the civil sector raise problems that defy a simple application of discriminate and overwhelming force. Other instruments of national power in addition to military force are required. For the military, this often means that combat service support units and regional and language expertise can be as valuable in operations other than war as the latest weapons technology.[8] Despite the fact that operations other than war involve political constraints on the application of technology, that adversaries design strategies to avoid our technological prowess, and that the applicability of technological solutions is constrained by the need to work with third parties, advanced technology is an important component of the U.S. response to operations other than war. Frequently a new technology is the most efficient and effective means of solving an operational problem in the environment short of war. For example, better area-surveillance and bomb-detection technologies can partially compensate for the large target sets available to terrorists. Americans will always be inclined to pursue such remedies if they prove efficient at substituting matériel for human costs. Before considering the efficacy of Information Age technologies for addressing specific low-intensity conflict missions, it is important to consider how they are going to change the nature of the threat in the environment short of war and the response options available to the United States.

How Will Information Age Technologies Change the OOTW Environment?

> Due to the ease with which modern arms and equipment can be obtained from outside sources, it can be expected that, in the future, irregulars will have weapons and equipment equally as effective as those of the intervening forces. Except for aviation, therefore, the decided advantage in arms and equipment enjoyed by intervening troops in the past will seldom obtain in the future.
> *Small Wars Manual*, chapter 2, p. 5.

A diminishing qualitative edge for technologically advanced nations intervening in the affairs of less developed countries is not a new prediction, but a durable observation. Over the past hundred years, the ability of poorer and technologically unsophisticated forces to obtain some modern weaponry has improved steadily.[9] During the Marine occupation of Haiti (1915–39), the loss of even one machine gun to the insurgent forces was considered a catastrophe. Now the general availability of automatic weapons to all infantry units, regular or irregular, is a given. Similarly, the decision to arm the Afghani Mujahideen with *Stinger* missiles was considered an extraordinary exception in the early 1980s. Now the presence of such missiles is not unusual. U.S. military forces disembarked from Mogadishu by boat rather than aircraft, for example, because it was feared that Somali faction leader Muhammed Aideed might have surface-to-air missiles.

Operations other than war occasionally require U.S. forces to face organized military units that might be much smaller than U.S. forces but better armed than irregular units. Worldwide trends for conventional forces suggest continuing decreases in military manpower and increasing emphasis on smaller, better trained, high-tech, rapid-reaction forces with improved tactical mobility, precision-guided munitions such as anti-tank guided missiles, and improved tactical communications. There will be a reduction in maintenance-intensive heavy equipment and hybridization of older weapons systems with new Western technology in order to postpone obsolescence. Some of these trends will also affect irregular forces, which will selectively access advanced weapons, tactical communications, and improved training.

In general, U.S. forces must be prepared to face adversaries with varying levels of military technology and training at their disposal. The phenomenon of Agrarian Age warriors armed with Information Age weapons will be increasingly common as even the least-sophisticated paramilitary groups find access to some advanced military systems. More lethal portable surface-to-air missiles and anti-tank missiles, longer-range and more accurate mortars and sniper rifles, and anti-helicopter mines will be common. Most adversaries will be able to benefit from targeting systems that draw upon the Global Positioning System (GPS). In the not-too-distant future our foes could possess laser rifles and non-nuclear electromagnetic pulse weapons capable of destroying the unprotected circuitry upon which most U.S. military systems depend.

Information Age technology is changing the operating environment for operations other than war in other ways that cannot be ignored. The explosion of communication media throughout the world, easy access to video cameras, and the gradual spread of cable television and broadcast satellite receivers ensure a global audience for nearly instantaneous video coverage of events around the world. The parochialism of Neville Chamberlain's 1939 reference to German designs on Czechoslovakia as a "quarrel in a faraway country between peoples of whom we know nothing" seems ever more anachronistic in a world united by global communications.

The influence of television images on decisions to intervene in places like Somalia is sometimes overstated. While undeniably a factor in decisionmaking, grisly photos of suffering and destruction from around the world seldom are sufficient to bring about intervention by the United States. More to the point is the influence of real-time video coverage of operations once a decision to intervene has been made. The exponential increase in video imagery, which cannot be capped or controlled, means that military operations will face unprecedented scrutiny in the future. Beginning with Vietnam, the American public increasingly has had access to video images of U.S. military operations, with a consequent impact on policy. In the days following the introduction of U.S. troops to Haiti in 1994, bloodshed in the streets of Port-au-Prince was broadcast live, leading to immediate White House decisions to redefine the responsibilities of U.S. soldiers to control civil strife. Even mundane issues, such as the delayed entry of U.S. forces into Bosnia by the swollen Sava river, become extended topics for the nightly news when accompanied by video images.

In addition to the proliferation of video news coverage, the rapid, worldwide increase in other communications media (such as facsimile machines, Internet connections, broadcast satellite receivers, and cellular telephones) will transform the operating environment for operations other than war.[10] Access to the Internet and other on-line databases by computer-savvy adversaries will ensure that they are well informed on a variety of fronts, not the least of which is U.S. domestic politics. Captured documents demonstrated the sophistication of the Sendero Luminoso revolutionaries who were able to keep abreast of congressional debate on U.S. assistance to Peru. Muhammed Aideed reportedly received U.S. publications by fax within thirty minutes of their arrival at newsstands. Mexico's insurgent Zapatistas lobby the U.S. public and Congress through the Internet. Public relations will be complicated in the future by adversary misinformation campaigns using audio manipulation technologies and video morphing spread over the Internet, and commercially available satellite imagery pulled off the Internet will make it all the more difficult to conceal the disposition of U.S. forces operating overseas. Increasing use of international e-mail networks for organizing political movements and communicating in code will assist the growth and management of subversive organizations. As commercial methods of encryption become more readily available, secure, lightweight, and reliable tactical communications in urban environments will become commonplace for terrorists and insurgents, helping them operate without detection and offsetting some advantages traditionally enjoyed by security forces. The ability to operate more effectively without detection in urban environments takes on greater importance with the increasing rate of urbanization throughout the world and the growth of large populations of displaced persons attracted to cities in search of basic services. U.S. forces, which historically avoided built-up urban areas, must prepare to operate in them as a matter of course, and to do so with an increasing array of legal and policy restrictions.

In short, operations other than war will take place in a future environment marked by a much more rapid and comprehensive flow of information, and with adversaries who may lack a full panoply of modern weaponry, but who will have access to selected pieces of the most sophisticated light armaments available. This means information management and force protection will become increasingly complex and important missions for military forces engaged in operations other than war, presenting both opportunities as well as challenges. This survey of future trends suggests these mission areas should be included in any American strategy for leveraging technology in operations other than war. The following section sustains and elaborates on the argument.

How Should the U.S. Leverage Technology in OOTW?

> It can be assumed that the Fleet Marine Force in the Marine Corps, and the reinforced infantry or cavalry brigade in the Army, will be the basic organizations for small wars operations. Major changes in their strength, organization, armament, and equipment are neither essential nor desirable. However, some slight modification in armament and equipment may be advisable, and the proportion of supporting arms and services attached to the force may vary from the normal.
> *Small Wars Manual*, chapter 2, p. 43.

Realistic plans to leverage advanced technology in operations other than war must begin with the assumption of modest resources. Because of an understandable focus on developing and safeguarding warfighting capabilities, the Pentagon will not devote large amounts of resources to developing specialized capabilities for operations other than war per se. Nor is there any reason to do so, since the overwhelming majority of capabilities required by operations other than war – particularly low-intensity conflict requirements – are resident in the warfighting force structure. This is all the more true as we improve our ability to deliver conventional weapons with ever-greater discrimination.

Previously, conventional forces were incapable of strictly limiting damage to specified, individual targets, which is a fundamental requirement in low-intensity conflict. Today, advanced weapons systems are increasingly capable of holding collateral damage and unintended casualties to a minimum, and even recording the results on video so that propaganda attempts to assert the contrary may be deflated. Recently, the deputy secretary of defense asserted that the accuracy of American bombers over Bosnia was such that they were actually able to select aiming points within individual military targets. Pilots train immediately prior to their missions on virtual reality simulations that translate satellite imagery and other data into detailed real-life computerized pictures, showing pilots in their simulator cockpits exactly what the terrain surrounding their target will look like. These virtual-reality simulations, paired with other real-time intelligence sources while on mission, greatly reduce the probability of human error and increase the accuracy of guided munitions.[11]

It is also true that there are very few requirements in operations other than war that differ absolutely from – that is, have no relevance to – warfighting requirements. Most military tasks are only modified by the environment short of war, or remain the same but must be performed to a much higher degree of proficiency. Defeating surface-to-air missiles is a warfighting requirement that is modified in operations other than war. During war slow-flying cargo planes normally operate to and from secure bases where friendly forces control all the territory surrounding the airfields they use. In low-intensity conflict this often is not the case. C-130s flying in and out of Mogadishu needed defenses against shoulder-launched surface-to-air missiles when they were most vulnerable, flying slow and low in preparation for landing or on take-off. Countering snipers was a warfighting requirement that had to be performed with much greater proficiency in Somalia. Disrupted operations and casualties from snipers were intolerable given limited U.S. objectives in Somalia. Highly proficient countersniper efforts were accordingly a priority and, in some cases, tactics were modified to account for the environment. For example, low-flying helicopters with countersniper personnel patrolled Mogadishu at night to engage enemy snipers at close range and limit collateral damage.[12]

Because low-intensity conflict requirements often are just modifications of warfighting requirements, and because those modifications may depend upon specific circumstances, the military prefers to seek ad hoc solutions to operational problems in the environment short of war. If a particular operational problem seems especially deserving of a longer term solution, occasionally one will be applied ex post facto in reaction to lessons learned. The U.S. Army decision to purchase better armored vehicles as a hedge against command-detonated mines following the Somalia experience is an example.[13] In general, however, only very limited resources are allocated to operational capabilities specifically addressing requirements in operations other than war as a matter of deliberate planning, mostly in the area of combating terrorism as a result of our extended engagement in counterterrorist capabilities over the last several decades.

To secure such scarce resources for low-intensity conflict capabilities, it is essential to identify requirements that are critical for overall mission success rather than those merely desirable for marginal operational advantages. The general requirements for mission success in operations other than war and how they differ from warfighting have been touched upon above and amply discussed elsewhere.[14] The summary that follows demonstrates the congruence between historic requirements for success in low-intensity conflict and the survey of technology trends, which pointed toward information management and force protection as increasingly important missions areas for operations other than war. These operations differ from warfighting in that the immediate objective is not to take terrain and destroy forces, but to alter political relationships and adversary policies. In comparison with warfighting these objectives can take much longer to secure, making patience and perseverance cardinal virtues. Protracted engagements in which less-than-vital national interests are at stake also make it imperative that costs – human, material, and political – be kept low. As a result it may be advisable to work through third parties and by clandestine or covert means. In addition, the focus on political relationships means that operations other than war require popular support and the use of all national instruments of power rather than reliance on military force. Consequently, when military force is used it is constrained by political considerations even down to the tactical level.

Military forces that can operate effectively in such an environment must be able to use force with discrimination, work with other national agencies, and have the language and cross-cultural skills to work with other foreign forces and populations. The requirements to limit costs, exercise discriminate force, and work closely with foreign forces and populations often combine to make the success of small-unit actions critically important in operations other than war. The British acknowledge this fact when they refer to low-intensity conflict as "corporals' war." For the same reasons operations in the environment short of war often depend upon intelligence directed at social and political indicators rather than tables of organization and equipment.

Comparing a combat reconnaissance patrol in war with an urban reconnaissance patrol in an operation short of war highlights why force protection, limited force, and command and control are more complicated in low-intensity conflict. The combat patrol will use cover, concealment, and camouflage to avoid contact while reconnoitering an area and engaging in passive observation. It will be able to identify the enemy easily and, if discovered, operate with standard rules of engagement, use military tactics for self-defense, lay down fields of fire, and accept collateral damage as unavoidable. It will operate under general guidance from the regional commander-in-chief and be responsive to the tactical military chain of command. It will operate under the Geneva convention, taking and becoming prisoners of war if captured.

By contrast, an urban reconnaissance patrol in a low-intensity conflict will often seek to establish its presence and authority by overtly patrolling an area, engaging in active investigation, and interacting with civilians and local law-enforcement personnel. It will operate under constrained rules of engagement, avoiding collateral damage. It will be responsive to local civil and criminal law, using some police tactics for self-defense, such as applying lethal force only when threatened with the same. It will cooperate with local officials, and be responsive to the concerns of the local U.S. ambassador. It will have difficulty identifying the enemy and, if captured, members of the patrol are more likely to become hostages than be treated according to the rules of the Geneva convention.

In summary, technology trends affecting the environment short of war and the special requirements for success in that environment suggest that the nucleus of a strategy for leveraging technology in operations other than war ought to include the mission areas of force protection, proportional and discriminate use of force, intelligence, psychological operations, and command and control. The remainder of this article examines why these mission areas are more demanding in operations other than war, identifies specific military tasks of special importance in each area, and suggests some possible technological solutions that merit further exploration.

FIVE CRITICAL MISSION AREAS FOR MILITARY FORCES IN OPERATIONS OTHER THAN WAR

Force Protection

> A Force Commander who gains his objective in a small war without firing a shot has attained a far greater success than one who resorted to the use of arms. While endeavoring to avoid the infliction of physical harm to any native, there is always the necessity of preventing, as far as possible, any casualties among our own troops. *Small Wars Manual*, chapter 1, p. 18.

Force protection is more demanding in operations other than war because it is more difficult to identify the adversary. Even if an adversary can be located, the enemy may be operating from sanctuaries which cannot be attacked for political reasons. In such circumstances, it is difficult not to surrender the initiative to the enemy and rely more on passive defenses. Most importantly, however, casualties are less sustainable in operations other than war. The general public's intolerance for casualties is often overstated. It depends on the how various interest groups interpret the national interests at stake, their perceptions of progress toward stated objectives, and the costs of pursuing the objectives – mostly in terms of lives, but to a lesser extent in matériel resources as well. Nevertheless, it is true that in operations short of war vital national interests are usually not at stake, and the likelihood of a protracted engagement and ambiguous results is greater. Consequently, the general public's willingness to accept a high rate of casualties is low.[15]

In recent operations other than war, command-detonated mines, snipers, "shoot and scoot" mortars, and shoulder-fired surface-to-air missiles (SAMs) have created the greatest force-protection challenges. All these weapons allow an adversary to target U.S. facilities or forces carefully from a distance and either quickly abandon the location of the attack before U.S. forces can respond, or fire the weapons from another position altogether. Reducing the footprint of U.S. forces, for example by operating as much as possible from offshore platforms, would reduce their vulnerability. However, in many circumstances, maintaining presence for political effect is often an implicit objective of the operations.

A variety of emerging technologies have possible applications to countering these threats: robotics; lasers and non-nuclear electromagnetic pulse devices; non-lethal weapons; ultra-lightweight body armor; and mine-resistant vehicles. Hovering unmanned aerial vehicles (UAVs) that can constantly monitor an area without being easily detected, and which may return fire with precise lethal or non-lethal means to avoid collateral damage, are attractive countersniper and countermortar option. For a near-term option, technology has already been developed that can automatically locate snipers by projecting backward the tracked ballistic trajectories of the bullets they fire. Using machine guns mounted on fast, precise gimbals, the system can adjust to the exact coordinates of the target and return fire less than one second after a sniper attack. Robotic vehicles or hovering UAVs that could precede convoys and detect hidden mines by their chemical or electromagnetic signatures also are possibilities.

Developing reliable counters to shoulder-fired SAMs are a major technological challenge. Two of the more attractive possibilities are directed-energy defenses such as lasers to jam infrared-guided missiles, and directional electromagnetic pulse weapons that could destroy the circuitry of the incoming missile. These systems could be deployed on aircraft or set up around the perimeter of airfields to protect aircraft when they are most vulnerable.

The ability to protect individual soldiers and limit fatalities is a less exotic but no less important means of enhancing force protection. Following the Ranger raid in Somalia on October 3, 1993 that produced nearly a hundred American casualties, modern medical capabilities and modular operating rooms proved their value. Only three of the sixty-three wounded soldiers who reached these medical facilities were lost. Following the firefight, the Army also quickly ordered special body armor suits designed to protect extremities left vulnerable by older-generation flak jackets.[16] In the future, chameleon camouflage that adapts to the soldiers' surroundings, and artificial flesh that can be quickly applied to stabilize wounds, could enhance the survivability of individual soldiers.

Proportionate and Discriminate Force

The responsibility of officers engaged in small wars and the training necessary are of a very different order from their responsibilities and training in ordinary military duties. In the latter case, they simply strive to attain a method of producing the maximum physical effect with the force at their disposal. In small wars, caution must be exercised, and instead of striving to generate the maximum power with forces available, the goal is to gain decisive results with the least application of force and the consequent minimum loss of life.
Small Wars Manual, chapter 1, pp. 31-32.

The importance of strictly limiting the use of firepower in operations other than war has long been insisted upon by specialists in these types of operations. Of course, the U.S. military avoids harming non-combatants and limits the use of force to what is necessary to accomplish the military task at hand in all its operations. Yet during war, the requirements to discriminate between combatants and non-combatants and to use force proportionate to the military objective are not absolute requirements; they are to be pursued in so far as they do not compromise the success of the military mission. In operations other than war, however, the requirements for proportionate and discriminate use of force are not subordinate to, but rather prerequisites for, mission success. Collateral damage and unintended casualties can fatally undermine critical U.S., indigenous, and international support for an operation. Thus, while other goals and objectives may be obscure, the requirement for minimum force remains essential:

> Frequently the commander of a force operating in a small wars theater of operations is not given a specific mission as such in his written orders or directive, and it then becomes necessary for him to deduce his mission from the general intent of the higher authority, or even from the foreign policy of the United States. In any event, the mission should be accomplished with a minimum loss of life and property and by methods that leave no aftermath of bitterness or render the return to peace unnecessarily difficult.[17]

Neutralizing adversary assets with minimum casualties and damage is a major challenge in operations short of war, however. There are two especially difficult tasks in this regard: controlling large, hostile crowds without lethal force; and disrupting an adversary's communications, utilities, and transportation infrastructure during a raid or limited intervention without gross, permanent damage to the targets. In both cases casualties and collateral damage must be kept to a bare minimum in order not to alienate the populace or drive up the costs of the operations. As noted above, the increasing precision of lethal weapons has been a boon to efforts to control collateral damage in general, but any weapons that destroy their targets through blast, penetration, or fragmentation are likely to produce some collateral and permanent damage when directed at crowds or infrastructure targets.

Non-lethal anti-personnel and anti-materiél weapons offer an attractive potential solution to these problematic tasks. Non-lethal options such as tear gas are not new, but recent advances in technology promise greater operational utility for non-lethal weapons. Low-frequency acoustic signals, malodorous substances, or directional microwave weapons may temporarily incapacitate crowds, allowing agitators to be subdued with sting nets or various types of "soft shots" without causing permanent casualties. The U.S. Marines responsible for the evacuation of UN peacekeepers from Somalia in early 1995 took along an assortment of rudimentary non-lethal weapons for the purpose of crowd control, and U.S. Army forces in Bosnia have been similarly armed.[18]

Sticky foams or anti-traction agents that make bridges impassable for days, or electromagnetic pulse weapons that short-circuit critical communication targets (such as radio stations) without permanent damage, would be of immense strategic utility. Limiting damage to national infrastructure is a critical objective in brief "coup de main" operations such as the U.S. invasions of Grenada, Panama, and the one planned for Haiti, prior to the last-minute agreement permitting the peaceful entry of U.S. troops into that country. Since protecting our own forces and apprehending key opposition figures takes precedence, however, strategic infrastructure targets must be attacked in order to cripple organized resistance and cut off avenues of escape. The advantage of non-lethal weapons is that they may be able to accomplish these objectives with no permanent damage to the targeted structures or the environment.

Intelligence

[The intelligence section] must keep in close touch with all other staff sections and is responsible for...not only information of (sic) the military situation, but the political, economic and social status

of the occupied area, together with the attitude and activities of the civil populations and political leaders insofar as those elements may affect the accomplishment of the mission.... In no type of warfare is the latest current information more vital.
Small Wars Manual, chapter 2, pp. 19-20.

Intelligence support in operations other than war is a more complex and perhaps more critical task than during war.[19] In war the intelligence community can focus on a standard set of primary indicators: enemy disposition, composition, and movement. Usually the most likely wartime adversaries are known well in advance of hostilities so the enemy's order of battle is a familiar collection target. In operations other than war intelligence often is required on short notice and for a broad set of social, political, and military subjects. Just assessing the civil dimension of the problem that precipitates the intervention can be a demanding task. In Somalia it was well understood that the critical requirement was facilitating the distribution of humanitarian assistance from the ports to the interior of the country. In Haiti the problem was not distribution of humanitarian assistance but rather jump starting the dysfunctional Haitian government ministries, so that the international reconstruction and assistance effort could get under way.

New technology can potentially assist with the requirement for esoteric information on short notice about complex political-military environments. One possibility is to make far greater use of open source information by accessing on-line databases and the Internet. The Internet makes it possible to access information from international aid workers, missionaries, government workers, academics, and others who may have extraordinarily detailed and current information about an area of interest. On-line databases managed by private firms and international organizations also provide rich detail on economic, social, and political developments. The reliability of information obtained through such open sources is problematic but manageable by many of the same techniques used to screen or qualify the reliability of any intelligence source. By accessing on-line databases and other open sources it could be possible to quickly develop detailed profiles of the environment in an area of interest. Classified intelligence collection could then focus on information that is not freely available.

Operations other than war also can require a "finer grain" of intelligence. Instead of tracking the movement of tanks, for example, the objective might be to record the faces of agitators in a crowd for later identification. Advanced information-processing systems can store, sort, and retrieve enormous amounts of data about adversary groups if the means of collection are in place. Identifying and understanding an obscure adversary requires detailed and timely information collection in order to disrupt enemy supply, penetrate enemy organizations, and reduce popular support for an adversary. The small-unit engagements that characterize low-intensity conflict – especially hostage rescue or other personnel recovery operations – also require extremely detailed and perishable information on the subjects' location and surroundings.

In general the whereabouts and intentions of even a small number of adversaries can be critically important in operations other than war. Since it is not possible to protect every lucrative target against an adversary who is often willing to attack noncombatants, it is also important to have as much advance notice as possible of adversary plans. Such advance notice usually requires effective human sources of intelligence, which take time to cultivate. Human sources are even more important when the adversary does not use weapon and communication systems with signatures susceptible to technical means of collection.

A short list of the most critical tasks in operations other than war that are dependent on accurate intelligence would include advanced notice of terrorist attacks, locating enemy caches, and locating enemy personnel and contraband. The Army is interested in devices that can help soldiers in urban terrains see undergound, through walls, and around corners.[20] Microsensor networks are another possible future technological solution to some of these problems. Millions of tiny, inexpensive sensors created using micro-electromechanical systems technology could be dropped over a wide area, by manned or unmanned, aerial- or ground-based platforms. The sensors could detect acoustic, seismic, magnetic, chemical, and other signatures. They would be inherently "smart" and automatically organize themselves into networks. An airborne platform with a GPS receiver would examine each microsensor so that signals detected by the sensor could be located accurately. Such networks would make it difficult for insurgents and terrorists to pass through barriers or hide contraband without detection. A more likely near-term solution would be placing modular sensor packages specially configured for low-intensity conflict missions[21] on long-loitering, low-observable manned or unmanned aerial vehicles[22] to accomplish the same purpose as the microsensor networks.

Psychological Operations (PSYOP)
The great importance of psychology in small wars must be appreciated. It is a field of unlimited extent and possibilities, to which much time and study should be devoted.... The resistance to the intervention comes not only from those under arms but also from those furnishing material or moral support to the opposition. Sapping the strength of the actual or potential hostile ranks by the judicious application of psychological principles may be just as effective as battle casualties.
Small Wars Manual, chapter 1, pp. 18–19.

"PSYOP: don't leave home without it." Thus advised a senior Marine Corps general in a Pentagon debriefing on mission requirements in Somalia. Shortly thereafter, a U.S. Senator took the unusual step of publicly encouraging the use of Pentagon PSYOP aircraft to influence Serbian behavior in the Bosnian conflict.[23] Senator Levin argued that PSYOP assets, which proved their worth in the Gulf War in inducing desertions from Iraqi forces, were valuable tools with applicability to post-Cold War threats like Bosnia. Such attestations from the Gulf War and Somalia experience seem to have won over some skeptics of psychological operations. PSYOP is now much more widely accepted — especially, but not exclusively, in the Pentagon — than at any time previously.

The importance of influencing foreign audiences with messages supportive of U.S. policy, particularly in operations other than war where the populace renders critical support to the protagonists, may be self-evident. Less understood is why PSYOP is more challenging in operations other than war. PSYOP is much more complicated in the environment short of war because it must be immediately responsive to tactical developments. After firefights in Somalia, it was important to broadcast the U.S. version of events quickly — and, when the U.S. was responsible for civilian casualties, to assert regret and explain that reparations were being made. Policy can shift quickly in operations other than war and PSYOP must keep pace. Senior civilian and military participants in the Somalia operation often recount one particular instance in which a PSYOP unit was not alerted to policy changes. As a result, U.S. officials meeting with Aideed to negotiate for the release of an American captive reportedly were showered with leaflets asserting Aideed's status as a criminal and the need to capture and bring him to justice. Continuous and rapid reaction to tactical and strategic developments and shifts in policy are particularly difficult when coordination with third parties is required, as it most often is in operations other than war.

Minimizing resistance and maximizing public support for U.S. policy objectives are critical tasks where the U.S. military can most easily take advantage of Information Age technology. The rapid expansion of communications technology and media can enable a multimedia PSYOP campaign against U.S. adversaries. PSYOP messages will be strengthened by repetition through different media. Using fax, electronic mail, amateur radio, and cellular phones to complement the traditional PSYOP tools of radio, television, and leaflets will reinforce perceptions favorable to the U.S. interpretation of facts, and also allow for more focused targeting. Messages designed to influence elite or even individual opinion can be faxed, phoned, or sent by e-mail to specific addresses. Such discrimination in targeting would be useful for sowing suspicion and discord within terrorist and other subversive organizations.

According to some sources, the forerunners of complex multimedia PSYOP campaigns have already taken place. Reportedly, PSYOP operations in Haiti distinguished between as many as twenty target groups, and included phone calls and e-mail messages to selected members of the Haitian oligarchy.[24] In another example of using modern communications to further state objectives by influencing public opinion, the United States and Australia are sponsoring a project to make data on Khmer Rouge atrocities in Cambodia available through the Internet. The data includes maps of prisons and mass grave sites, as well as photographs of victims.[25]

As noted above, modern communications technology also offers powerful tools for disinformation, such as audio manipulation and video-morphing technologies, which can create high-quality false messages and images to mislead an audience. These false messages can also be broadcast as part of a psychological campaign, and even broadcast worldwide via the Internet. U.S. PSYOP experts, insisting that "truth is our best weapon," generally agree that such an approach would be counterproductive for the United States, undermining the credibility of highly effective overt PSYOP programs.[26] However, since audio manipulation and video-morphing technologies are readily available, the United States must be ready to counter them.[27]

Command and Control

> The military strategy of small wars is more directly associated with the political strategy of the campaign than is the case in major operations.... The political authorities do not relinquish active participation in the negotiations and they ordinarily continue to exert considerable influence over the military campaign. The military leader in such operations thus finds himself limited to certain lines of action as to the strategy and even as to the tactics of the campaign.
> *Small Wars Manual*, chapter 1, p. 11.

Several days before the October 3, 1993 clash between U.S. forces and militia loyal to Muhammed Aideed in Mogadishu, U.S. newspapers reported two interesting trends. The *Boston Globe* – citing CIA and military sources in Mogadishu – noted that Aideed was consolidating his position, able to move with increasing ease, and capably targeting U.S. helicopters. The Globe added that "the efficacy of the U.S. Army Ranger...teams sent in to track Aideed was decreasing by the day." At the same time, the *New York Times* reported that U.S. leadership was arguing with UN Secretary-General Boutros-Ghali over the U.S. desire to shift the focus away from capturing Aideed, and toward reinvigorating the search for a political solution. After the Ranger raid went awry, U.S. newspapers reported that the secretary of state and the president were surprised that such military operations were taking place. It would seem that either senior political leadership was unaware of the risks inherent in the military efforts to capture Aideed, or the military officers in charge of the raid were unaware of the political initiative to de-emphasize the military option.[28]

In operations short of war, policy must repeatedly and carefully be translated into realistic operational requirements, and operational plans must be carefully tailored to support policy objectives. Close coordination of policy and operations requires clear policy objectives, thorough knowledge of operational capabilities and limitations, and recurring dialogue between policymakers and policy implementers.[29] A second and only somewhat less challenging command and control issue is the requirement to deal with a wide variety of disparate actors in operations other than war. The requirement to apply all instruments of national power, instead of relying primarily on military force, means that operations short of war demand interagency involvement. The fact that they also frequently require coordination with other states and international and non-governmental actors, with different objectives and standard operating methods, makes command and control all the more complicated.

At first blush, achieving maximum unity of effort from all actors supporting a fast evolving and complex political-military operation without compromising security or the chain of command would seem like a task tailor-made for the latest communications technology. Video-teleconferencing could put field commanders in touch with Washington interagency decision-making bodies, where the broad outlines of policy and operations could be coordinated. On-line databases could provide critical and timely information to a wide variety of actors in the field, allowing coordination of disparate activities consistent with security requirements and general policy. For example, aid workers could be apprised of military activities that will support or require modification of their routines – e.g.

locations and timing of security provided, transportation available, or areas where access is limited.

Individual soldiers equipped with hand-held GPS locators, laser designators, cellular communications, video and real-time interactive voice communications, and overhead UAVs linking their communications with other units and the chain of command, could better coordinate small-unit engagements and call in precise fire support to limit collateral damage. Their superiors, able to pinpoint the location of friend and foe and to see the engagement from numerous vantage points, will be able to choose more quickly and wisely which fire-support requests to honor. Repetitive small-unit training in virtual-reality simulations based on known geographical areas of interest, in likely adversarial situations that include combatants and civilians, could improve command decisionmaking under stress.

Many of these promising technological aids to command and control are currently being explored. Many are prohibitively expensive, and some technically impractical. The biggest obstacle to major change in this area, however, is organizational inertia. Flattening decisionmaking pyramids, compromising security in favor of broader information sharing, and (most radically) acknowledging the legitimacy of political influence on even the tactical details of military operations, would require major changes in attitudes. Many warfighting commanders are uncomfortable with operations short of war. The tendency is to define problems in terms of the capabilities with which one is familiar, and to use those capabilities regardless of how the problem is defined.

∼

CONCLUSIONS

It is important not to overestimate the importance of technology as a means of securing victory in operations other than war, or to think that its overall impact on our ability to control outcomes will be as dramatic as the improvements that advanced technology can make in warfighting capabilities. It also is important to realize that political and bureaucratic realities argue against devoting large amounts of increasingly scarce defense resources to specialized capabilities for operations other than war.

Nevertheless, operations other than war do require military capabilities beyond those designed for warfighting, some of which should exploit emerging Information Age technologies. A better process for self-consciously weighing the costs and benefits of pursuing or ignoring advanced technological solutions to low-intensity conflict problems and associated changes in organizational and operational concepts would be helpful. Far more important, however, is the need first to isolate the operational requirements that are critical to mission success in low-intensity conflict. As the references in this article to the half-century old Marine Corps *Small Wars Manual* are meant to suggest, when it comes to understanding critical requirements in operations other than war, much has already been learned – and forgotten.[30] In this sense, we might agree with Goethe that "Everything has been thought of before, but the problem is to think of it again." After thinking of the critical mission requirements in low-intensity conflict again, we are more likely to address them with effective and appropriate technological solutions.

ENDNOTES

1. This and subsequent notes are drawn from U.S. Marine Corps, *Small Wars Manual* (Washington, D.C.: Government Printing Office, 1940). Reference is made to this classic work throughout the article to illustrate that while the subject is revolutionary technology, the general requirements toward which the technology is applied often remain remarkably consistent.

2. For an exception, see Steven Metz and James Kievit, *The Revolution in Military Affairs and Conflict Short of War* (Carlisle Barracks, PA: U.S. Army War College, Strategic Studies Institute, 1994).

3. Low-intensity conflict (LIC) and its traditional categories of counterinsurgency and insurgency, counterterrorism, peacekeeping, and contingency operations (sometimes including counternarcotics) are subsumed under operations other than war (OOTW), the currently preferred term in military doctrine. (See Joint Pub 3–07, "Joint Doctrine for Military Operations Other Than War," 16 June 1995.) In addition to the traditional LIC categories, OOTW includes arms control, enforcement of sanctions, enforcement of exclusion zones, humanitarian assistance, support to civilian authorities, noncombatant evacuation operations, protection of shipping, recovery operations, show of force operations, strikes and raids, and what now are referred to generically as peace operations. Many of these operations that are adversarial in nature arguably could be classified under the old low-intensity conflict category of contingency operations. In this article the terms "low-intensity conflict" and the "environment short of war" are used in addition to operations other than war for accuracy and editorial convenience.

4. See David Tucker and Christopher J. Lamb, "Peacetime Engagements," in Sam C. Sarkesian and Robert E. Conner, eds., *America's Armed Forces: A Handbook of Current and Future Capabilities* (Westport, CT: Greenwood Press, 1996), p. 298; and "Unconventional Military Instruments," in *Strategic Assessment 1996: Instruments of U.S. Power* (Washington, D.C.: National Defense University, Institute for National Strategic Studies, 1996), p. 143. For what I consider to be an overstatement of the continuing importance of low-intensity conflict, see Martin van Creveld, *The Transformation of War* (New York: The Free Press, 1991). See also Ralph Peters, "The Culture of Future Conflict," *Parameters* Vol. XXV, No. 4 (Winter 1995-96).

5. Mr. Charles Swett of the Office of the Assistant Secretary of Defense, Special Operations, and Low-Intensity Conflict, was the executive secretary and principal researcher for the task force. He has contributed elsewhere in this volume. The Department of Defense Advanced Research Projects Agency also has conducted a valuable study on the applicability of future technology to operations other than war. See DOD Advanced Research Projects Agency, "Report of the Senior Working Group on Military Operations Other Than War (OOTW)" (Arlington, VA: May 1994).

6. The views expressed herein are those of the author, and do not necessarily reflect those of the Department of Defense or the U.S. Government.

7. These basic principles are now codified in U.S. military doctrine. See Joint Pub 3–07: *Joint Doctrine for Military Operations Other Than War* (16 June 1995), p. viii.

8. See the discussion in Tucker and Lamb, "Peacetime Engagements," pp. 303 and 329ff.

9. Some date the 1898 battle of Omdurman, in which an Anglo-Egyptian force of twenty-six thousand with superior firepower defeated an indigenous force of forty thousand, as the high-water mark of European military technological advantage over their native adversaries. In a few hours Lord Kitchener's force suffered five hundred casualties while inflicting ten thousand killed and taking five thousand prisoners.

10. Vint Cerf, the "father of the Internet," recently estimated that by the year 2000 there would be some 200 million computers in 180 countries, including five million networks, linked to the Net in cyberspace, compared to thirty million computers and eighty-five thousand networks in use today. See http://www.csis.org/ for CSIS News (Autumn 1995), p. 4.

11. See Deputy Secretary of Defense John White's remarks to the Air Force Association Business Session, Washington, 18 September 1995, in *Defense Issues,* Vol 10, No. 89; Dana Priest, "For Bosnia Pilots, Virtual Reality is Reality," *Washington Post* (12 December 1995), p. 3; "Bosnia Action Helps Focus Battle Intelligence Picture," *Washington Post* (27 September 1995), p. 23; and James Kitfield, "Space War II," *National Journal* (23 December 1995), pp. 31, 41. See also William Matthews, "Bombing That Hit Its Mark," *Navy Times* (2 October 1995).

12. Tony Capaccio, "U.S. Snipers Enforced Peace Through Gun Barrels," *Defense Week* (31 January 1994), p. 1.

13. Sean D. Naylor, "Beefed-up Humvees are Headed for Somalia," *Army Times* (13 December 1993), p. 8.

14. For example, see James Gallagher, *Low-Intensity Conflict: A Guide for Tactics, Techniques and Procedures* (Harrisburg, P.A.: Stackpole Books, 1992); and Tucker and Lamb, "Peacetime Engagements," pp. 329–335.

15. Some even complain that force protection has become an end in itself at the expense of other national objectives. A soldier courtmartialed in Haiti for conducting an unauthorized inspection of the Haitian National Pentitentiary complained publicly on this score, deriding the prosecution's assertion that force protection was priority number one during the operation. Lawrence P. Rockwood, "When Robots Take Over the Military," *Philadelphia Inquirer* (29 July, 1995), p. 9.

14. See John Lancaster, "Combat in Mogadishu Posed a Challenge for Small U.S. Army Hospital," *Washington Post* (20 October 1993), p. 36; and Andrew Weinschenk, "After Urgent Request, Troops In Somalia Got Special Body Armor," *Defense Week* (13 December 1993), p. 3.

17. Small Wars Manual, chapter 2, p. 2. Pfc Matthew Knopf of Bradenton, Florida, who was among the first wave of troops into Haiti, seemed to paraphrase this passage when he reportedly said, "We don't know what our job is, what our mission is, and for how long it's supposed to last. We've just been instructed not to shoot anybody," in Jack Kelly and Judy Keen, "Like Somalia, Goal Difficult to Define," *USA Today* (20 September 1994).

18. See "Unconventional Military Instruments," *Strategic Assessment* 1996, p. 152, and Mary Greczyn, "Army Prepares to Ship Nonlethals to Bosnia," *Defense Week* (20 May 1996).

19. See Joint Pub 3-07: *Joint Doctrine for Military Operations Other Than War*, chapter IV, p. 2; Office of the Assistant Secretary of Defense, Special Operations and Low-Intensity Conflict, "Intelligence Support to Operations Other Than War" (White Paper, 1994); and James B. Motley, "The Army's Need: A Relevant LIC Environment," *International Journal of Intelligence and Counterintelligence*, Vol. 4, No. 3 (1990).

20. See "Army Seeks Mine Detection, Other Peacekeeping Equipment," *Tactical Technology* (16 February 1994), p. 6.

21. Surveillance platforms have been configured for low-intensity conflict in the past; for example, OV-10Ds could locate people on the ground through their body heat. These aircraft have been passed from the Department of Defense to the Bureau of Alcohol, Tobacco, and Firearms. Jerry Seper, "ATF Gets 22 Planes to Aid Surveillance," *Washington Times* (18 July 1995). Some low-intensity conflict surveillance aircraft are currently available, but the norm is to focus airborne surveillance on warfighting requirements. In Somalia the most valuable intelligence collection platform was a system designed for a cold war mission and

pressed into service for the exigencies of Mogadishu. More recently the JSTARS ground-surveillance radar, designed to locate enemy ground vehicles, was put to use monitoring movement around suspected mass grave sites in Bosnia. Tony Cappaccio, "JSTARS Watches Atrocity Site For Crimes Tribunal, Perry Says," *Defense Week* (29 January 1996).

22. Some experimentation in this regard is already taking place. See "Army Battle Lab Examines Peacekeeping Equipment," *Tactical Technology* (2 February 1994), p. 3.

23. Senator Carl Levin, "Use Propaganda Weapon: Broadcast Truth of War to Bosnian Population," *Defense News* (27 June–3 July 1994), p. 24.

24. Douglas Waller, "Onward Cyber Soldiers," *Time* (21 August 1995), p. 38.

25. Barbara Crossette, "Effort to Record Atrocities in Cambodia to Go on Internet," *New York Times* (25 September 1995), p. 5.

26. Douglas Waller, "America's Persuader in the Sky," *Time* (21 August 1995), p. 43.

27. Some commentators find PSYOP capabilities troubling, noting that they might be considered "un-American" at best, or at worst, that they will be turned on domestic audiences. See Metz and Kievit, "The Revolution in Military Affairs," p. 15. A greater problem, in my estimation, is how to separate foreign from domestic audiences. As news coverage develops a global audience, it is increasingly difficult to target foreign audiences with radio and television messages without having them inadvertently relayed to the U.S. public.

28. On Clinton's surprise, see Walter Clark and Jeffrey Herbst, "Somalia and the Future of Humanitarian Intervention," Study No. 9 (Princeton Unviersity: Center for International Studies, 1995), p. 3.

29. For a longer discussion of this subject, see Tucker and Lamb, "Peacetime Engagements," pp. 319–321.

30. Shortly after the events of October 3, 1993 in Somalia, then Secretary of Defense Les Aspin commented on the need to learn from the experience. He observed that, "Because these operations require our forces to perform tasks that are substantially different from those on the battlefield, the equipment might include other kinds of capabilities than we have now." He also noted the increased importance of human intelligence, civil affairs, and psychological operations in peace operations, and announced a series of studies to identify the new capabilities. "Pentagon Eyes New Equipment for Peacekeeping," *Defense News* (19 October 1993), p. 95; and "Americans Want Troops to Stay Home," *Washington Times* (19 October 1993), p. 12.

chapter fourteen
The Role of the Internet in International Politics: Department of Defense Considerations

Charles Swett

THE POLITICAL PROCESS is moving onto the Internet. Individuals, interest groups, and even nations are using the Internet to find each other, discuss issues, and further their political goals. Local, state, and national governments are establishing an Internet presence, both for disseminating information to the public and for receiving feedback. Candidates for elective office conduct debates over the Internet. Organizers of domestic and international political movements mobilize support through the Internet. In the Gulf War, the attempted coup in Russia, the conflict in the former Yugoslavia, and in challenges to authoritarian controls in Iran, China, and other oppressive states, the Internet has played an important role.

The last few years have witnessed the transformation of the Internet into a household topic. After a long period of relative obscurity when it was solely the domain of technically oriented individuals, the Internet has burst onto the national scene, affecting an ever-widening spectrum of activities that involve an exponentially increasing number of people. With tangible effects on the social, cultural, economic, and political lives of millions, the evolution of the Internet is leading in directions completely unanticipated by its original designers. Rather than merely enhancing pre-existing social processes, the Internet is actually transforming the nature of the processes themselves.

As it is for others, the Internet can be a useful tool for the Department of Defense (DOD). By monitoring public message traffic and alternative news sources from around the world, electronic early-warning systems could outpace more traditional means of warning. Commentary placed on the Internet by observers on the scene of low-intensity conflicts could be useful to U.S. policymaking. During large-scale conflicts, when other conventional channels are disrupted, the Internet may be the only means of maintaining communication intact. Internet messages from regions under authoritarian control could enhance current intelligence and play an important role in counterintelligence. The Internet could also be added to the repertoire of psychological operations tools and help achieve unconventional warfare objectives. In short, when used creatively as an integral asset, the Internet can facilitate many DOD operations and activities. This chapter will highlight current trends in the evolution of the Internet, and analyze its role in domestic and international politics and conflict. The aim is to provide some relevant predictions about the future of the Internet and derive implications and recommendations for the Department of Defense.

WHAT IS THE INTERNET?

The Internet is an enormous global network of computers. Often called a "network of networks," it integrates thousands of dissimilar computer systems worldwide through the application of uniform technical standards. Individuals connected to the Internet through desktop computers are able to exchange electronic mail (e-mail) with other users at any location; participate in discussion groups both on-line (in real time) and off; log on to remote computer sites worldwide; read complex documents; and view multimedia images of text, graphics, sound, and video. There is no central authority managing the Internet, and participation is voluntary and cooperative. The Internet Society in Fairfax, Virginia plays an integrating role and sets the technical standards. Funding for the communication links is provided mainly by non-governmental institutions, such as universities and corporations.

Although accurate numbers are difficult to obtain, current figures estimate twenty million Internet users worldwide. Projections indicate that approximately one hundred million people will have access to the Internet by the turn of the century. This vast increase is fueled by a variety of factors. First, user-friendly improvements in technology replaced arcane operating systems, allowing non-technical individuals to become highly sophisticated users. Second, the proliferation of commercial Internet access providers now makes possible on-line connections from virtually any location with a telephone hook-up. The concomitant reductions in the cost of access has made the Internet affordable to a large segment of the population, who may now communicate over long distances at the price of a local phone call. And as the number of users has grown, so has the volume of useful and entertaining information available over the Internet. As a result, increasing momentum has created a new electronic marketplace of ideas, goods, and services that is cost effective and useful for both for information providers and those logging on.

CURRENT TRENDS ON THE INTERNET

One important trend is the growth in the proportion of professionals with personal e-mail addresses on the Internet. Increasingly, business cards include not just phone and fax numbers, but Internet addresses. This trend is so strong that, rather than considering an Internet address to be a luxury, not having one is viewed as a handicap, comparable to not having a fax. Individuals and organizations without Internet access increasingly risk being left out of important discussions and processes taking place on-line. Additionally, these individuals and organizations bring vast knowledge to the Internet. Millions of experts in various fields, from medicine to plumbing, conduct business over the Internet and use it for recreation and information exchange, creating a great storehouse of specialized knowledge.

Federal, state, and local governments are rapidly establishing a presence on the Internet. Dozens of federal agencies provide public information on-line. These agencies are all reachable through a service in Virginia called Fedlink. Fedlink acts as a gateway through which the general on-line public can reach any agency system. The Office of the Assistant Secretary of Defense for Public Affairs has just implemented a World Wide Web service containing news releases, daily summaries, press advisories, transcripts, and contracts. However, information on this service flows one way – from DOD to callers. Provisions have not been made to accept feedback from callers. The Office of the Assistant Secretary of Defense for Command, Control, Communications, and Information (OSD C^{3}I) has built its own World Wide Web page, an Internet entity that provides graphics-based information publicly over the Internet. This system provides OSD organizational information and, for official users, an on-line version of the "Early Bird," the Pentagon's daily newspaper clipping circular. Additionally, local governments are increasingly establishing on-line information services open to the public, known as "freenets." These services provide local government documents and news, and are a medium for discussion of local issues.

Commercial on-line databases containing every form of information imaginable are now accessible, mostly for a fee, via the Internet. Open-source intelligence originates largely from these databases. Public library catalogues, including the one belonging to the Library of Congress, are available for free over the Internet. Increasingly, authors of magazine and newspaper articles also include Internet addresses in their bylines, allowing readers to contact them directly to give reactions or obtain additional information.

Internet users interested in particular subjects log on to electronic "conferences." These conferences are collections of messages that become extended discussions. Currently, there are roughly sixteen thousand conferences available on the Internet in various forms. Conferences exist for virtually every subject, are easily accessible, and operate at low cost. Some of the most energetic types of conferences are those devoted to current events and political debate. Opinions span the entire political spectrum, from far left to far right, and originate in many nations. Whenever an important event occurs, such as a national election, a major conflict, or even a natural disaster, there is an almost deafening roar of responses on the Internet. Participants in the international conferences include journalists, professors, political analysts, and politicians. As a result, Internet conferences provide a unique medium for interpersonal communication on a massive scale. Many of the issues addressed focus on current military operations in which DOD is involved. Often, electronic conference statements include incorrect presentations of fact, misrepresentations of the United States position on an issue, and gross distortions of reality —

which is not altogether surprising. However, the vast size of the audience for such mis-statements amplifies the magnitude of their effect on public opinion.

In global terms, Americans are by far the heaviest users of the Internet – and the proportion of American homes with personal computers and modems is increasing quickly. In Europe, Internet use is less prevalent but still significant, and is increasing rapidly. In the less-developed world, particularly in the nations where future conflicts are likely to occur, few individuals other than government officials, business persons, educators, and some professionals have access to the Internet. However, all South American nations and nearly two-thirds of all African nations have at least some Internet connectivity.[1] There is currently an international project to spread the Internet to the undeveloped world, but progress is likely to be slow.

The threat from "hackers" and computer viruses is always present. Internet security is one of the greatest concerns of the organizations using it, particularly the Department of Defense. Malicious tampering with government computers could seriously disrupt operations if sufficient countermeasures are not built in. A strategy called "firewalls" has been developed, whereby a second computer is placed between an organization and the Internet communication lines, to help control access and prevent computer break-ins. With respect to viruses, there is a kind of arms-race spiral, whereby anti-virus software writers improve their software to protect against a newly discovered type of virus. The virus writers respond by creating a new virus that can circumvent that new protection, and so on.

~

THE INTERNET AND DOMESTIC U.S. POLITICS

The Clinton administration has embraced the Internet as a means of direct political communication with the electorate. Using the president's e-mail address, president@whitehouse.gov, anyone can send a message to the White House staff. Some five thousand e-mail messages are sent to the White House every week. Interns read every message, tally them by issue and opinion expressed, and send a standard response. They see interaction with the public via the Internet as a positive force. This direct, two-way interaction between the pinnacle of the federal government and ordinary citizens bypasses congressional representation, poll takers, and the news media. White House staffers believe the direct communications may help counteract any distortions or filtering that those entities might otherwise add. If this unprecedented phenomenon continues to grow over the long term, it may fundamentally alter the political process. However, there is no telling to what extent future administrations may emphasize the electronic medium.

It is not only the American public that uses the Internet to communicate with the White House. On February 4, 1994, Swedish Prime Minister Carl Bildt sent an e-mail message to President Clinton, becoming the first head of state to do so:

> Dear Bill: Apart from testing this connection on the global Internet system, I want to congratulate you on your decision to end the trade embargo on Vietnam. I am planning to go to Vietnam in April and will certainly use the occasion to take up the question of the MIAs.... Sweden is – as you know – one of the leading countries in the world in the field of telecommunications, and it is only appropriate that we should be among the first to use the Internet for political contacts and communications around the globe. Yours, Carl.[2]

Speaker of the House Newt Gingrich has established a program to make electronic versions of all draft legislation available on the Internet. This will allow the subset of the electorate with Internet access to evaluate legislation for themselves, and thus offer informed opinions to their representatives in Congress. It will also weaken the position of those without Internet access; they will be less knowledgeable of the details of legislation or unable to ascertain its significance independently.

The theme of the Internet as a threat to the established mass media is increasingly common in recent literature. Wide access to electronic information endangers the media's role as the nation's information gatekeeper. The public can now choose what they want to read and independently share their own experiences and opinions. They can tap into electronic wire services at will, call up expanded versions of news stories, and then directly discuss their political aspirations or cultural passions. The Internet not only carries news and forges communities, it shapes values and public opinion without help from the gatekeepers, who traditionally decided what information was important and how it should be perceived.[3]

Many newspapers and magazines are timid about going on-line. Others, believing that they had better go on-line to retain their relevance, are finding for the first time in their entire history that they are subject to strong, serious criticism. On-line media conferences provide a forum for challenging journalists. The public can now directly question reporting and editing decisions.

> Time [magazine]'s on-line effort is intensely interactive, generating more than two million on-line visits in its first eight months. Editors and writers regularly make on-line appearances for drubbings by displeased readers who want to go a few rounds about gun control or women priests.... Time's on-line message boards contain some of the most vigorous democratic debate on social issues in any modern medium.... More importantly, users sense that Time, hardly a bastion of populist journalism, is changing as a result, becoming a bit less aloof, more in touch.[4]

Another popular concept emerging is "electronic democracy," whereby American citizens can become more influential participants in government decisions by making their views known via the Internet. It is inspired by the desire to bypass bureaucratic inconvenience — by making government information available at the touch of a button — and by the desire to make politicians answerable and accessible to their constituents.[5] Some advocates of electronic democracy envision on-line elections and referendums, in which voters cast ballots from their homes. The ease of voting would presumably increase participation, making ballot referendums and polls more common and meaningful.[6] Other observers are more skeptical of the possibilities of electronic democracy. They fear the political process will become captive to uninformed Americans. Still others fear the potential for "big brother" control of the political process, in which electronic information is used to manipulate constituents as well as inform them. In this view, detailed databases make the public vulnerable to sophisticated, well-targeted information campaigns. The security and anonymity of balloting on-line is questioned; suspicions arise of computer hackers rewriting elections for profit, politics, or a prank.[7]

The Internet has already played an important role in several local elections. In these elections, the candidates were essentially forced on-line and put under the spotlight of determined questioning by voters. In another episode, a software developer from Washington state discovered on-line support for his dislike of Rep. Tom Foley. "Within weeks a 'De-Foley-ate Congress' campaign had used the Net and commercial on-line services to find supporters and donors. Foley might have lost anyway, but news of [the] effort helped spread the notion of the Speaker's vulnerability — and brought help from national Republicans."[8] Many other political activists have discovered the utility of the Internet for sharing information and organizing activities. For example, LatinoNet uses America Online to help Latino organizers cooperate and lobby government officials. The success of this network sets the stage for other electronic ethnic lobbyists, such as a Serbo-CroatNet, SlovakNet or BelarusNet.[9]

One activist has actually published advice for on-line political activists, in the form of ten rules:

Rule One: Decide what issues are worthy of your time.

Rule Two: Don't automatically assume you must work within a traditional group.

Rule Three: Be realistic about the possibility of payback.

Rule Four: Know how to scout the Internet effectively – and where to post your own messages.

Rule Five: Don't be intrusive or otherwise boorish.

Rule Six: Write for the medium.

Rule Seven: Tell the truth.

Rule Eight: Turn flaming [insulting postings] to your advantage.

Rule Nine: Provide a way for people to take action.

Rule Ten: Don't forget to communicate with the media – and the policymakers.[10]

The Internet's ability to reach large numbers of individuals efficiently who are potential political actors plays to the strengths of special interest groups and political action committees. The Internet is thus highly attractive to activists who value a populist approach to politics. Examples of on-line political activism abound. In one instance, electronic messaging quickly spread word of gun-control rallies scheduled around the country in the fall of 1995. Gun rights activists seized the opportunity to mobilize their own supporters on-line, and effectively overshadowed the gun control events.[11]

Another somewhat startling example of on-line activism was a message posted on the Internet on December 16, 1994, calling for nationwide protests against the Republican Party's Contract with America. The message accused the Contract with America of being a class war, race war, gender war, and generational war. It urged recipients to "mobilize thousands of demonstrations in local communities across the nation, fill the jails by engaging in acts of civil disobedience, and engage in other dis-ruptive actions."[12] Yet another example is a message posted on the same date entitled, "Protest: GOP `96," which began the process of organizing mass protests against the 1996 Republican National Convention in San Diego. The message stated:

> With the GOP's historical opposition to women's equality, lesbian & gay civil rights, and freedom of choice, and with the party's support for Prop 187 [preventing access to many government programs in California to illegal immigrants in the state], insensitivity to environmental issues, and hawkish pro-war stances, the possibilities for expressing popular dissent against Republican policies are virtually endless. For that reason, a local committee is forming to help facilitate the largest number of protests and demonstrations for the broadest range of issues possible.... Called "Protest: GOP `96," the committee seeks to serve as a local point of contact for organizations from across the country intending to demonstrate during the GOP Convention in August of 1996.[13]

Still other types of interest groups have moved on-line. Groups of conspiracy theorists exchange e-mail explaining their often bizarre theories about conspiracies conducted by the United States government in general, and DOD in particular. One well-organized group, the Mutual UFO Network (MUFON), has its own computer network with a gateway to the Internet. Much of the traffic on this network refers to U.S. military oper-ations that members believe relate to investigations and cover-ups of UFO-related incidents, and other messages con-tain details on MUFON's efforts to conduct surveillance of DOD installations and to obtain information on UFOs that they believe exists in classified form. Some of the other fringe groups that are beginning to exploit the Internet include:

- The National Alliance, a white supremacist organization that circulated a missive on the Internet exhorting peo-ple to oppose welfare mothers, homosexuals, Jews, illegal aliens, and "minority parasites;"
- The Gay Agenda Resistance, "dedicated to the struggle

against the sexual deviancy forces;"
- The Michigan Militia Corps, a private group that is training to combat an "inevitable takeover" by federal armed forces;
- The National Association for the Reform of Marijuana Laws;
- Earth First!, a loosely affiliated group of environmental extremists; and
- People for the Ethical Treatment of Animals, which is preparing an on-line forum to promote its militant approach to animal rights.[14]

According to the *Wall Street Journal,* "the more a group is shut out of the mainstream, the more likely it is to go on-line.... The Simon Wiesenthal Center, which monitors hate groups...has tracked about 250 hate groups in the United States and says fifty or more communicate on-line. Other experts believe the number is considerably higher."[15]

THE INTERNET AND INTERNATIONAL POLITICAL ACTIVISM
Numerous commentators and activists believe that the Internet will play a catalytic role in international affairs. Former U.S. presidential candidate John Anderson envisioned a "supranational" political era in which current conceptions of state sovereignty might become outmoded. He viewed the Internet as a potential global support network for the United Nations, an important source for measuring world public opinion, and a possible early-warning system for monitoring developing regional conflicts.[16]

One highly significant effect of Internet use overseas has been to circumvent the informational controls imposed by authoritarian regimes. Citizens can gain access to alternate forms of information, as well as reach others to express points of view that differ from the official stance. Censorship can be bypassed by distributing home-produced books or manifestos worldwide.[17] During the student protests in Tiananmen Square and the attempted coup in Moscow, dissenters used computer networks to communicate with kindred spirits around the world. The Chinese and Russian autocrats knew how to censor radio, television, and the print media; however, they could not shut down these computer networks.[18] "'During Tiananmen Square, students were getting the news out and were fundraising through Internet,' [said] Tom Mandel.... 'There were a bunch of us hungrily reading newsgroups, stuff we weren't getting from reporters.'"[19]

In Sarajevo, 150 residents under siege were able to e-mail friends and relatives using one computer and a single phone line over the course of three months. During the upheaval in Moscow in 1991, protest mail sent over the Internet helped secure the release of dissidents arrested by the police, perhaps saving their lives.[20] One Internet e-mail, intercepted during the same period, expresses the crucial role of the electronic network:

> I've seen the tanks with my own eyes. I hope we'll be able to communicate during the next few days. Communists cannot rape the Mother Russia once again! ... Don't worry, we're ok, though frightened and angry. Moscow is full of tanks – I hate them. They try to close all mass media, they stopped CNN an hour ago, and Soviet TV transmits opera and old movies.... Now we transmit information enough to put us in prison for the rest of our life...maybe you'd write me what do they say on your (American) TV about the situation, as we can't watch CNN now.... You can't even imagine how grateful we are for your help and support during this terrible time! The best thing is to know that we aren't alone.... Don't worry; the only danger for us is if they catch and arrest us, as we are sitting at home and distributing all the information we have.... Thank heaven, these cretins (KGB) don't consider us mass media! Please stop flooding the only narrow channel with bogus messages with silly questions. Note that it's neither a toy nor a means to reach your relatives or friends. We need the bandwidth to help organize the resistance. Really good news. Right now we're listening to Radio Russia (without any jamming); they told that the eight left Moscow, no one knows where...[21]

Similar exchanges of information and experience took place during the Gulf War. Israelis under siege by *Scuds* communicated in real-time with the United States, and live reports from Baghdad catalogued the damage of bombing raids.

Another significant dimension of the Internet is its use by international protest groups and political activists. In instances where a protest movement does not have significant means to reach potential constituencies, they seek stronger organizations to donate modems and connections to reliable phone lines — often the most difficult part of establishing a network connection. Once these hook-ups are achieved, a movement can make contact with millions of people worldwide via international computer networks, often unnerving authoritarian regimes. In Africa, some regimes bristle at organizations that use more advanced technology than the government. In India, a modem cannot be connected to a phone line without official permission.[22] Other examples of Internet use for protest include:

- *Counterev-L*, a French group dedicated to the cause of traditional monarchy and counterrevolution.[23]

- The use of electronic mailboxes by neo-Nazi groups in Germany to propagandize and organize rallies. The neo-Nazi network is becoming so sophisticated that German officials warn that they may lose critical time in trying to detect and intervene in extremist operations.[24]

- A Mexican underground group, the Zapatista National Liberation Army (EZLN), utilizes portable laptop computers to issue orders to other EZLN units and maintains international media contacts.[25] In some cases, they used the Internet to publish accounts of government attack, rape, and pillage that could not be substantiated by reporters in the region.[26]

The largest and most active international political groups using the Internet appear to be the Institute for Global Communications (IGC) and the Association for Progressive Communications (APC), both based in San Francisco. As such, an overview of the IGC can provide a good perspective on the breadth of DOD-relevant information available on the Internet. According to a text file placed on the IGC's publicly accessible Internet site, the group reaches twenty-five thousand activists and organizations in more than 130 countries. Its networks – PeaceNet, EcoNet, ConflictNet and LaborNet – together with APC partner networks, are dedicated to environmental preservation, peace, and human rights. The Institute organizes private conferences to facilitate internal group decisionmaking, task-sharing processes, or sensitive communications.[27] Although IGC/APC is clearly a left-wing political organization, without actually joining IGC and reading its message traffic it is difficult to assess the nature and extent of its members' real-world activities.

The IGC is also the most comprehensive source for alternative news, playing a significant, if slanted, role in filling gaps in reports issued by the mainstream news media. It offers many region-specific services, such as weekly reports from Latin America and the Caribbean, updates on trouble spots in Africa, alternative opinions on peace in the Middle East, coverage of Eastern Europe and various factions in the former Yugoslavia, and digests of economic and political news from across Asia.

SOME PREDICTIONS FOR THE FUTURE OF THE INTERNET

Given the exponential growth of the Internet in the past few years, and the power of its services, careful assessment of its future development is essential. The following predictions reflect this author's vision of the next five to twenty years.

New political parties operating through the Internet will emerge. The convergence of large numbers of people of similar political persuasion through the Internet will eventually spur the development of political blocs whose only means of interaction is through the Internet. Virtual conventions will be held over the Internet, where party platforms are agreed upon and candidates for office are determined by vote. These activists will then interface with the "physical" world by running for elective office, representing an electronic constituency. Virtual political parties of this type will be ad hoc, and may not be institutionalized for long periods of time. They may be oriented toward a single issue or group of issues and may dissolve once these issues are resolved to their satisfaction. They will defy political and geographic boundaries, transcending local, state, and even national borders. Membership in and activism on behalf of these parties will occur on a global scale. They will increasingly make their presence felt in the internal political affairs of nations and in international affairs. The proliferation of such parties will also make the political scene more complex, triggering political wars in cyberspace. Due to the almost instantaneous transmission of news about current events to members, and the very rapid development of responses to them via e-mail, these parties will be able to react almost immediately to developments that relate to their interests. This reactive speed will afford them a disproportionate degree of influence relative to their actual numbers.

Although it will be nearly impossible to enforce party discipline in these semi-formal, loosely defined organizations, considerable political momentum will be achieved when large groups support particular positions. Single-issue coalitions between different parties with common interests will add to their potency. Financing will be problematic, since members may be reluctant to transmit funds to a virtual treasurer for a party that might go out of existence without warning. However, these parties will have modest financial requirements compared to more traditional political parties, since most of their operations will occur over the Internet. The only significant costs will be incurred by activities through which party leaders interface with the "real world" of Congress and the White House or non-U.S. governments. Lobbying, advertising, membership drives, polling, and most other party activities will occur almost exclusively on the Internet at almost negligible financial cost.

Political groups whose operations are coordinated through the Internet will be vulnerable to having their operations disrupted by false messages inserted by opposing groups. This will encourage the proliferation of encrypted messages. However, these groups will face the dilemma that encrypting their messages excludes the wider audience, from which they hope to elicit sympathy and support.

The monopoly of the traditional mass media will erode. No longer will the news editors and anchors of newspapers and television networks solely determine what the mass audience learns and thinks about current events. Raw news reports from local, national, and international newswires and alternative news sources, and from unaffiliated individual observers on the scene of events, will be accessible to all Internet users. The filtering of the news, currently performed by traditional media, will partially give way to direct consumption of un-analyzed information by the mass audience, diminishing the influence now enjoyed by the media. An increasingly skeptical audience will be able to compare raw news reports with the pre-digested, incomplete, out-of-context, and sometimes biased renditions offered by television and newspapers. Some of the mass media will attempt to reassert their traditional roles on the Internet, and will fail because they will have no advantage over their audience. The average consumer of news on the Internet will also have much wider cognizance of current events worldwide and will be more likely to have an opinion on overseas situations. This is not to imply, however, that the traditional mass media will lose their audience and become insignificant. They will continue to play a major role in the national news flow. Yet, they will lose considerable ground to alternative sources and interpretations circulating on the Internet.

Members of Congress and federal agency officials will be inexorably drawn into the Internet. When members of Congress discover the power of their rivals' presence on the Internet, they will want to join themselves. This will intensify as they are attacked in electronic debates and discover there is no one in cyberspace to defend them or, even worse, that they are not being discussed at all. Remaining out of the Internet will be seen as a strategic weakness, a sign of being behind the times. The same phenomenon will affect officials in the executive branch. Increasing demands for public accountability will draw them into the Internet, beyond simply posting news releases and other documentation on-line. Members of Congress and senior federal officials will require staffs simply to monitor and respond to Internet traffic.

Text-oriented e-mail will be replaced by video/audio messages. As a result of reductions in the size and cost of high-quality video cameras and improvements in video data compression technology, all personal computers in the future will be equipped with small video cameras, much as each computer today has a mouse. At the same time, the capacity of the communication links connecting personal computers to the Internet will greatly expand, due to the replacement of twisted-pair copper telephone wires with fiber-optic cables. These two trends will allow Internet users to compose messages consisting of compressed full-motion color video images. To send a message, users will simply prepare a script and then speak the words for the camera while reading them from the computer screen, like a teleprompter. The resulting data file will then be uploaded into the Internet and played back by all recipients using standard video playback hardware/software with which all computers will be equipped. Although some users will prefer the anonymity of text-oriented e-mail, many others will find the urge to let the world see them irresistible. The addition of the visual and audio dimensions to computer-mediated communications will greatly expand the content of messages, since facial expression, tone of voice, body language, race, nationality, gender, and age all convey contextual information. Full-motion color video with sound will magnify the emotional impact and intensity of political debate on the Internet. As a result, political groups will discover the propaganda potential of video on the Internet, and will produce and disseminate video clips supporting their point of view. Internet users will encounter a wide variety of political advertisements in the form of video files. Opposing groups will engage in video propaganda wars entirely within the medium of the Internet.

The Internet will be used as a tool of statecraft by national governments. The recent use of the World Wide Web by the Peruvian and Ecuadorian governments to wage a propaganda war during their recent military confrontation is highly significant. Those nations, not renowned for their technological sophistication, have been the first to bring international diplomacy officially on-line. Although many governments currently have an official presence on the Internet, they provide only standard embassy-type public affairs statements, with information about their populations, cultures, industries, and businesses. In the future, as more governments recognize the strategic value of this new medium for conveying their message, they will use it as an additional tool in the political process.

The information currently placed on the Internet by official government organizations will be supplemented with politically-oriented material conveying argumentation favorable to their respective positions. When one country involved in a dispute begins to use the Internet in this way, a catalytic effect will occur, whereby all involved countries will feel compelled to enter the electronic debate.

The Internet will play an increasing role in international conflict. Political discussions among the members of the on-line public, national leaders, political parties, interest groups, commercial enterprises, and world bodies such as the United Nations will be energized by the Internet. Current information about conflicts placed on the Internet in real time by on-the-scene observers and alternative news sources will be devoured voraciously by the world audience and will have an immediate and tangible impact on the course of events. Video footage of military operations will be captured by inexpensive, hand-held digital video cameras operated by local observers, transferred unedited into data files, and then uploaded into the global information flow, reaching millions of people in a matter of minutes. Public opinion and calls for action – or calls to terminate actions – may crystallize before national leaders have a chance to develop positions or to react to developments. These factors will greatly add to the burden on military commanders, whose actions will be subjected to an unprecedented degree of scrutiny.

ASSESSMENT OF THE INTERNET'S IMPACT ON U.S. POLICYMAKING AND THE DEPARTMENT OF DEFENSE

Political Roles. While the Internet has already become a powerful political tool both domestically and internationally, there is likely to be a significant increase in the scale and sophistication of such use in the coming years. The Internet is likely to be most powerful in directly influencing public opinion in the United States. In other parts of the developed world, such as Europe, its impact will be less significant. However, in less-developed countries, individual activists are likely to capitalize on the Internet connection through laptop computers plugged into a telephone line. Information brought into less-developed countries through a small number of Internet access points can be spread locally through more traditional methods such as print, radio broadcast, and word of mouth. Activists will also be able to use the Internet to disseminate information to the rest of the world and to help coordinate their activities.

The Internet is clearly a significant long-term strategic threat to authoritarian regimes, one that will be difficult to counter effectively. News from the outside world brought in by the Internet will clash with official government versions, eroding the credibility of authoritarian regimes. Direct e-mail communication between people living under such governments and people living outside will also help achieve more accurate understanding on both sides, and further undermine authoritarian controls. Information about violations of human rights and other forms of oppression will be conveyed to the outside world by the Internet, helping to mobilize external political forces on behalf of the oppressed.

According to some analysts, the concepts of "national sovereignty" and "nation-state" are becoming less relevant due to greatly increased economic, political, and cultural linkages that cut across national boundaries. To the extent that this is true, the Internet will play an important role, since it is the medium through which an increasing volume of these types of linkages will take place.

Intelligence. The Internet is a potentially lucrative source of information for DOD. Intelligence that can be drawn from the Internet includes reports on current events, analytic assessments by observers on or near the scene of a conflict, and information about the plans and operations of politically active groups. John Anderson's concept for using the Internet to provide early warning of impending security threats has a great deal of merit. Internet message traffic on developing situations tends to precede news and intelligence reporting, since the individuals are not constrained by the resource limitations under which news and intelligence organizations operate. These organizations must prioritize their efforts, focusing on what appears to be the most important items of the moment. Individual observers overseas, with access to the Internet, can write about anything that interests them. It is likely that routine monitoring of messages originating in other countries would help provide strategic warning of developing security threats that would be of concern to the United States.

At the same time, it should be noted that a great deal of the message traffic on the Internet is idle chatter with no intelligence value whatsoever, a veritable "tower of babble." Monitoring Internet traffic needs to be supported by automated filters that retain only messages satisfying certain relevance criteria. It is also important to note that the accuracy of much of the raw information on the Internet is suspect. Thus, new means of validating information received in this way are needed. Alternatively, news reports on the Internet could be used to cue higher-confidence means of U.S. intelligence collection, by highlighting potentially important factors and allowing us to orient and focus intelligence collection more precisely.

Beside its usefulness in identifying general trends and areas of unrest, the Internet can also help generate highly specific intelligence. Networks of human sources with access to the Internet could be developed in areas of security concern to the United States. These sources could be oriented to pinpoint critical information. If constructed and managed correctly, such a system could be much more responsive and efficient than the complex, unwieldy intelligence tasking and collection processes we now use. It is even worth considering cultivating the capability to perform strategic reconnaissance by modem. This approach could never replace official DOD intelligence collection systems or services, but could be a useful adjunct.

The Internet can also serve counterintelligence purposes. For example, a message posted in an Internet discussion group for left-wing political activists repeated for their benefit an Associated Press article about an upcoming U.S. Army Special Operations Command training exercise directed at the empty St. Moritz Hotel in Miami Beach.[28] However, if it became widely known that DOD were monitoring Internet traffic for intelligence or counterintelligence purposes, individuals with personal agendas or political purposes in mind, or who enjoy playing pranks, would deliberately enter false or misleading messages. Intelligence analysis would need to account for this.

Support to Policymaking. The insights and analyses of thoughtful overseas observers – such as educators, former politicians, local journalists, and foreign government officials – could also be very useful to U.S. policymaking. E-mail discussions about the likely consequences of various policy approaches to security problems could help improve policy decisions. A great deal of brain power is accessible through the Internet and, if harnessed and channeled for productive purposes, might be a useful addition to DOD's informational and political assets. Any such use, of course, would have to be protected by appropriate security measures.

Support to Civil Affairs Programs. The Internet has substantial value to the civil affairs community in helping to establish closer working relationships with non-governmental organizations. In pursuit of the goal of minimizing government's role in executing civil-sector programs in favor of a stronger role by non-military organizations, the Internet can be used to accelerate and strengthen the coordination of activities among all parties. In addition, a project is underway to identify public on-line information bases accessible through the Internet that contain data useful to civil affairs programs. A substantial volume of relevant information has been found.

Offensive Uses of the Internet. Just as the United States could be vulnerable to e-mail disinformation campaigns, political groups using the Internet could be vulnerable to deceptive messages introduced by hostile persons or groups. Far-right groups and far-left groups tend to watch each other, and it is likely that "moles" will obtain access to another camp's network for the purpose of disrupting operations. This would tend to weaken the protection afforded by coding or encrypting messages.

Increasingly, officials in national governments, foreign military officers, business persons, and journalists are obtaining access to the Internet and establishing individual e-mail addresses. There is even a commercial service that will soon offer access to an on-line database of the names, organizational titles, phone/fax numbers, and Internet e-mail addresses of virtually all government officials worldwide. Using this information, it would be possible to employ the Internet as an additional medium for psychological operations. E-mail conveying the United States' perspective on issues and events could be efficiently and rapidly disseminated to a very wide audience.

The United States might be able to employ the Internet offensively to help achieve unconventional warfare objectives. Information could be transmitted over the Internet to sympathetic groups operating in areas of concern, allowing them to conduct operations that the United States might otherwise have to send special forces to accomplish. Although such undertakings would have their own kinds of risks, they would reduce the physical risks to special forces personnel and limit the direct political involvement of the United States, since the actions would be carried out by indigenous groups.

Roles During Conflict. Even if the actual presence of the Internet in a conflict is limited, widespread access to the Internet in the United States and other parts of the developed world will provide a medium through which political debate and activism related to that conflict can occur. Thus, the Internet can indirectly play an important role in the way the world deals with a conflict, without having substantial physical presence within the conflict.

The Internet can play an important positive role during future international crises and conflicts. Under the chaotic conditions of such situations, normal government and commercial reporting channels are often unreliable or unavailable, and the Internet might be one of the few means of communication present. Some of its uses might include extracting news from the region, transmitting information from the United States and other nations into the region, and cultivating political and even operational support for the United States.

RECOMMENDATIONS FOR THE DEPARTMENT OF DEFENSE

Clearly, the Department of Defense would benefit from taking a proactive approach towards capitalizing on the Internet. Of course, any involvement in the Internet must be guided by full compliance with the letter and the spirit of U.S. laws and protection of the privacy of the nation's citizens. Within these guidelines, Internet capabilities could be capitalized upon in a number of ways:

- All DOD professional and support personnel should have Internet e-mail addresses with convenient access and a user-friendly interface.
- Individual analysts in DOD intelligence agencies should

routinely monitor Internet traffic related to their responsibilities.

- DOD intelligence agencies should investigate the role of
the Internet in coordinating the operations of political
activists and paramilitary groups in regions of interest.

- An early-warning capability should be established uti-
lizing Internet traffic to help identify developing
situations overseas that could lead to security threats.

- Officials planning and conducting DOD civil affairs programs overseas should be informed about any activists
working in their vicinity who use the Internet.

- The Office of the Assistant Secretary of Defense for
Public Affairs site on the Internet should accept feedback from callers and should provide responses.
Although it would be impractical to provide an individual reply to every incoming e-mail message, statistical
profiles of opinions conveyed by large volumes of messages could be used to compose periodic DOD bulletins
addressing general issues. This would help provide a
semi-interactive environment within resource limitations.

- Subject to appropriate security and propriety precautions, DOD officials involved in formulating DOD policy
should be given access to the advice and thinking of
people on the Internet with relevant expertise.

- The Internet should be incorporated into psychological
operations planning.

- Offensive uses of the Internet, in support of unconventional warfare objectives, should be explored.

- Senior DOD officials should be kept aware of domestic
U.S. political developments on the Internet that relate to
DOD interests.

To use the Internet most productively for these purposes, DOD must address the Internet as an integral asset, rather than as an uncontrollable element of the environment whose role is determined by happenstance or as an afterthought. Once it is viewed as a resource that can be systematically and effectively integrated into DOD planning and operations, the Internet can make important contributions to conflict management and help assure the success of U.S. foreign policy.

ENDNOTES

1. Howard Fineman, "The Brave New World of Cybertribes," *Newsweek* (27 February 1995), pp. 30–33.

2. Evan I. Schwartz, "Power to the People," *Wired* (December 1994), pp. 88–92.

3. John Katz, "The Times Enters the Nineties; Doesn't Like it Much," *New York* (June 27 to July 4, 1994), pp. 26–29.

4. John Katz, "Bulletin Boards: News From Cyberspace," *Rolling Stone* (15 April 1993), pp. 35–77.

5. Unattributed article, "The PEN is Mighty," *The Economist* (1 February 1992), pp. 96. See also Richard J. Varn, "Jeffersonian Boom or Teraflop?" *Spectrum* (Spring 1993), pp. 21–25.

6. Author unattributed, *The Internet Unleashed* (SAMS Publishing, 1994).

7. Author unattributed, *The Internet Unleashed* (SAMS Publishing, 1994). See also Varn, *Spectrum* (Spring 1993), and Andre Bacard, "Electronic Democracy: Can We Retake Our Government?" *The Humanist* (July/August 1993).

8. Howard Fineman, "The Brave New World of Cybertribes," *Newsweek* (27 February 1995), pp 30–33.

9. Unattributed article, "The War of the Webs," *Washington Technology* (23 February 1995), pp. 3.

10. *The Internet Unleashed.*

11. Dave Kopel, "Defend Your Rights," *American Hunter* (Undated), pp. 14–70.

12. E-mail message, "A Call to Action," 16 December 1994 from rich@pencil.cs.missouri.edu.

13. E-mail message, "Protest: GOP '96," 16 December 1994 from rich@pencil.cs.missouri.edu.

14. Jared Sandberg, "Fringe Groups Can Say Almost Anything and Not Worry About Getting Punched," *Wall Street Journal* (8 December 1994), pp. B1–4.

15. Sandberg, *Wall Street Journal.*

16. Marion Long, "We Are the World," *Net Guide* (December 1994), pp. 55–66.

17. See Howard Rheingold, *The Virtual Community: Homesteading on the Electronic Frontier* (New York: Harper Collins, 1993), and Jolyon Jenkins, "Cyberthreat," *New Statesman & Society* (7 May 1994), pp. 29–30.

18. Andre Bacard, "Electronic Democracy: Can We Retake Our Government?" *The Humanist* (July/August 1993), pp. 42–43.

19. Kevin Cooke and Dan Lehrer, "The Whole World is Talking," *The Nation* (12 July 1993), pp. 60–64.

20. Long, "We Are the World," *Net Guide.*

21. Larry Press, "Wide-Area Collaboration," *Communications of the ACM* (December 1991), pp. 21–24. Emphasis added.

22. Mike Holderness, "Power to the People – by Modem," *The Independent*, as reproduced in *World Press Review* (February 1993), p. 44.

23. See Christina Maxwell and Czeslaw Jan Grycz, *The New Riders' Official Internet Yellow Pages* (Indianapolis, Indiana: New Riders Publishing, 1994).

24. U.S. Army Intelligence, "Computer Links Strengthen German Neo-Nazis" (Unclassified) (15 December 1994).

25. U.S. Army Intelligence, "Technical Applications for Insurgents," (Unclassified) (3 August 1994).

26. Tod Robberson, "Mexican Rebels Using a High-Tech Weapon; Internet Helps Rally Support," *Washington Post* (20 February 1995).

27. All information regarding the Institute for Global Communications (IGC) was taken from an Internet file placed on-line by the IGC.

28. E-mail message, "Special Forces Practice Assaults in Miami," 25 December 1994 from a newsgroup article.

chapter fifteen

PSYOP and the Revolution in Military Affairs

Carnes Lord

PSYCHOLOGICAL OPERATIONS — PSYOP in the time-honored acronym — deal largely with information; and information is at the very core of the contemporary revolution in military affairs. One might reasonably conclude that the subject of psychological operations has assumed greater importance in current debates on the future of warfare, and that PSYOP as a discipline has profited from these debates in furthering its own doctrinal and operational renewal and in integrating more closely with the other elements of military power. Unfortunately, both conclusions would be wide of the mark.

Why should this be so? A standard answer might go somewhat as follows. The revolution in military affairs is above all a technological phenomenon, reflecting the radical improvements of the last several decades in the electronic gathering, manipulation, and communication of information for the purpose of enhancing traditional warfighting. PSYOP, by contrast, remains to a very large extent a low-tech enterprise. Indeed, its major tools — leaflets, balloons, loudspeakers, radio broadcasting — are almost laughably old-fashioned. Moreover, the impact of military PSYOP is either very diffuse and hard to demonstrate or else essentially tactical, while the revolution in military affairs affects the entire conflict spectrum, with decisive results for strategy and the overall conduct of war. Finally, and most fundamentally, the revolution in military affairs reduces, if not actually eliminates, the need for PSYOP. To the extent that this revolution enables the United States to apply crushing and decisive force against any plausible adversary and thereby avoid bloody and protracted conflict, there would seem little point in worrying about employing techniques of persuasion. To paraphrase the Vietnam-era adage: if you have them where you want them, their hearts and minds will follow.

This standard view is not altogether wrong, but it seriously understates the case for PSYOP, or rather for a broader function one might call (in the absence of any other accepted or less cumbersome term) *psychological-political warfare.*[1] Before examining the recent and future role of PSYOP and related activities, though, some general observations are in order concerning the emerging strategic environment and the nature of the contemporary revolution in military affairs.

THE EMERGING STRATEGIC ENVIRONMENT

In some respects, it can be argued, the revolution in military affairs belongs to the past rather than the future.[2] It was born in a strategic context of rigid alliance systems, peer military rivalry, and the prospect of high-intensity general war. From the point of view of the United States, it was the core of a more or less consciously pursued competitive strategy aimed at offsetting Soviet advantages in men and materiél with American strengths in high technology – especially (though not only) microelectronic technology. As the Gulf War convincingly demonstrated, advanced American military capabilities provide high leverage against conventional armed forces of the Soviet type. Yet the Gulf War also occurred in a strategic context quite different from a U.S.-Soviet test of arms, and it can be argued that America's capabilities in that conflict were only imperfectly harnessed to its strategic purposes and requirements.

There is, of course, an important sense in which the revolution in military affairs remains to be achieved.[3] Analysis of military-technical revolutions in the past suggests that technology is only one of their principal components. These revolutions almost always involve significant change as well in military systems, operational concepts, and organizational forms. In all of these areas, the implications of the ongoing revolution in information technologies have yet to make themselves fully felt. Some foresee a battlefield of the future that will dispense with large systems and platforms, as well as with centralized command and control hierarchies. Others argue that the information-dominated battlefield will essentially collapse the traditional distinction between tactical, operational, and strategic levels of war.[4] It is as yet far from clear when, how, or to what extent such developments will transform current American military practice. What does seem clear is that they will unfold in a strategic context that imposes imperatives of its own – and ones not always or simply compatible with the technology driven imperatives of the revolution in military affairs as generally understood.

What are the key features of this strategic context? The following would appear to be the most obvious and fundamental: absence of a peer competitor, more fluid and weaker alliance relationships, less stability and predictability in domestic as well as international politics, heightened prospects for regional conflict and for mid-intensity conventional warfare (with the possibility of unconventional excursions), the persistence of low-intensity internal warfare, and international lawlessness. Perhaps less obvious but no less important for present purposes are commercially-driven developments in the international communications environment, especially the growing availability of global television with real-time reporting capabilities. There can be little doubt that what is sometimes called the "CNN factor" has not only greatly magnified the political impact of violence, but in complex ways also affected decisionmaking processes and diplomacy in times of crisis and war.[5] Coupled with a declining external threat and the uncertainty of the stakes involved in any potential military involvement by the United States, this factor is a kind of strategic wildcard whose potency is still inadequately appreciated. While clearly a source of strategic vulnerability for this country, it is a two-edged sword that also opens up certain strategic opportunities.

The rise of global television needs to be seen against the backdrop of the decades-long American commitment to an overseas information effort specifically targeted against the Soviet bloc. The mainstay of this effort was the short-wave radio broadcasts of Radio Free Europe/Radio Liberty and the Voice of America. Though widely discounted at the time as an element of Western security policy, these broadcasts unquestionably made a major contribution to the political and ideological decay of the foundations of communism (particularly in Eastern Europe), and therewith the eventual collapse of Soviet rule. In retrospect, given the high credibility and wide listenership of these American radio stations, it seems certain that they could have played a role of prime importance in any war-threatening crisis in Europe, generating political turmoil that would greatly have

complicated any Soviet decision to go to war.[6] They were plain-
ly a major factor in the Soviet decision not to intervene militarily
to crush the Solidarity movement in Poland in 1980. A careful
analysis of media (especially CNN) coverage of the continuing
civil war in the former Yugoslavia would almost certainly show
a persistent story of television's strategic impact on the course
of the conflict.

If anything, the importance of the psychological-political
dimension of conflict is greater today than it was in the strategic environment of the Cold War. However critical the "war of
ideas" between East and West, no one doubted that the key
security challenge then was to thwart Soviet military power in
a high-intensity struggle approximating Clausewitz's model of
pure war. Today, the key security challenge is to be able to wage
limited and politically constrained warfare in a glare of pub-
licity by which unaccustomed factors – ethnic and cultural
sensitivities, human rights outrages, environmental concerns
– can unexpectedly assume political importance, and in an
international environment where weak leadership and domestic political instability is increasingly the rule rather than the
exception.[7]

In the psychological-political dimension of conflict, the
United States has potential vulnerabilities, but also significant
advantages. The key vulnerability is our susceptibility to what
has been called *political attrition*, a decline in popular support
for military involvement as a result of such factors as unexpected losses (the bombing of the Marine barracks in Beirut),
atrocities (the My Lai massacre), or prolonged military stalemate. The role of the popular press is of course important here,
though it is sometimes overstated. As the Gulf War showed,
the military-media relationship, though inevitably a tense one,
can nevertheless be managed effectively, though perhaps not

to the satisfaction of all concerned. Perhaps more important and worrisome is the still unresolved tension between the president and Congress over war powers, as the Gulf War also showed – and as we have seen recently in the debates over committing American peacekeeping forces in Bosnia.

But consider the advantages the United States enjoys here. Its military forces are disciplined, professional, highly educated, technically competent, and morally and culturally sensitive. Moreover, especially following the Gulf War, they enjoy an unparalleled reputation for overall military excellence. Thus, while their own vulnerability to psychological operations is low, their potential for conducting effective PSYOP is very high, particularly against their likeliest adversaries – Third World military establishments that lack most of these same qualities. It is also important to bear in mind the vulnerabilities of Third World political leaders. While not generally subject to the kind of political attrition American officials must worry about, these leaders, poorly supported as they are by staff work or intelligence, are apt to have highly distorted views of the world and to think in conspiratorial terms; and they are frequently suspicious – often with reason – of their own military high command. These are vulnerabilities the United States should be prepared to exploit.[8]

RETHINKING THE PSYOP CONTEXT

It is impossible to think intelligently about PSYOP without considering it in the context of a much broader category of psychological-political capabilities, a category cutting across the responsibilities of all the major agencies in the national security establishment. The first task of any effort to improve the effectiveness of military PSYOP in the narrow sense must be to rethink its relationship to four traditional disciplines or activities: public diplomacy, public affairs, covert psychological-political warfare, and what has been called military persuasion – that is, the deliberate use of military combat capabilities to create psychological-political effects.[9] In addition, PSYOP need to be situated properly with respect to the new concept of command and control warfare (C^2W), which proposes to integrate PSYOP with other capabilities in a comprehensive attack on an adversary's decisionmaking and military communications, as well as the related but much broader notion of strategic information warfare.[10]

Thinking about PSYOP in this larger context is necessary in the first place because of the impact of the revolution in military affairs, with its acceleration of the tempo of military operations, its potential for radical psychological shock, and its tendency to collapse the levels of warfare. No less important, it is necessary as a result of the increasing transparency of the modern battlefield and the near-real time reporting of military operations by the global media. Both of these developments have increased the strategic salience of psychological operations. But by so doing, they have also increased the urgency and importance of a more careful delineation of the area(s) of responsibility of military PSYOP, and of better coordination with related disciplines.

Anyone familiar with the postwar history of military PSYOP knows that the issues of definition and coordination have long been contentious, reflecting the bureaucratic weakness of PSYOP within the national security establishment as a whole.[11] Public affairs personnel within the Defense Department have always tried and generally succeeded in keeping PSYOP out of their business. Relations with the foreign affairs agencies have been episodic at best. During Operation Desert Shield, PSYOP was essentially derailed by confusion over the handling of (arguably) covert portions of the PSYOP plan developed within the Defense Department. PSYOP planning and command and control within the uniformed military have often been problematic. During the Gulf War, most of these problems were eventually overcome, and PSYOP proved highly effective when fully engaged. But significant systemic change has yet to occur.

An adequate discussion of this complex and poorly understood history is not possible here, but a few key points needs to be made. One of the critical lessons of both Operation Just Cause and Operation Desert Shield is that PSYOP planning cannot be usefully done in purely military channels and without taking due account of PSYOP requirements in pre- and post-combat environments. In order to position PSYOP to play an effective role in a pre-combat crisis situation, however, a well-understood and accepted system is needed for the planning, coordination, and management of PSYOP activities in peacetime and with due regard for the interagency environment. A second key lesson is that PSYOP must be securely coupled with policy at a relatively high level – and not only within the U.S. government. The Gulf War demonstrated beyond question the importance of the coalition dimension of PSYOP and related activities. The strategic salience of PSYOP was much more evident in Riyadh and Cairo than it was in Washington.

The fluidity of alliance relationships during the Gulf War is in fact a strong argument for an enhanced role for PSYOP-related activities in post-Cold War conflict generally. Saddam Hussein's efforts to split the allied coalition through propaganda and political warfare enjoyed considerable initial success, and the United States and its partners were slow to counter these efforts. Part of the reason for this was that this task was thought to exceed the scope of PSYOP as a military function; yet other elements of the U.S. government were not prepared to take it on. The result was the reconstitution of a public diplomacy staff within the Defense Department with the mandate of conducting (in coordination with the U.S. Information Agency) counter-propaganda and counter-disinformation operations throughout the Muslim world. This is one of the unsung success stories of the war.

STEPS TO BE TAKEN

If the United States is to engage effectively in political-psychological warfare in a post-Cold War context, fundamental changes are needed not only in the conceptualization of this instrument but in its organization and management. The first and most fundamental point is that PSYOP need to be integrated within the Defense Department with public diplomacy, public affairs, and overall national policy in a way that transcends coordination in the normal bureaucratic sense. The most effective solution to this long-standing deficiency would be to create a (let us call it) Strategic Information Staff housed at a high level within the office of the Under Secretary of Defense for Policy, and made up of civilian as well as military personnel representing all of the areas just mentioned as well as the intelligence community. This staff would be responsible for developing and validating plans and programs for military PSYOP and defense-related public diplomacy across the conflict spectrum, and coordinating activities in these areas through appropriate public affairs and other operational loops both within the Defense Department and at the national level. At the same time, a focal point for strategic information should be created within the National Security Council to help ensure policy and operational coordination across all relevant agencies. A key priority for such a national-level effort must be to develop agreed policy, doctrine, and procedures governing the relationship between overt and non-overt psychological-political warfare and the respective responsibilities in this area of the Department of Defense and the Central Intelligence Agency. There is also a need for a stronger focus on the relationship between traditional PSYOP and the use of other combat capabilities for conducting sophisticated command and control or information warfare, as well as the varieties of military persuasion. In a battlefield environment where the United States maintains electronic dominance, many possibilities open up for the direct exploitation of electronic systems for psychological purposes, and therefore for close cooperation between the disciplines of PSYOP and electronic warfare. With adequate intelligence, there is no reason why PSYOP could not be more surgically targeted at an enemy's military command structure; there are also interesting possibilities for interactive communication with enemy troops and leaders. At the same time, more systematic efforts could no doubt be made to interrupt or degrade non-military communications traffic and national broadcast media during or prior to a military conflict. Many questions remain to be answered, however, regarding the offensive use of information technologies by the United States against state or societal assets of a hostile power and the particular role of PSYOP in such an endeavor.

These are some examples of new operational concepts for PSYOP that could profitably be pursued. Other innovative possibilities exist in the more traditional areas of responsibility of military PSYOP personnel. At the battlefield level, given the increasingly compressed timeframe of operations and the opportunities afforded by the shock and disorientation of frontline enemy troops (as in the Gulf War), it can be argued that PSYOP personnel should be more fully integrated with combat units and have a larger role at an earlier stage of certain kinds of ground actions. There is also considerable work to be done in devising PSYOP approaches to the use or threatened use of weapons of mass destruction on the future battlefield.

Finally, there is clearly room for improvement and innovation in PSYOP systems, which have generally received very low priority in defense procurement. The greatest technical failure of PSYOP in the Gulf War was our inability to get an adequate radio signal into Baghdad. This reflected in particular the limitations (and vulnerability) of *Commando Solo* (formerly *Volant Solo*), an EC-130 aircraft configured for radio and television broadcasting principally for PSYOP purposes. Though repeatedly modernized, this platform will soon have to be supplemented or replaced with a new aircraft possessing significant self-defense capability, and perhaps a powerful ship-borne mobile radio. The use of unmanned aircraft for leaflet dissemination and possibly broadcasting is beginning to receive attention and should be seriously explored. Consideration should perhaps also be given to the development of a highly agile aircraft for information gathering and broadcasting in support of defense public affairs, public diplomacy, and PSYOP requirements in low threat environments and operations other than war.

It needs to be reiterated, however, that the key to future improvement in American performance in psychological warfare remains at the conceptual and organizational levels. Only when we have gained greater clarity as to what PSYOP actually is, what objectives it can reasonably be expected to achieve, and how PSYOP campaigns are to be planned, organized, and implemented, will this capability come fully into its own as an integral component of American military power and an accepted tool of our national security policy.

ENDNOTES

1. The emerging concept of strategic information warfare overlaps in some ways with this term, but is more narrowly focused on the use of information technologies as an autonomous instrument of warfare. See Roger C. Molander, Andrew S. Riddile, and Peter A. Wilson, *Strategic Information Warfare: A New Face of War*, RAND Report No. MR-661-OSD (Santa Monica, CA: The RAND Corporation, September 1995). For a vigorous statement of this case see Ralph Peters, "After the Revolution," *Parameters* 25 (Summer 1995), pp. 7-14.

2. For what follows see especially Jeffrey Cooper, *Another View of the Revolution in Military Affairs* (U.S. Army War College, Strategic Studies Institute, 15 July 1994).

3. See Douglas A. MacGregor, "Future Battle: The Merging Levels of War," *Parameters* 22 (Winter 1992/93), pp. 33-47.

4. Frank J. Stech, "Winning CNN Wars," *Parameters* 24 (Autumn 1994), pp. 37-56 is an excellent and well-documented account.

5. See especially Henry S. Rowen, "Political Strategies for General War: The Case of Eastern Europe," in Carnes Lord and Frank R. Barnett, eds., *Political Warfare and Psychological Operations: Rethinking the U.S. Approach* (Washington, D.C.: National Defense University Press, 1989), pp. 169-97.

6. Some of these themes are developed in Carnes Lord, "The Role of the United States in Small Wars," *Annals of the American Academy of Political and Social Science* 541 (September 1995), pp. 89-100.

7. See Alvin H. Bernstein, "Political Strategies in Coercive Diplomacy and Limited War," in Lord and Barnett, pp. 145-59.

8. See Stephen J. Cimbala, "Military Persuasion and the American Way of War," *Strategic Review* 22 (Fall 1994), pp. 33-43; and *Military Persuasion* (State College, Penn.: Pennsylvania State University Press, 1994).

9. PSYOP are critical in command and control warfare, which is the integrated use of operations security, military deception, PSYOP, electronic warfare, and physical destruction, supported by intelligence, to influence, degrade, destroy, or deny information to adversary command and control capabilities and to protect friendly command and control against such actions. Jeffrey B. Jones and Michael P. Mathews, "PSYOP and the Warfighting CINC," *Joint Force Quarterly* 8 (Summer 1995), p. 31. (This article, by the recently departed commander and deputy commander, respectively, of the 4th Psychological Operations Group (Airborne), provides a good snapshot of the current state of the discipline)

10. Fundamental for what follows is *PSYOP at War: Psychological Operations in Recent Conflicts* (Institute for National Strategic Studies, National Defense University, 1993), SECRET (with unclassified summary). This study (of which the present writer was director and principal author) was based on interviews with military and civilian participants at all levels from a variety of agencies and covers Operation Just Cause as well as Operation Desert Shield/Desert Storm. See also Carnes Lord, "The Psychological Dimension in National Strategy," as well as Alfred H. Paddock, Jr., "Military Psychological Operations," in Lord and Barnett, pp. 13-37 and 45-65.
11. Worth particular emphasis here is the intelligence dimension. The timely and effective use of declassified intelligence information in support of policy is currently no one's primary responsibility; yet this is a function that can assume great importance in crises and wartime.

chapter sixteen

Public Affairs, the Media, and War in the Information Age

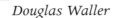

Douglas Waller

IN THE PAST DECADE, the media have undergone revolutionary changes in the way they report on the United States military and the wars it fights. Covering wars had once been a slow and cumbersome affair. Before the radio and telephone, military correspondents spent days and sometimes weeks relaying dispatches from the front, either by messenger or over the same telegraph system the military used. Civil War correspondents, for example, depended on the goodwill of military commanders to dispatch their stories. In many instances the stories (or the accurate stories) never made it from the battlefield. Journalistic standards were almost non-existent. Rather than true reporters, war correspondents were often propagandists and, in some cases, even spies.

Even with telephone and radio communications, World War II correspondents had to rely on the military to provide the logistics and clearances for stories transmitted back to home networks or newspapers. Had they possessed the means to transmit stories independently, World War II correspondents would not likely have filed different stories. Support for the war was practically universal, even in the press. Save for a few critical stories, most of the war reporting was what the U.S. military wanted Americans to hear.

For most of the Vietnam War, the news media was also captive of the military. Print correspondents generally did not have the ability to transmit their stories without the help of the U.S. military. Because their video and audio equipment was so bulky, broadcast journalists had to rely on military trucks and planes to get their gear to the front. Throughout most of the war, the vast majority of journalists relied on handouts from public affairs officers in Saigon for the bulk of their reporting on the conflict. A few journalists braved the jungles on their own to ferret out the real news that the Army was losing the war. But it was not until the latter stages of the war that the press showed more independence in its coverage – not so much because the technology for reporting had improved, but because public opinion back home, which the press followed as much as anyone, had turned against the war.

The media today have become far more independent and skeptical in their coverage of the Defense Department and its wars. This change is due partly to cultural changes and partly to technology. Vietnam, Watergate, Iran-Contra, and wasteful defense spending have all bred distrust in the media about the U.S. national security community. To this day, there are editors who see covert CIA operations behind every U.S. foreign policy initiative overseas, even though the agency's covert action budget is minuscule. Generals and admirals are still viewed by a large share of reporters as bloodthirsty war mongers – even though, in many interagency battles, the Pentagon is usually arguing *against* deploying U.S. troops.

The same technology that is revolutionizing the way the Pentagon fights wars is also changing the way the media cover them. The media can now provide viewers, listeners, and even readers almost instant access to a battlefield. With lighter video cameras, smaller portable computers, cellular phones, their own aircraft, and worldwide electronic linkups, the media can report on any battlefield no matter how remote and no matter how many restrictions the Defense Department tries to place on coverage. During the Gulf War, much of the press initially had to rely on the briefings in Riyadh and the Pentagon pool system – primarily because the Saudi government would not allow thousands of Western journalists to roam the country freely, but also because a conventional desert war was difficult for the press to cover on its own. Reporters get lost in the desert.

But if the war had lasted much longer, the rigid Pentagon pool system would quickly have broken down and the media would have begun covering the conflict on their own. CNN was already broadcasting from Baghdad (which, ironically, U.S. intelligence appreciated for the glimpses the network offered inside Iraq). By the time the ground war had begun, the media were straining at the leash and working around the public affairs officers. Some reporters rented Land Rovers and sneaked up to the border on their own. One such excursion landed CBS correspondent Bob Simon in an Iraqi jail. When colleagues in Riyadh were barred from visiting Air Force pilots based nearby, I managed to track down telephone numbers for their quarters – not only in Riyadh, but also in Bahrain – in order to interview them on the air war.

In the future, technology will give journalists even more independence. The media already have their own satellites for sending video and audio. They may soon have imagery satellites to take pictures of the war below. With Global Positioning System receivers commercially available – sold for as low as $200 in mail-order catalogues – reporters will no longer have to worry about getting lost in the desert, or anywhere else for that matter. News organizations now buy body armor and armored vehicles for their correspondents. Ideas are already afloat for media outlets to have their own command and control planes to cover wars. Reporters may even be able to develop portable, secure communications packs that could more easily bypass Pentagon censors during a conflict. Every major U.S. military command center already has CNN blaring from a television all day, simply because the media have demonstrated they can often get to conflicts and crises faster than U.S. national security organs.

The changing nature of war – more low-intensity conflicts, no neat lines of attack, no forward edges of battlefields – is also making it more difficult for the Defense Department to control the media during a conflict. The distinction between combatant and non-combatant is blurring. Battle zones have become porous; reporters are able to cover both enemy and friendly forces. The Pentagon told news outlets that the Defense Department would not put together a media pool to be flown to Bosnia with the soldiers. Bosnia already was swarming with reporters who probably knew more about the territory and the conflict than the American troops coming in.

But the Pentagon has not been standing still during this media revolution. During the past decade, the Defense Department has built a vast public-affairs bureaucracy – larger than that of any other agency in the federal government. Each of the military services has public-affairs operations that rival any national news organization in size. Practically every military command, no matter how small, has a public-affairs staff. Dealing with the media is now a major component of modern-day battle plans. Unit commanders, in many cases down to the battalion level, are trained to handle reporters. Almost every general and admiral has a public-affairs aide. Like other branches of the service, the Pentagon's public-affairs bureaucracy has schools for public-affairs officers (PAOs); in some services, public affairs has been given status as a military occupational specialty. With the advent of CNN, Pentagon public-affairs shops have become twenty-four-hour operations. For the sixty thousand NATO troops deployed in Bosnia, there are several hundred public-affairs officers. Pentagon public affairs has its own experts. Today an officer can reach the two-star flag rank solely through the public-affairs career track.

Even with this vast buildup on both sides, tensions remain between the media and the Pentagon over war in the Information Age. The media will inevitably clash with military public-affairs officers because the two have different roles to play. A PAO's job is to tell his organization's story. A reporter's job is to tell the story. The two stories may sometimes be the same, but not always. I chuckle when cheery public-affairs officers try to convince me that they really want to help me get what I'm after. We both know that's the case only if what I'm after will please their boss. As any public-affairs officer would privately admit, his or her loyalty is first to the immediate commander, second to the unit, third to the unit command, fourth to the service, fifth to the Pentagon, and sixth — if there's any loyalty left — to helping the reporter get at the truth. Any PAO who walks into a general's office and says, "Boss, I'm here to make sure the press gets everything it wants and let the chips fall where they may," is likely to find his or her career abruptly shortened.

I have made many friends among public-affairs officers. A few have even braved the wrath of their bosses to help me get the true story, rather than just the organization's story. And the military as a whole is doing a better job of releasing bad news and taking its lumps rather than trying to cover up. But

I, like other experienced defense correspondents, recognize that working with public-affairs officers is always a marriage of convenience; there will still be clashes.

This is not to say that both sides can't improve on the relationship. With no draft for almost two decades, fewer reporters have military experience. Too many reporters, photographers, camera operators, and producers who cover the military are abysmally ignorant of its operating procedures, traditions, protocol, and mores. This explains why Marines landing in Somalia were practically blinded by television camera lights. One idea worth considering is to send inexperienced reporters for a week of indoctrination training on how to live with the military in the field.

There have been other disturbing trends in the media. All three networks air trashy magazine shows that constantly push the edge of the envelope in terms of sound journalistic ethics. Sensationalized coverage once found only in supermarket tabloids has crept into established news outlets. All the news organizations sunk to a new low in their coverage of the O.J. Simpson trial. Attitude journalism – writing outside the editorial pages with a barely concealed point of view – has become trendy. Television networks have discovered that info-entertainment – news coverage that's short, entertaining, and visually attractive – is far more profitable than programs heavy on substance and public policy. In my own medium, magazine journalists and editors are too often guilty of deciding how a story should be told, or packaged, before conducting the research.

On the military side, handling the press has become too big a business in the Pentagon. The Defense Department's vast public-affairs bureaucracy can often be stifling for reporters. Public-affairs officers can open doors for reporters – many service members won't talk to the press unless a PAO is present –

but they can also get in the way of reporting. I'll never forget interviewing several wives of sailors aboard a ship for a feature story on life in the Navy. I was crammed into a small room with the three wives, three public affairs officers, a technician operating a large tape recorder, and the command's chaplain. The terrified women, of course, said little.

The irony is that the military will trust a general officer with billions of dollars of equipment and the lives of thousands of soldiers, but not to speak to a reporter alone. The excuse usually is that the public-affairs captain acts as a witness to protect the general in case of misquotation by the reporter. Somehow, if the captain says there has been a misquote, it is deemed more credible than if the general makes the same claim.

The Defense Department continues to classify too much information. There are legitimate national security secrets that the Pentagon needs to keep from enemies. But mixed in too often are political secrets the Pentagon wants to keep from the American people. The intelligence community believes that classifying everything will better protect the inner core of true national security secrets. I received one Pentagon document stamped SECRET that was nothing more than press guidance drafted by public-affairs officers containing sample questions they expected from reporters.

The "classify everything" approach breeds dangerous cynicism in the media, which often stumbles upon the inner core secrets. Most reputable reporters and editors will not print secrets that will compromise ongoing operations or result in casualties to soldiers. Overclassification, however, can make it more difficult to be responsible. When a journalist is asked by the Pentagon not to print a story, questions immediately arise: Are lives, or politics, at stake? Is the Pentagon trying to protect itself, or the troops? With so much abuse in classification, the journalist becomes reluctant to give the Pentagon the benefit of the doubt.

Senior officers can become too obsessed with spin control in a military conflict. During the Gulf War, military planners were preoccupied with how their operations would play out in the media. The Pentagon did not want to repeat what it perceived to be the mistakes of Vietnam, where (it believed) its reputation had been tarnished because of unbalanced media coverage. (It has taken more than two decades for many senior officers to realize that the military's reputation was tarnished because of poor strategy and tactics employed in Vietnam, not because of media coverage.) In the Gulf War, senior Pentagon officers ultimately allowed a large part of Saddam Hussein's army to escape unscathed because of their overriding concern that public sentiment would turn against a war that was not concluded quickly and with the fewest possible casualties – or that was pursued by means of allied warplanes chasing fleeing Iraqis across the desert. In Somalia, aerial gunships were not sent to protect U.S. soldiers because senior officials feared the press and public would view their use as a buildup of American forces. During the final disastrous Mogadishu raid, U.S. Army Rangers were stranded with inadequate air cover.

As the Pentagon expands its capability to wage information warfare, there will be even more conflicts with the media. Information warfare has as many definitions as it does advocates. Tactical information warfare has been practiced for a long time. It includes electronic warfare, deception operations, battlefield psychological operations (PSYOP), and attacks on enemy command and control centers. At the tactical level, there is little disagreement among defense experts, and even among the media, that information warfare should be a major part of U.S. military operations. The media did not complain when the Iraqis were deceived into thinking that the Marines planned an amphibious attack on the shores of Kuwait – even when the media inadvertently played a part in the deception.

But there is considerable debate among defense experts, and certainly among journalists, over information warfare at the strategic level. Strategic information warfare includes such measures as computer hacking to disable a country's financial, transportation, and utility service; PSYOP to influence a nation's leaders or its population; and broad-based information control or distortion to change the politics of a foreign country. Setting aside computer warfare for the moment, strategic information warfare intended to influence people and politics abroad is difficult for a democratic society, with a free press, to wage. In tomorrow's global village, it may be impossible to wage.

Many Pentagon officials I have interviewed are deeply concerned about not only the feasibility but also the ethics of strategic information warfare. During the Gulf War, a proposal to launch a broad-based strategic PSYOP campaign against Iraq never made it out of the thicket of interagency review. Senior Pentagon and White House officials feared that any such effort would quickly leak and the administration would be accused of trying to manipulate the media. The skepticism was, and still is, understandable. With so many media outlets in the world, it would seem almost impossible for the United States to control the information flow into any country. Just as some bits will likely always get past electronic jamming, information contrary to the PSYOP plan will make it through as well. Strategic PSYOP planners would face too much competition from multiple media outlets that now have the technology to circumvent Pentagon control.

In a strategic campaign, the line between information warfare waged against a foreign country and information warfare waged against Americans back home also could easily be blurred. In tomorrow's wars, the American media may be able to cover the enemy as well as they cover U.S. forces. Deceiving a foreign country may involve deceiving the American media as well. The Pentagon may have developed an impressive capability to tell its story to the media; but it has learned from painful experience that telling a false story has severe consequences.

There may be some instances in which a strategic information warfare campaign can be successful. The United States launched what came close to a strategic PSYOP campaign in Haiti before the U.S. intervention, with the Air Force's *Commando Solo* plane broadcasting speeches from President Aristide. But Haiti was a tiny, backward, and isolated country that could easily be overwhelmed by a PSYOP campaign from a superpower. Such a campaign would likely be far more difficult to wage in most other countries. Strategic information warfare sounds intriguing on paper. It makes for good reading in a conspiracy novel. But in real life, strategic information warfare poses many dangers for the Pentagon and for the democratic values it is supposed to protect.

Conclusion

A Framework for Discussing War in the Information Age

Gregory J. Rattray
Laurence E. Rothenberg

PRECEDING CHAPTERS PROVIDE A VARIETY OF PERSPECTIVES on war in the Information Age, ranging from strategic national security concerns to leadership and training for an expanded battlespace. Each author focuses on a piece of the complex puzzle that confronts U.S. national security policymakers in a rapidly changing environment. This concluding chapter synthesizes the analyses in a framework that examines war in the Information Age on three levels: as a revolution in security affairs, a revolution in military affairs, and a military-technical revolution.[1] The chapter identifies and expands on themes discussed in previous chapters, and offers ideas for future consideration of U.S. national security policy in the Information Age.[2]

THE REVOLUTION IN SECURITY AFFAIRS
The new global strategic environment emerging with the end of the Cold War, together with the development of sophisticated information technologies, has led to a revolution in

security affairs (RSA) that will transform the nature of conflict and how the United States thinks about its security. In the changing international security environment, there are new actors with advanced capabilities, and there are new vulnerabilities created by our own society's dependence on information systems for both commerce and military operations. These changes require a rethinking of national security strategy.

The basic outlines of the new global security environment are drawn by Robert Pfaltzgraff and Richard Shultz. They depict a "bifurcated" system consisting of the traditional state-centered paradigm and a sub-state stratum involving actors such as terrorists, ethnic separatists, and international criminal organizations; upon this framework is superimposed the impact of information technology. Tim Thomas's research illustrates that, for the most part, Russian analysis of the post-Cold War security environment parallels the views of American commentators, although the Russians demonstrate greater unease regarding their own vulnerability. Richard O'Neill comments in his chapter that information technologies are creating a "continuum from peace to war" as the barriers between crime, terrorism, and war crumble. Within this context, he argues, the United States must redefine its concept of national security from one based on territorial impregnability to one focused on the idea of "connectedness." In other words, we must recognize that our society relies on the continuous functioning of our government, financial, and economic institutions, as well as our public utility, safety, and disaster-response infrastructures. National security depends on maintaining the viability of this connected loop of institutions, and protecting the information systems that link them.

Despite common acknowledgment of fundamental changes in the strategic environment, little agreement exists about how information technologies will further affect it. Many commentators speak of the rise of information warfare (IW), but there is no agreement on precisely what constitutes IW. Winn Schwartau, for example, argues that IW is a non-lethal way to attack an enemy's civilian infrastructure as a means of waging war. He notes that using computers as weapons does not require a military presence, state sponsorship, or large amounts of financial or human resources. He believes that information warfare may provide an alternative to traditional means of conflict. In contrast, Michael Vickers points to the Department of Defense definition of information warfare, in which future conflict will become significantly more lethal than current warfare because of the contribution of precision guidance and strike technologies to find and destroy targets. In yet another view of IW, Carnes Lord sees information technologies as tools to accomplish strategic psychological warfare. Christopher Jon Lamb describes how such technologies will enhance U.S. capabilities for force projection and information management in operations other than war (OOTW), increasingly common endeavors in the post-Cold War world.

A cogent way of resolving the disparity in these views is to identify "independent" versus "integrated" information warfare. Independent IW can be an alternative to war, as, for example, when civilian targets and information systems are attacked by terrorists; or it can be used in preemptive strikes on systems supporting military operations. At the same time, integrated IW can be viewed as part of the transformation of battlefield military operations, in which information technologies are used to support traditional military objectives by providing enhanced situational awareness for conducting operations, with all the attendant changes in organization and doctrine that this will require. These two kinds of IW can be conducted simultaneously or separately, depending on who is engaged in a conflict.

Just as there are many different ways to conduct information warfare, the revolution in security affairs has resulted in a proliferation of actors capable of waging it. Again, there are several ways to understand the unfolding situation. Numerous analysts cite Alvin and Heidi Toffler's taxonomy of "agrarian, industrial, and post-industrial"[3] societies as one guide to the spectrum of potential adversaries. In this conception, information technologies can become a "great equalizer" for both state and non-state actors fighting against advanced societies. Less-advanced societies, and individuals and groups within them, may be able to leapfrog over existing technologies to obtain state-of-the-art information systems. Industrial and post-industrial societies reliant on information systems may then be vulnerable to attacks from individuals, groups, or states with pre-industrial, agrarian societies. Moreover, industrial and post-industrial societies may find that their information-age capabilities are less useful in conflicts with agrarian societies, which lack significant information-dependent targets, such as communications, transportation, and economic infrastructures.

Michael Vickers, on the other hand, points out that this taxonomy might be too limited. He believes that a five-tiered spectrum of potential adversaries will emerge, possessing a range of capabilities for waging either independent or integrated IW. Large peer competitors such as Russia or China, for example, may be able to modernize their forces enough to take advantage of some of the information-enhanced weapon systems the United States now possesses. Smaller, regional states might not be able to build and sustain a totally Information Age force, but could buy certain systems and capabilities on the open market, while sub-state actors will likely use independent IW to attack states with which they are in conflict. Meanwhile, both high-tech and low-tech states without IW capabilities will still pose conventional threats to the United States.

Regardless of which taxonomy one may prefer, the growing diversity of actors and capabilities in the new security environment raises major challenges for U.S. defense planning. First, it is critical to examine how the Information Age may affect U.S. strategy. Contributors to this volume generally agree that formulating strategy in the age of information warfare requires national coordination across disciplines, agencies, departments, and sectors of society. O'Neill, for example, describes the need for "cumulative" strategies on a national level that can integrate economic warfare, political warfare, psychological warfare, and covert operations. Both Schwartau and Lord stress the need for a strategic information policy, reflecting a similar desire for a coordinated, interagency, national security strategy.

Deterrence, one of the cores of American strategic thinking, is already moving away from reliance on purely military instruments toward a combination of capabilities – military, political, and economic – and this shift is likely to become more pronounced given the growing appreciation for information technologies. For example, information campaigns designed to reduce tension or to communicate U.S. advantages in an impending conflict may be critical tools for conflict avoidance. Information technologies can provide the capability for greatly enhanced surveillance of potential adversaries and incipient crisis situations. In the early phases of a crisis, advanced communications capabilities could play a key role in psychological operations aimed at discouraging aggressive action by the enemy. The capability to shut down or otherwise impair the functioning of civilian information infrastructures, to degrade enemy civilian and military communications, and to attack enemy battlefield information systems could enhance U.S. escalation dominance strategies. The speed, flexibility, and adaptability of IW technologies to a variety of missions make them ideal for the type of synergistic military, political, and economic deterrence posture the United States is adopting.

Information warfare might also be used as a deterrent against the United States. Adversaries who cannot compete with U.S. conventional or nuclear capabilities might instead focus their human, financial, and technical resources on developing IW in order to deter the United States from intervening in regional crisis situations where U.S. allies or friends would normally expect support. States anticipating a possible confrontation with the United States could develop less-costly forces that emphasize dispersal and defense to slow the pace of decision in a theater conflict. Such an opponent might even concentrate efforts on developing strategic information-strike capabilities against U.S. military and civilian information infrastructures. Had Saddam Hussein been able to use IW during the Gulf War, he could have attacked civilian information systems in the United States to erode public support for the war, or targeted the civilian systems critical to the deployment of troops. In this sense, IW could become the pauper's strategic deterrent, similar to chemical and biological weapons but without the higher retaliatory risk that chemical and biological weapons use might engender, especially given unresolved questions of how the United States would respond to an information attack.

In turn, deterring an IW attack may prove difficult. Just as U.S. deterrence strategists might plan an IW campaign as a prelude to conventional warfare, state or non-state actors could conduct their own IW against the United States before any planned traditional military assault or terrorist act. The situation would be further complicated if the attacker could not be identified, since the mechanisms of IW are often difficult to trace. Deterring IW in a security environment characterized by the wide availability of information technology is even more complex than countering the threat of weapons of mass destructions in a multipolar, multinuclear, dual-use technology world.

The Information Age may also alter U.S. strategies for forward presence. The Air Force, for example, has promoted the idea of "virtual presence" as a replacement for traditional forward-deployed forces.[4] Virtual presence advocates argue that, as the defense budget decreases and support for deployments abroad declines, forward presence will have to rely on remote-sensing capabilities to provide intelligence, and on private and publicly financed media to provide "information presence."[5] They contend that information technologies can provide early-warning capabilities equal to human sources, and that the military advantages produced can enable long-range strike assets and flexibly deployed forces to deter and fight as effectively as forces deployed close to potential areas of conflict. In addition, information technologies as part of psychological operations can be used to smooth the entry of U.S. forces into host countries or regions slated for peacekeeping missions. Virtual presence detractors, in contrast, argue that information-based substitutes for "classical presence" do not fulfill the crucial role of demonstrating the U.S. commitment to the defense of its allies, nor are they comparable to direct human contact, either for promotion of friendly and allied relationships or for intelligence gathering. Most importantly, virtual presence would be at least as vulnerable to exploitation for political purposes as forward-deployed troops, and would, in fact, be more vulnerable to information-based attack than physical presence. If, for example, U.S. presence in a region substantially depended on information assets, then any successful IW attack on those assets could delay, degrade, or even totally shut down U.S. operations there.

Another compelling challenge for the United States is to determine how IW may affect the organization of the U.S. national security apparatus. If independent IW can be conducted against civilian targets as part of a military campaign, then who is responsible for defending against potential attacks, locating an attacker, or punishing those responsible for an attack? Is it the Federal Bureau of Investigation, or the U.S. armed forces? Perhaps a new agency should be chartered to combine the analytical and technical skills – as well as the legal authority – of different branches of the national security community concerned with IW. Some analysts have urged the creation of a specialized information security agency as a new arm of the intelligence community. Alternatively, others argue that integrated defense may be possible only through proper interagency coordination. These questions are critical for the defense of the United States from both independent and integrated information warfare, during peace, crisis, and war.

Problems of organizing for IW involve not only the government, but relations between the government and civilian society. In peacetime, the national information system functions primarily under civilian control but must account for vulnerabilities to possible terrorist attacks or criminal use. The U.S. government is becoming increasingly concerned about the viability of the national information infrastructure as the likelihood of attack by an information-warfare capable opponent grows. In future conflicts, the integrity of the information infrastructure will become a national priority. Communication links with forces in the field and the smooth functioning of information-dependent infrastructures, such as transportation and energy, will prove vital to sustaining a war effort and generating public support. The civilian and government sectors will need to determine who is responsible for protecting and operating the system as the United States confronts different conflicts and crises. Will the federal government be empowered to assume greater control as an international conflict becomes more intense? How would such a plan be implemented organizationally and technologically?

This increased need for coordination between the government and the civilian sector in areas relevant to information and national security may prove difficult. One source of potential disagreement might be on the tradeoff between access and security. While awareness of the need for security is growing in all sectors of society, there is tension between civilian desires to maximize the efficiency and lower the costs of information infrastructures – such as the public-switched network – and government desires to build safeguards that may limit accessibility and raise costs. Who will be responsible for assuring hardware and software integrity for newly produced and installed systems? Might the government be empowered to monitor or inspect the production and installation processes of components of the national information infrastructure deemed vital to national security? Can the government afford such activities – and are they legal? Asserting the government's right to monitor communications for national security purposes will prove even more contentious. The current debate over the Clipper Chip and Pretty Good Privacy (PGP) encryption software highlight the tradeoffs between U.S. citizens' right to encrypt for privacy purposes versus the government's need to provide law enforcement and security in the Information Age that may require monitoring computer-based communications.[6] The policymaking mechanisms and implementation responsibilities for such difficult decisions, including the role of the Department of Defense, have yet to be addressed.

Whatever the result of the changes in current American strategy and defense organization brought about by the revolution in security affairs, there is little doubt that the Information Age will bring additional challenges to the use of information itself. Charles Swett addresses some of these concerns in his essay, most importantly, the use of this new medium for spreading propaganda by extremist groups and disinformation about U.S. activities. Developing a U.S. information policy for national security will prove all the more difficult because the problems involve systems, institutions, and persons not subject to the authority of the U.S. government. Increased digitization of communications and use of satellites and other networked telecommunications systems magnify the difficulty of separating national and global information infrastructures. A single message can take multiple paths as the information is transmitted over networks that reach into space and cross national borders. Many of the assets of the global information infrastructure, such as the communications satellites controlled by INTELSAT and GLOBESTAR, operate under international or commercial authority. The volume of information transmitted over these networks is already so great that monitoring the activity to sort out illegal and threatening activities seems an impossible task.

The global information infrastructure will expand access to intelligence resources, once monopolized by the United States and the former Soviet Union during the Cold War, particularly through commercial satellite imaging systems.[7] The commercial systems planned by the United States, Russia, France, and other countries offer increased resolution and global coverage. Other satellite systems under national or international control provide accurate navigational data and global communications links. The Clinton administration announced in March of 1996 that the Department of Defense would be required, within the next ten years, to end its practice of giving only degraded Global Positioning System data to commercial users. The advantages currently enjoyed by the United States in creating battlespace transparency may thus be decreased by the presence of a fully functioning global information infrastructure without which the U.S. military itself cannot operate effectively. Douglas Waller notes that the international media further complicate U.S. military operations, since many journalists already use information technologies to reduce their reliance on the military for reporting their stories. As many commentators have pointed out, this immediate access and independence fosters transparency in international affairs, benefiting all actors, including America's adversaries.

An alternative approach to national monitoring and control of information flows may exist in the form of international cooperative arrangements similar to efforts designed to control physical armaments during the Cold War and earlier periods. Decisions to engage in such discussions, however, will require the United States to determine whether too much valuable information about our current capabilities and doctrine would be compromised by participating. How would one orchestrate discussions of the international control of information technologies and their employment for national, rather than commercial, advantage in peace, crisis, and war? To whom should the United States talk first? How will cooperation with our allies proceed in planning for information warfare? If we hesitate to engage in such discussions, what are the possibilities for an "arms race" occurring in the field of information warfare?

The need to monitor information flows highlights the impact of the Information Age on the intelligence community. In order to develop new strategies, military options, and policy choices for the emerging security environment, we must fully understand the processes by which other states and groups could use information systems, both hardware and software, against U.S. interests. The U.S. National Security Strategy states, "[T]he threat of intrusions to our military and commercial information systems poses a significant risk to our national security and is being addressed."[8] Some analysts, commenting on the diffusion of IW capabilities, commonly assume that recipients will have the necessary expertise to use these technologies effectively or, alternatively, that such technical expertise would be available for hire. However, important questions must be answered regarding the ability of societies to assimilate and use information technologies quickly. Actors who can exploit one type of information technology may be less capable in another. Some types of information technology, such as computer hacking, might be much more rapidly obtained and integrated into a state's or group's plans to influence the United States than would other information technologies necessary for the creation of a long-range, precision-strike capability based on sophisticated networks of sensors, command and control, and weapon systems.

Cultural influences impact the ability to assimilate information technologies as well. Many of the states that the United States may face as adversaries will have (or already have) difficulty coping with the social implications of modern information systems. Iran, for example, has tried to ban private possession of satellite dishes, and China is attempting to restrict Internet access for its citizens. How would such societies utilize sophisticated information technologies and capabilities? Intelligence resources will need to be devoted to analyzing the human and technical IW capabilities of potential adversaries, and the asymmetric strategies they might employ, particularly since other states and non-state actors – including terrorists, transnational organized crime groups, or religious movements – would likely adopt information strategies quite dissimilar to those of a technologically advanced state.

Understanding how others will use information systems to compete with the United States must also be combined with greater knowledge of the environment in which future conflicts may occur. The electronic, binary world of computers and telecommunications is a strange place for most of those involved with national security and military operations.[9] Fundamental questions about how to depict information attacks and measure system vulnerability are only beginning to receive attention. Military commanders will have to comprehend how sensors may win or lose battles for information dominance through a hide-and-seek competition of increasingly sophisticated computer algorithms.[10] Understanding the mindset of whiz kids, programmers, and hackers – who will design, operate, and disrupt the information systems that are increasingly essential to our national military capabilities and economic well-being – may prove as challenging as understanding how other state and non-state actors approach conflict in the Information Age. Thinking about the revolution in information may differ significantly from thinking about the Industrial Revolution, in terms of both the impact of technology and its human dimensions.

THE REVOLUTION IN MILITARY AFFAIRS

Along with the revolution in security affairs, it appears certain that an information-based revolution in military affairs (RMA) is also occurring. In his essay, Vickers defines RMAs as "major discontinuities in military affairs" caused by changes in "militarily-relevant technologies, concepts of organization, and/or resources," which transform the conduct of war and increase military effectiveness by an "order-of-magnitude or more." RMAs in history have included the development of artillery, the use of the telegraph and railroad, and the development of nuclear weapons. The RMA in information technology appears to affect four areas: the expansion of the battlespace, the creation of a transparent battlespace, an enhanced ability to operate inside the enemy's decision cycle, and a shift in the nature of command.

The expansion of battlespace is, as Vickers explains, a common feature of RMAs. The submarine and the aircraft, for example, added two new dimensions to warfare. Vickers asserts that in the emerging RMA, long-range precision strike and the information aspects of war will fundamentally transform war on land, sea, and in the air, while adding two new warfare areas: space warfare and information warfare, both independent and integrated. The common theme will be the overlapping of battlespace and multidimensionality, creating integrated air, land, sea, space, and information operations. In this situation, Vickers writes, the boundaries between levels of war will be blurred, and military planners will need to think less about strategic versus tactical assets; rather, their focus will be directed to the purposes to which different assets are applied.

Significantly, Vickers argues that nuclear weapons will continue to have a "truncating effect" – theater wars may remain limited as long as there are strategic sanctuaries and robust nuclear deterrents. In his conception, the availability of strategic sanctuaries will mean that the ability to sustain theater conflicts will become a critical national asset. This is a controversial argument, however. One of the key assertions about the power of information warfare is its utility for intruding on the strategic sanctuary of even nuclear powers such as the United States. As nuclear weapons become a less-credible deterrent, and the strategic sanctuary they once assured is seen as vulnerable to information-warfare techniques, the threat of an IW attack upon U.S. civilian infrastructures might deter the United States from intervening in certain situations. This problem highlights, again, the importance of integrating both offensive and defensive IW into the U.S. deterrent posture.

Another controversial argument posits that the emerging RMA will create a transparent battlefield in which commanders, and even troops in field units, will be able to see the whole battlespace in real time. Creating battlespace transparency through sensor technologies is variously referred to as "situational awareness," "battlespace awareness," or achieving "dominant battlespace knowledge (DBK);"[11] James McCarthy's essay presents an operational concept for achieving DBK, the WarNet. There are, however, some disputes about how DBK may work in practice. Some analysts have pointed out that DBK may not be possible to the extent that is generally assumed. Conflict with a low technology enemy may lead to "visual-blind" battles in which U.S. forces have battlespace transparency but the battlespace is opaque to the enemy. On the other hand, critics argue that conflict is also possible with an enemy who has equivalent information capabilities, resulting in "visual-visual" battles in which both sides achieve battlespace transparency. In addition, as Vickers notes, the battlefield of the future may not be fully transparent because of advances in stealth technology. Such technology can be applied not only to aircraft but also to surface naval vessels, unmanned aerial vehicles, and even ground assets, such as armor. Chris Lamb also points to this problem, saying that the low-technology adversaries likely to be encountered in OOTW may be able to develop indirect methods of aggression that circumvent U.S. capabilities. Other analysts have noted that the global media may help increase transparency for U.S. opponents. In fact, instead of total DBK, periods of relative transparency may occur that can be exploited for operational advantage. As such, U.S. forces must be able to operate in an environment where opponents are blinded only temporarily or in a certain locale.

Similar problems may occur in the attempt to achieve decision-cycle dominance. Many commentators assume that battlespace transparency will lead to U.S. ability to "operate inside the enemy's decision cycle" because U.S. forces will have a shorter "observe" phase. The capability to see what the enemy

is doing in real time, it is argued, will allow U.S. forces to predict an enemy's next move and develop any number of plans
in anticipation. John McDonald notes, however, that technology does not guarantee decision-cycle dominance. There are
many ways to defeat technology, as he points out: low-technology enemies might not provide signatures for our systems to
track, thus slowing the U.S. observe phase; enemy forces may
use built-up areas and close terrain as force multipliers, degrading the utility of U.S. sensors; and, finally, an enemy may
operate defensively, leading to difficulties in identifying the
patterns of activity that make anticipatory planning possible.
In visual-visual battles, of course, the enemy will be also able
to observe the movements of U.S. forces, which must therefore
act defensively to prevent the enemy from operating within
our decision cycle. This will include the need for attacks on
their command and control networks.

Other complications may arise from the use of enhanced
information systems as a means of achieving decision-cycle
dominance. Political issues, for example, may become critical.
McDonald points out that the ability to detect, target, and hit
an enemy position rapidly – that is, linking the "observe" phase
to the "act" phase in an automatic response – may not allow
for adequate consideration of the political implications of certain offensive measures. At the same time, too much information
about battlefield operations may lead to micromanagement by
both political and military leaders, slowing the decision cycle.
Finally, nearly all of the commentators in this volume have noted
that too much information can result in a friendly electronic
fog of war, where there is so much information that commanders
cannot decide among the many options for action with which
they are presented. These caveats are crucial to keep in mind
when discussing the presumed benefits of technology for bat-

tlefield operations. They reinforce the point that the effects of technology are not clear, and should not be taken for granted.

Perhaps the least controversial area of military procedure that is expected to be changed by the RMA is the nature of command. Most observers agree that military hierarchies will become "flatter" as information is transmitted to lower echelons. This will lead, analysts predict, to the creation of guidelines allowing subordinates to adapt to conditions, yet still communicate a commander's goals. McCarthy believes, for example, that all echelons will be able to see a commander's intent visually, generating higher levels of understanding, increased operations tempo, and greater opportunities for success. Frederic Brown explains that, in the past, information available at the division and battalion level determined the actions of subordinate. In the future, however, unit commanders will possess far more information. Commanders will rely less on set movement procedures to maintain control; instead, they will seek to develop guidelines that free subordinates to react to conditions and alter their movements, while fulfilling their commanders' goals. McCarthy envisions that warriors will be able to exploit situations without direct tasking from the commander because they will understand their leaders' intentions. Such an approach might require a redefinition of the idea of "unity of command." This diffusion of information, however, will require many new tasks, both for commanders and soldiers. As McCarthy points out, commanders will be required to assess their warfighters' information needs, and then format, prioritize, edit, and transmit such information. At the same time, flatter organizations require better judgment at lower levels. Thus, training and education must be improved in order to staff these new organizations.

Given these changes, "anticipatory planning" will be the future basis of successful operations, according to Huba Wass de Czege. Commanders will need to understand how and what the enemy can do, what can be done to preempt the enemy, and how sufficient flexibility can be maintained to enable the commander to change plans as circumstances demand. Such planning will be aided by the proposed WarNet system and the flatter organizational structure. These, in turn, will lead to better exploitation of initiative, further increasing battlefield success.

THE MILITARY-TECHNICAL REVOLUTION

The current revolution in security affairs and the revolution in military affairs are joined by a third level of transformation, the military-technical revolution (MTR). The MTR focuses on enhancing warfighting tools and tactics using the new technological advances. As with the RMA, new systems will allow for more effective achievement of traditional objectives, but will also require revised methods of operation and training for officers and soldiers.

At the heart of the MTR is the impact of enhanced warfighting tools, what Wass de Czege calls the "enabling technologies" that increase combat power: large numbers of precision-guided munitions (PGMs) that can be used simultaneously; sensors to target the digital communications of PGMs; and information-processing systems that facilitate anticipatory planning. Bob Wood details the new systems available to his unit, the 3rd Infantry Division (Mechanized) Artillery at Fort Stewart, that provide the division with technologies characteristic of the Information Age. Specifically, the M109A6 *Paladin* howitzer — equipped with communication, fire control, and other capabilities — can operate independently yet achieve massed fires with others in its unit. No longer is it necessary to mass weapons on a "line of metal," since the same effects can be achieved from howitzers dispersed for survivability or other needs. Information systems permit decentralized operation, horizontal integration of fire support with other battlefield operating systems, and self-location.

The core concept of the MTR is addressed by William Hartzog and Susan Canedy in their discussion of "precision." Precision, they assert, permits the use of weapons that hit and kill only legitimate military targets, reducing collateral damage. It facilitates rapid, effective, and economical maneuver on the battlefield. Precision also simplifies logistics, enhancing its usefulness to warfighters. The Army's modernization effort, as described by John Rose, goes a long way toward establishing the primacy of precision. Most importantly, the modernization program relies on a horizontal technology integration (HTI) program to ensure that dissimilar information and weapon systems have common information technology, thus providing for standardization, simplified maintenance, and increased efficiency.

Taking this idea a step further highlights the potential for an alternative model of force modernization for the next century. Wood states that the howitzer will be the division artillery system for the foreseeable future, since it is unlikely that the Army will be able to afford to buy a new mobile howitzer system for more than a decade. However, if U.S. defense planners begin to think in terms not of changing the physical capabilities of platforms, but rather of providing better information flows to weapons systems platforms so as to maximize effectiveness, a new view of systems such as the *Paladin* could develop. While the gun tube and tracked vehicle of the system may not change for an extended length of time, the munitions, communications, computing, and display systems that determine how they are used may be altered dramatically. The ways in which today's weapons are operated, and their use in combat, will probably change so much in twenty years that they will effectively become different systems. The evolution of the Air Force employment of the B-52, now in use for nearly forty years, is illustrative of this model. The challenge for acquisition planners may be to think flexibly about the procurement of expensive weapon systems platforms. In many cases, information hardware and software drivers can instead be quickly adapted in ways that completely transform the original concept for the platform.[12]

Like the RSA and RMA, the MTR will most likely change the battlespace, and several authors in this volume describe their vision of the effects on the battlespace that can be traced to this sweeping revolution. Vickers, for example, discusses how future military forces will be increasingly able to attack concentrations of land or naval forces at long ranges. In such a lethal environment, close-combat maneuver operations will take on new forms. Units will need to be smaller and more information-intensive. Most importantly, we will think of the battlefield less in spatial terms, and more in temporal ones. Operational advantage, then, may come from exploiting relative periods of advantage. Thus, "the paradigm of protection" will shift from the physical to the informational realm as information becomes a key asset for troops engaging the enemy. Wass de Czege illustrates that information technologies now allow commanders to track and control multiple systems within the battlespace, but the mobility and flexibility of their assets means that there are more "moving parts." At the same time, deep and simultaneous attack of the enemy may become easier, with responsibility for execution devolving to the battalion level and synchronized at the division level. Maneuver on the battlefield will likely change. Elements such as tanks and helicopters will be critical for exploiting earlier attacks by PGMs, to take advantage of confusion and produce cascading effects. The impact of maneuver tactics, therefore, will increasingly occur in the temporal or psychological realm rather than in the spatial realm, a point related to the idea discussed above of operational advantage in periods of relative transparency.

As with the RSA and RMA, caveats should be noted when considering the effects of the MTR on military operations. Perhaps the most important of these is the danger of "information overload." As discussed earlier in this chapter, commanders must now manage information flows and soldiers must face the "human challenge" of visualizing the complex nature of war in the Information Age. Brown, for example, emphasizes that officers and troops will be under stress, and must be trained in how to use information – and not be used by it. He argues that this challenge will be greatest below brigade level because the leaders of these echelons are less experienced, less informed, and have smaller staffs. These levels are involved in actual fighting, and are therefore focused on personal survival and mission accomplishment. Their access to information is also likely to be disrupted by any number of combat factors. He urges that the introduction of information systems should be proceed at a cautious pace. Most military personnel, Brown argues, are able to perform required physical tasks and operate weapons systems, but they are not highly proficient in handling information systems and processing. Again, the conclusion is inescapable that military operations and training for the Information Age will need to be adjusted.

Training is integral to helping troops deal with the changes brought about by the growing importance of information and information systems in the battlespace. The implications of the MTR for training will affect both officers and enlisted personnel. In discussing advances in artillery systems, for example, Wood notes that the most comfortable soldier in Information

Age warfare is the new enlistee, who does not need to adjust or be reeducated to new tactics, techniques, and procedures. To a certain extent, then, he disagrees with Brown. Wood suggests that the average soldiers in the U.S. armed forces can handle the new information and information-based systems being placed in their hands. In fact, he claims the computer generation's young enlistees have the technical skills required to operate the systems, but they need to develop and hone – over time and through rigorous training – the analytical skills and judgment necessary for the effective employment of these skills. On the other hand, those with longer military experience will face a different challenge. They have developed the analytical skills and judgment needed for combat situations, but must learn to integrate those abilities into the new doctrines and procedures created by state-of-the-art systems.

Leader development must also be a focus of training. As noted earlier, commanders will be responsible for new, information-related tasks. They must learn to filter information to their warfighters, providing only the data necessary to achieve their objectives. Officers should be trained to ask not, "Who does what?" but rather, "Who can provide me with the information I need to accomplish my unit's task?" At the same time, however, the skills of battle command must not be lost, since tension and terror in combat will always be present and will require leadership to achieve a unit's objectives. Brown cautions against creating officers trained to use computers who cannot lead soldiers through minefields. Officers need to be able to make decisions in the worst of times, not just the best, and they must be able to deal with "digital default" – when their information systems fail. Training that includes worst-case scenarios will force officers to maintain their manual tactical abilities. Battle command skills, in combination with information management skills, will provide the synergy to take advantage of the advances in firepower and protection to increase combat power.

CONCLUSIONS

This summary chapter creates a framework for debate of the difficult issues raised by the emergence of the Information Age and its impact on national security. Analysis of warfare in the Information Age through the lens of the revolution of security affairs, the revolution in military affairs, and the military-technical revolution focuses discussion of a subject that is too often addressed in general terms and without analytic rigor. Thinking about the Information Age and its impact on national security should begin with a taxonomy linking related facts and concepts.

First, through the revolution in security affairs, the United States can leverage its advantages in telecommunications, precision targeting, and satellite technologies to create the world's most information-enhanced military force. However, as national power in the next century becomes dependent on information, the United States also faces new vulnerabilities for both civilian society and the armed forces. Second, the emerging information-based revolution in military affairs will affect military operations at all levels and demand new operational concepts, although it is probably too early in the RMA to determine what these might be. Systems such as WarNet and attendant reforms in command structure to "flatten" hierarchies are part of this RMA. Finally, advanced weapons systems, and the changes in tactics, techniques, and procedures they require, fuel the military-technical revolution. The MTR may allow for more precision and lethality of weapons, but dependence on technology can also increase the danger of succumbing to periods of "digital default." In short, applying this three-tiered framework to the broad subject of war in the Information Age will structure the debate, eliminate superficial analysis, and encourage further research on the intellectual foundations and policy implications of the Information Age.

ENDNOTES

1. This framework was devised by Mr. Jeffrey Cooper, director of the Center for Information Policy and Strategy at Science Applications International Corporation (SAIC).

2. The authors wish to thank Dr. Ray Macedonia and Mr. Tim Thomas for their comments on conference presentations.

3. Alvin and Heidi Toffler, *War and Anti-War: Survival at the Dawn of the 21st Century* (Boston: Little, Brown and Co., 1993).

4. See, for example, Sheila E. Widnall and Ronald R. Fogelman, "Global Presence," in *Joint Forces Quarterly*, No. 7 (Spring 1995), pp. 94–99.

5. This idea is also discussed in Joseph S. Nye, Jr. and William A. Owens, "America's Information Edge," *Foreign Affairs*, Vol. 75, No. 2 (March–April 1996), pp. 20–36.

6. See Stuart J.D. Schwarzenstien, "Export Controls on Encryption Technology," *SAIS Review*, Vol. XVI, No. 1 (Winter-Spring 1996), pp. 13–34, for an overview of the equities and trade-offs involved in encryption control policies.

7. See Vipin Gupta, "New Satellite Images for Sale," *International Security*, Vol. 20, No. 1 (Summer 1995), pp. 94–125, for a thorough review of projected commercial imaging systems and their capabilities.

8. The White House, *A National Security Strategy of Engagement and Enlargement*, February 1996, p. 13.

9. Nicholas Negroponte, in *Being Digital* (New York: Alfred A. Knopf, 1995), provides an analysis of some of the characteristics of a binary, digital environment.

10. See Martin E. Libicki, *Mesh and the Net* (Washington, D.C.: National Defense University Press, 1994).

11. See Stuart E. Johnson and Martin C. Libicki, eds., *Dominant Battlespace Knowledge: The Winning Edge* (Washington, D.C.: National Defense University Press, 1995).

12. Eliot A. Cohen proposes a similar concept in "A Revolution in Warfare," *Foreign Affairs*, Vol. 75, No. 2 (March-April 1996), p. 45.

Contributing Authors

Lt. Gen. Frederic J. Brown, USA (Ret.) retired in 1989 after thirty-three years of service commanding units in the United States, Germany, and Vietnam. Most recently, he was Chief of Armor and Cavalry, Commanding General Fort Knox, and Commander of Fourth Army. He holds *license* and doctorate degrees from the Graduate Institute of International Studies in Geneva, Switzerland and has published widely including *U.S. Army in Transition II: Landpower in the Information Age* (1993), *U.S. Army in Transition* (1973, co-author), and *Chemical Warfare: Restraints in War* (1968).

Dr. Susan Canedy is Special Assistant to the Commanding General, U.S. Army Training and Doctrine Command (TRADOC) and is TRADOC historian. She holds a doctorate in American history from Texas A&M University. She is Adjunct Professor of History at Christopher Newport University, Old Dominion University, and Thomas Nelson Community College.

Major Mark J. Eschelman, USA is assigned to Headquarters, Department of the Army as a Force XXI Integration Division Staff officer, supporting the Office of the Deputy Chief-of-Staff for Operations and Plans. He holds a master's degree in strategic intelligence from the Defense Intelligence College, and two masters' degrees in military art and science from the U.S. Army Command and General Staff College and the School for Advanced Military Studies at Ft. Leavenworth.

Major Robert M. Evans, USA (Ret.) retired in 1995 as a Senior Analyst in the Army Information Warfare Office. He is currently employed as an information warfare consultant for Booz, Allen & Hamilton, Inc. in Falls Church, Virginia.

Lt. Col. Jack Gerber, USA (Ret.) supports the Assistant Deputy Chief of Staff of the Army for Operations and Plans, Force Development in developing and executing horizontal technology integration programs. Mr. Gerber has twenty-seven years of experience in managing personnel, equipment, time, and budgets for diverse military organizations, dealing with many facets of the logistics management system.

General William W. Hartzog, USA is Commanding General of the U.S. Army Training and Doctrine Command (TRADOC). Previously, he was Deputy Commander-in-Chief and Chief-of-Staff of the United States Atlantic Command, Norfolk, Virginia; Commanding General, 1st Infantry Division at Fort Riley, Kansas; Commanding General, U.S. Army South, Fort Clayton, Panama; and J-3 for the United States Southern Command in Panama during Operation Just Cause. General Hartzog holds a master's in psychology from Appalachian State University and has completed advanced course work at the U.S. Army Infantry School, the U.S. Marine Corps Command, and the U.S. Army War College.

Dr. Christopher Jon Lamb is Director of Policy Planning, Office of the Assistant Secretary of Defense for Special Operations and Low-Intensity Conflict. He is currently serving in the Department of State as the Deputy Director for Military Development on an interagency task force that is developing and executing a plan to train and equip Bosnian Federation military forces. He is the author of *How to Think About Arms Control, Disarmament, and Defense* (1988); *Belief Systems and Decision Making in the Mayguez Crisis* (1989); and, with David Tucker, "Peacetime Engagements" in *America's Armed Forces: A Handbook of Current and Future Capabilities* (forthcoming).

Dr. Carnes Lord is currently the John M. Olin Professor of Civilization and Statecraft at the Fletcher School of Law and Diplomacy. He is a political scientist with interests in international relations, strategic studies, and political philosophy. He has served as assistant to the Vice President for national security affairs, and was distinguished fellow of the Institute for National Strategic Studies at the National Defense University in Washington. His most recent book is *The Presidency and the Management of National Security* (1988).

General James P. McCarthy, USAF (Ret.) is Olin Professor of National Security at the U.S. Air Force Academy. He retired from the Air Force in 1992 after thirty-five years of service. His last command was Deputy Commander-in-Chief, European Command, Stuttgart, West Germany, where he was responsible for all forces in Europe. General McCarthy served as Director of Legislative Liaison, Office of the Secretary of the Air Force as well as Deputy Chief-of-Staff for Programs and Resources at Air Force Headquarters, responsible for Air Force programming, manpower, and foreign military sales.

Mr. John W. McDonald is Assistant Vice President and Division Manager in the National Security Studies and Strategies Group of Science Applications International Corporation (SAIC) where he focuses on national military policy and strategy issues. Mr. McDonald previously served as Executive Assistant to the Commander-in-Chief of the U.S. Army Southern Command. He holds master's degrees from the American University and from the Institute of Political Studies, University of Grenoble, France.

Captain Richard P. O'Neill, USN is the Deputy for Strategy and Policy, Directorate of Information Warfare, Office of the Assistant Secretary of Defense for Command, Control, Communications and Intelligence. Previously, Captain O'Neill was Assistant Commander for Operations on the staff of the Commander, National Security Group (NSG) Command, as well as Commander of NSG Activity, Kunia, Hawaii. Captain O'Neill received a master's in international relations from the Naval War College and also holds master's degrees from Georgetown University and the Naval Postgraduate School.

Dr. Robert L. Pfaltzgraff, Jr., is Shelby Cullom Davis Professor of International Security Studies at the Fletcher School of Law and Diplomacy, Tufts University. He is also President of the Institute for Foreign Policy Analysis (IFPA) of Cambridge, Massachusetts and Washington, D.C.. His recent publications include: *Contending Theories of International Relations: A Comprehensive Survey* (4th ed. 1996, co-author); *Roles and Missions of Special Operations Forces in the Aftermath of the Cold War* (1995, co-editor); *Ethnic Conflict and Regional Instability: Implications for U.S. Policy and Army Roles and Missions* (1994, co-editor); and *Transatlantic Relations in the 1990s: The Emergence of New Security Architectures* (1993, co-author).

Major Gregory J. Rattray, USAF is a Ph.D. candidate at the Fletcher School of Law and Diplomacy, Tufts University, and a Research Associate at the Institute for Foreign Policy Analysis. His last Air Force assignment was as Deputy Director of the USAF Institute for National Security Studies and Assistant Professor of Political Science at the U.S. Air Force Academy. Major Rattray has served as an intelligence officer at Kadena AFB, Japan and Strategic Air Command HQ, Offut AFB, Nebraska. He also holds a master's degree from the John F. Kennedy School of Government, Harvard University.

General Dennis J. Reimer, USA became the 33rd Chief-of-Staff of the U.S. Army in June, 1995. Previously, he was Commanding General of the United States Army, Forces Command, Fort McPherson, Georgia. He served in the Pentagon as the Deputy Chief-of-Staff for Operations and Plans for the Army during Desert Storm, and as Army Vice Chief-of-Staff. His previous commands include an infantry company at Fort Benning, Georgia, an artillery battalion at Fort Carson, Colorado, and the division artillery for the 8th Infantry Division in Germany. General Reimer holds a master's degree from Shippensburg State University.

Brigadier General John P. Rose, USA is Director of Requirements (Horizontal Technology Integration), Office of the Deputy Chief-of-Staff for Operations and Plans, U.S. Army. Recently, he served as Chief of the Requirements and Programs Branch, Office of the Assistant Chief-of-Staff for Policy, Supreme Headquarters, Allied Powers Europe. He commanded the 94th Air Defense Artillery Brigade, U.S. Army, Europe and Seventh Army, Germany. He holds a master's degree from the U.S. Army Command and General Staff College and a Ph.D. in international relations from the University of Southern California.

Mr. Laurence E. Rothenberg is a Research Associate at the Institute for Foreign Policy Analysis, Inc. He holds a bachelor's degree in history, *magna cum laude*, from Amherst College and a master's degree from the Fletcher School of Law and Diplomacy, Tufts University.

Mr. Winn Schwartau is one of the country's leading experts on information security and electronic privacy. As President of Interpact, Inc., he provides security consultation to industry and government. He has testified before congressional subcommittees and appears regularly on television shows such as CNN's "Larry King" and ABC's "Nightline." Mr. Schwartau is a prolific author, with articles in such magazines as *Computer World, Infoworld, PC Week*, and *Info-Security News*. Among his recent books are *Information Warfare: Chaos on the Electronic Superhighway* (1994), and *Terminal Compromise* (1991).

Dr. Richard H. Shultz, Jr., is Director of the International Security Studies Program at the Fletcher School of Law and Diplomacy, Tufts University and Associate Professor of International Politics at the Fletcher School. He was Olin Distinguished Professor of National Security Studies at the U.S. Military Academy during the 1994-95 academic year. Recently, he authored *In the Aftermath of War: U.S. Support for Reconstruction and Nation-Building in Panama Following Just Cause* (1993), co-authored *Security Studies in the 1990s* (1993) and co-edited *Roles and Missions of SOF in the Aftermath of the Cold War* (1995) and *Ethnic Conflict and Regional Instability: Implications for U.S. Policy Missions* (1994).

Mr. Charles Swett is Acting Deputy Director for Low Intensity Conflict Policy, Office of the Assistant Secretary of Defense for Special Operations and Low Intensity Conflict (SOLIC). He was previously Operations Research Analyst in Strategic Programs at the office of Program Analysis and Evaluation, Office of the

Secretary of Defense working on program and cost-effective analysis of strategic nuclear weapons. During the 1980s, he was Chief, Plans Division in a White House-directed OSD Special Program, responsible for national security policy development, threat assessment, and operational planning. Mr. Swett holds a master's degree in systems science from Michigan State University.

Lieutenant Colonel Timothy L. Thomas (Ret.) is an analyst at the Foreign Military Studies Office at Fort Leavenworth, Kansas. He received a bachelor's degree from West Point and a master's degree from the University of Southern California. He has served as Director of Soviet Studies at the United States Army Russian Institute, now called the Eurasian Institute, in Garmisch, Germany; and as an inspector of Warsaw Pact tactical operations for the Conference on Disarmament in Europe. Mr. Thomas has written on Russian military-political events, ethnic conflict, and peace operations, among other subjects. He has extensive military contacts in Russia due to his travel there and to his escorting Russian military representatives in America. Mr. Thomas is an assistant editor of the journal *European Security*.

Mr. Michael J. Vickers is an Alexander Hamilton Fellow at the Johns Hopkins University's Paul H. Nitze School of Advanced International Studies where he is Associate Director of Strategic Studies for the 1996-97 academic year and is completing a doctorate. He has been a Strategic Studies Fellow with the Office of Net Assessment in the Office of the Secretary of Defense. Mr. Vickers served as a Special Forces Officer, commanded an elite counterterrorism unit, and was also a CIA Operations Officer. He holds master's degrees from both Johns Hopkins University and the Wharton School of the University of Pennsylvania.

Mr. Douglas Waller is National Security Correspondent for *Time* magazine. He works as part of a reporting team that covers defense, intelligence, and law enforcement for the magazine. His specialty is intelligence. Previously, Mr. Waller worked for *Newsweek,* where he reported on major military conflicts from the Gulf War to Somalia and Haiti. Mr. Waller is the author of four books, including *Commandos: The Inside Story of America's Secret Soldiers* (1994). He is currently working on a fifth book, on naval aviation.

Brigadier General Huba Wass de Czege, USA (Ret.) retired in 1993 after serving as Assistant Division Commander of the 1st Infantry Division at Ft. Riley, Kansas. He now works with the U.S. Army Training and Doctrine Command (TRADOC) on exploration of future technologies. He also headed the military analytical support team to NATO on the Conventional Forces in Europe negotiations and served as special advisor to the Secretary General of NATO during the implementation of CFE verification. He has completed graduate course work at the Kennedy School of Government, Harvard University and was an Assistant Professor of International Relations at the U.S. Military Academy at West Point.

Major Jo-Ann C. Webber, USA is currently assigned to the Army Information Warfare Office as Force Development Staff officer, supporting the Office of the Deputy Chief-of-Staff for Operations and Plans. Her prior assignments include Junior Officer Cryptologic Career Program at the National Security Agency, and Assistant Secretary of the General Staff, Headquarters, United States Army, Europe.

Colonel John R. Wood, USA is Commander of the 3rd Infantry Division Artillery. Previously, Colonel Wood served as Chief of the Strategic Plans and Policy Division in the Office of the Deputy Chief-of-staff of the Army for Operations and Plans.

Index

ABCS. *See* Army Battle Command System

Activism, political, Internet and, 287-95, 297-99

Addresses, Internet, 282, 283

AFCS. *See* Automatic Fire Control System
  See also Fire support systems

Afghanistan, 249, 251

Agrarian societies
  leapfrogging into Information Age, 228, 252, 334
  potential information warfare strengths of, 12-14
  See also Low-technology forces, Pre-industrial societies

Aideed, Muhammed, 252, 254, 268, 270

Air defense, 210
  See also Surface-to-air missiles (SAMs)

Air power, potential changes to, 36-37, 41

Air-to-air combat, decision-cycle theory and, 146-48

Air traffic control system, 17

Algeria, 22, 23, 249

Alliance relationships. *See* Coalition warfare

Ambush, deliberate attack methods and, 216-17

American Revolution, commander's decision cycle in, 230

Anderson, John, 290, 300

Anticipatory planning, 346, 348
  maneuver techniques and, 206-7, 208

Anti-satellite systems (ASAT), 38, 39

Architecture, information, 90-94

Army Battle Command System (ABCS), 232

Arsenal ships, 38

ASAT. *See* Anti-satellite systems

Asia, East, potential RMA in, 44

Assistant Secretary of Defense for Command, Control, Communications, and Information, Office of, 282
  See also Defense Department; Secretary of Defense

Assistant Secretary of Defense for
Public Affairs, Office of, 282
See also Defense Department;
Secretary of Defense
Attrition, virtual, 34
Baltin, Admiral, 75
Banks, 58
banking, banking system, 10, 24,
68, 76, 198
Battle command, 84, 85, 101, 111, 113,
171, 179, 204, 352
of 21st century force, 210-12
for field artillery leaders, 127-29,
139-40
Battlefield Combat Identification
System, 235
Battlespace, 129-30, 350-51
information warfare expanding, 4, 5,
9-10, 17, 33, 85, 344
synoptic view of, 154
warfighter's view of, 89-91
See also Battlespace transparency;
Decision-cycle dominance;
Dominant Battlefield Knowledge;
Situational awareness; WarNet
Battlespace transparency, 89-97
decision-cycle dominance and, 143-
68, 345-46
emerging RMA creating, 344-45
in operations other than war, 166
See also Battlespace; Decision-cycle
dominance; Dominant Battlefield
Knowledge; Situational awareness,
WarNet
Bildt, Carl, 285
Blitzkrieg, decision-cycle theory and,
149
See also World War II
Bosnia, 22, 93, 248, 249, 213
media coverage of, 253, 324, 325
non-lethal weapons in, 264
precision air power used in, 256
psychological operations and, 268
Boston Globe, 270
Boutros-Ghali, Boutros, 270
Boyd, John, 146-48

Brown, Frederic J., 84-85, 86, 99-119,
347, 351, 352
Bywater, Hector, 199
C^4I Directorate (J-6), 191
C-130s, 256-57
Cable News Network (CNN), 54, 189,
310, 311, 323, 325
Canedy, Susan, 171-72, 175-85, 349
Casualties, 12
limiting, 179, 180, 181, 232, 256,
260-64
public perceptions of, 260, 328
See also Fratricide
Censorship, Internet bypassing, 290-91
Chamberlain, Neville, 253
China, 41, 148, 279, 291, 334, 342
Central Intelligence Agency (CIA), 315
media's perception of, 322
CITV. *See* Commander's Independent
Thermal Viewer
Civil affairs programs, 301-2
Civil War
commander's decision cycle in, 230
information transfer in, 176-77, 321
Clarke, Arthur C., 50
Clausewitz, Karl von, 10, 150, 311
Clinton administration, 15, 54, 340
Internet embraced by, 285
Close-combat forces, 34-35, 222
CNN, *see* Cable News Network
Coalition warfare
emerging RMA and, 15, 16, 17-18, 64,
159, 160, 192
and psychological operations, 314-315
Cold War, 311, 340
economic warfare replacing, 48
low-intensity conflict during, 18, 19
radio broadcasts and, 310-11
technological advances during, 178
Collateral damage, 69, 259, 261, 349
precision operations and, 180, 181-82,
234, 256, 257, 264, 272
undermining operation support, 263
See also Casualties

Command and control,
  and artillery commanders, 138
  of fires, 122-23
  in OOTW, 270-73
  for tactical situational awareness, 101-3
  technology changing, 151, 157, 158, 170, 172, 173
  vulnerability to hackers, 68, 70
Commanders
  future tasks required of, 93-94, 101-104, 128, 347-48
  information training for, 114-15
Commander's Independent Thermal Viewer (CITV), 108
Commando Solo, 317, 330
Commercial information sources. See Databases, on-line;
Internet; Defense Department
Commercial off-the-shelf (COTS) procurement, 190, 197, 237
Communications, 25, 91, 177-78
  digital vs. analog, 110
  enhancing, 231
  Fire support systems and, 128-29
  See also Media
Computers, advances in, 178, 226-27
Computers at Risk report, 49
Conferences, electronic, 283
Contract with America, 288-89
COTS. See Commercial Off-the-Shelf
Counterattacks, 219
Counterproliferation strategies, 16
Covert operations
  computer viruses and, 39, 69
  disinformation and, 270
Credit bureaus, 10, 12, 17, 58
Cumulative operations/strategies, 157-58, 200, 335
Cyberspace, 4, 11, 15, 50, 53, 54, 55, 57, 58, 59, 294, 296
Databases, on-line, intelligence operations and, 266, 283
Data-transfer rates, 227
DBK. See Dominant Battlefield Knowledge

Deception operations, 210
Decision-cycle dominance, 86
  advantages of, 149-50
  challenges to, 150-55
  historical examples explained by, 146-49, 230
  leader development and, 168
  and precision, 183-84
  simplicity advantageous to, 167
  transparency and, 155-60, 345-47
  in visual-blind confrontation, 164-66
  in visual-visual confrontation, 161-64
  within OODA, 143-46, 148, 152
  See also Battlespace transparency;
    Dominant Battlefield Knowledge;
    Situational awareness; WarNet
Deep strike/attack, 35, 40, 102, 107, 133
  See also Long-range strike systems;
    Missiles, long-range
Defense, Department of (United States)
  commercial information sources used by, 90, 280, 282, 299-301, 303-5
  information distribution system of, 91
  intrusions on systems of, 198
  IW defensive strategy of, 194-98
  public affairs bureaucracy of, 324-28
  reliance on commercial systems, 190
  See also Assistant Secretary of Defense
    for Command, Control,
    Comunications and Intelligence;
    Assistant Secretary of Defense
    for Public Affairs; Secretary of
    Defense, Office of Defense
    Information Security Agency
    (DISA), 198
Defense Mapping Agency (DMA), 94
Defense Satellite Communications System (DSCS), 91
Defense Science Board, 94
Defense Science Board Summer Study (1994), 88

Defensive strategies
of 21st century force, 210, 217-22
of Department of Defense, 194-98
static and dynamic elements of,
221-22
Deliberate attack methods, 215-17
Democracy, electronic, 286-87
Desert Hammer, Operation, 101
Deterrence strategies, 74, 335-37
Digitization, 155, 229, 235, 340
Direct broadcast of information, 91-93
Disinformation
covert operations and, 270
on Internet, 283-84, 302
See also Deception operations
Doctrine, 83, 121, 131, 179
advanced weapons systems and, 85-
86, 140, 156, 171
descriptive, 126-27
Dominant Battlefield Knowledge (DBK),
84, 90, 345
See also Battlespace; Battlespace
transparency; Decision-cycle
dominance; Situational awareness;
WarNet
DSCS. *See* Defense Satellite
Communications System
Ecological damage, information
operations limiting, 66-67
Economic warfare, 48-54
Education, information
Russian, 73
for unit commanders, 114-15
See also Training
Elections, Internet and, 287, 294
Electromagnetic pulse weapons, 39, 70
for force protection in OOTW, 261,
262
permanent damage avoided with, 264
Electromagnetism, replacing chemical
propulsion, 34
E-mail, 227, 254, 282, 291, 303
Clinton administration and, 285
disinformation campaigns and, 302
Neo-Nazi's use of, 245, 292

video/audio messages replacing text,
296-97
Encryption
commercial methods of, 254
current debate about government
control of, 339
Enhanced Position Location Reporting
System (EPLRS), 125
ENIAC computer, 178
Environmental groups, 57-58
EPLRS. *See* Enhanced Position Location
Reporting System
Eschelman, Mark J., 225-39
Ethnic conflict, 19, 22
Evans, Robert, 225-39
F-86 aircraft, 146
FAASV. *See* Field Artillery Ammunition
Support Vehicle
Federal Aviation Administration (FAA),
88, 90
Federal Reserve System (United States),
vulnerability of, 4, 10
Fedlink, 282
Field Artillery Ammunition Support
Vehicle (FAASV), 124
Field Manual 100-5, 126, 127, 129
Fighter aircraft, 37, 146-48
Filtering information, 85, 94, 101, 107,
108, 109-12, 114, 116, 152, 167, 300,
352
using "presets" for, 110-11
Firepower
of 21st century force, 173, 204, 207-8,
222, 353
in operations other than war, 262-65
Fire support systems, 104, 122
Automatic Fire Control System
(AFCS), 123-24, 125-26
communication among, 128-29
positioning of, 130, 209
precision attack and, 160
Firewalls, 75, 89, 90, 172, 284
Flexibility, in defensive maneuvers, 221
Foley, Tom, 287

Force protection, 184
  in operations other than war, 255,
    257, 258-59, 260-62
Force XXI, 173, 179-85, 205-12, 225-26
  defensive maneuvers by, 210, 217-22
  goals for, 232-34, 237-38
  offensive systems of, 213-17
  risk management models for, 236-37
France, 23, 51, 188, 340
Franks, Frederick M., Jr., 127
Fringe groups, 50, 245
  on the Internet, 289-90
  See also Sub-state actors
Friendly fire. See Fratricide
Freenets, 283
Fratricide, 123, 173, 229, 231, 232
  Battlefield Combat Identification
    System and, 235
  precision reducing, 183
  "From the 'Cult of Secrecy' to An
    Information Culture" (Rubanov), 71
Funding, U.S. Army, 235-36
Genghis Khan, decision-cycle theory
  and, 147, 148
Geospatial temporal reference system,
  88-90, 94, See also Mapping
Gerber, Jack, 225-39
Gingrich, Newt, 285
Global Positioning System (GPS), 4,
  124, 230, 233, 235, 252, 267, 272
  expanded access to data, 340
Goethe, Johann Wolfgang von, 273
GPS. See Global Positioning System
Graphical control measures, in training
  exercises, 136
Greed, as motive for information
  warfare, 56
Grenada, 264
Gulf War, 11, 13, 15, 17, 31, 61, 64, 68,
  78, 91, 153, 175, 181, 189, 199, 192,
  209, 292, 309, 311, 312, 316, 336
  commander's decision cycle in, 230
  media coverage of, 189, 322, 323,
    328-29
  psychological operations and, 268,
    313-15, 317, 329

See also Iraq, Saddam Hussein
Hackers, 16, 51, 57, 235, 284, 287, 343
Haiti, 90, 114, 175, 178-79, 251, 253,
  264, 265
  psychological operations in, 269, 330
Hartzog, William W., 171-72, 175-85,
  349
Helicopters, increasing mobility of, 208
Hezbollah, 20
Horizontal Technology Integration
  (HTI), 174, 234-36, 238, 349
HTI. See Horizontal Technology
  Integration
Humanitarian assistance, 265
Hussein, Saddam, 13, 314, 336
  See also Gulf War; Iraq
ICE. See Interdiction and Counterfire
  Exercise
IFSAS. See Initial Fire Support
  Automation System
Industrial societies, 228
  vs. post-industrial information
    warfare, 13
Information
  controlling flows of, 341
  as economic asset, 48-49
  excess of, 153-54, 346
  filtering, 109-12, 167, 300
  government vs. civilian control of,
    338-39
  horizontal and vertical integration of,
    133
Information Architecture for the
  Battlefield, 88
Information policy (Russia), 71, 72-73
Information policy (U.S.), 59-60
Information revolution
  American vs. Russian attitudes
    toward, 6-7
  current RMA and, 32
  See also Revolution in military affairs

Information technologies
  anonymity offered by, 12
  counterproliferation strategies and, 16
  cultural differences impacting use of,
    342
  events compressed by, 178-79, 223
  increasing availability and impact of,
    11, 12-13, 252-53, 281, 341-42
  rapid replacement curve for, 190
  users of, 57-58, 342-43
Information warfare (IW), 3-4, 51-52,
    333
  American vs. Russian approaches to,
    6-7
  classifying, 52-56
  corporate, 53-54
  Defense Department's strategy for,
    194-98
  deterrence strategies and, 74, 335-37
  geographical boundaries transcended
    by, 9-10, 33, 344
  global, 54
  human abilities required for, 84-85,
    93, 94, 101-4, 113-14,
    347-48, 351-52
  independent, 39, 333, 337-38
  integrated, 39, 333
  motives behind, 56-58
  as non-lethal conflict, 333
  organizing the national security
    apparatus for, 337-339
  personal, 52-53
  Russian concerns regarding, 65-70
  Russian definition of, 63-64
  Russian responses to, 70-74
  strategic, 245-49, 315-16, 329-30
  winning (objectives necessary for),
    232-33
Initial Fire Support Automation System
    (IFSAS), 125
Intelligence, 54, 57, 65, 89, 94, 103-04,
    109, 111, 125, 129, 131, 134, 148,
    166, 172, 178, 180, 181, 194, 196
  Internet and, 266, 299-301
  and the media, 327
  in operations other than war, 265-68

new tasks for, 341-42
  for psychological operations, 315-316
  See also Cental Intelligence Agency;
    Real-time information
Interdiction and Counterfire Exercise
    (ICE), 133-35
International Information Academy, 73
Internet, 244-45, 279-305
  censorship bypassed by, 290-91
  current trends on, 282-84
  defined, 280-81
  Department of Defense's use of, 90,
    280, 282, 299-301, 303-5
  disinformation on, 283-84, 302
  fringe groups on, 289-90
  future of, 293-98
  in intelligence operations, 266,
    299-301
  political process (international) and,
    290-93, 297-99
  political process (United States) and,
    285-90, 294-95, 296, 298-299
  prevalence of, 279-80, 281, 284
  in psychological operations, 270, 302
Internet Society (Fairfax, VA), 281
Intervehicular Information System
    (IVIS), 108
IOC. See Organized crime, international
Iran, 16, 25, 51, 63
  advanced technology and, 279, 342
Iraq, 10, 16, 22, 63, 90, 189, 193, 268,
    323, 328, 329
  See also Gulf War; Saddam Hussein
Islamic radicalism, 21
  Algerian, 23
Israel, 20, 22, 51, 292
IVIS. See Intervehicular Information
    System
IW. See Information warfare
J-3. See Operations Directorate
J-6. See C^{4}I Directorate
Japan, 16, 22, 23, 50, 51, 56
  and World War II, 199-200
Joint Chiefs of Staff, 191-92
Joint Requirements Oversight Council,
    191

Joint Warfighting Capability
  Assessment (JWCA), 191-92
JWCA. *See* Joint Warfighting
  Capability Assessment
Khmer Rouge, 269
Kommunist (journal), 71
Korea, North, 11, 16, 63
Korea, South, 51
Korean War, air-to-air combat in,
  146-48
Kurdish Workers' Party (PKK), 20, 25
Lamb, Christopher Jon, 244, 247-78,
  333, 345
Lasers, for force protection in OOTW,
  244, 261, 262
Leader development, 113-114, 352-53
  advanced weapons systems and,
  85-86, 136-40
  decision-cycle dominance and, 168
Legislation on Internet, 285-86
Levin, Carl, 268
Library catalogues, 283
LICs. *See* Low-intensity conflicts
Logistics, precision operations and,
  184-85
Long-range strike systems, 34, 36, 337
  increasing sophistication in, 42
  stealth and, 40
  WarNet and, 95
  See also Deep strike/attack; Missiles,
  long-range
Lord, Carnes, 245-46, 307-19, 333, 335
Low-intensity conflicts (LICs), 4, 18, 19,
  23, 280, 324
  See also Cold War; Operations other
  than war
Low-technology forces, 4
  IW strategies of, 86, 334, 336, 346
  in visual-blind confrontation, 164-66
  See also Agrarian societies
Mandel, Tom, 291
Maneuver techniques, 203-23, 350-51
  chess analogy for, 204-5
  defensive methodology, 210, 217-22
  in field artillery, 130, 135, 234
  key elements of, 208-09

offensive methodology, 213-17
  precision in, 182-83
Mapping, digital, 94, 155, 218, 229, 234
  See also Geospatial temporal reference
  system
McCarthy, James P., 84, 87-97, 345, 347
McCluhan, Marshall, 50
McDonald, John W., 86, 143-68, 346
Media
  Defense Department, conflicts with,
  246, 322-23, 324-30
  as part of asymmetric strategy, 193
  increasing independence of, 246,
  321-24, 341
  Internet as threat to, 286, 295-96
  operations other than war and, 244,
  253-54, 269
  psychological operations and, 4, 67,
  310-11
  sensationalized coverage within, 326
  strengthening PSYOP through, 269-70
  used for strategic information
  warfare, 246, 329-30
Medical facilities, 262
"Medium is the Mess, The," 227
Microsensor networks, 267-68
Microwave weapons, 39, 70
Military Communications Satellite
  (MILSTAR), 91
Military-technical revolution (MTR),
  172, 192, 309, 331, 348-53
MILSAT. *See* Military Communications
  Satellite
Missiles, long-range, 33, 34, 35, 37
  See also Deep strike/attack; Long-
  range strike systems; Theater
  ballistic missile threat
Mongols, decision-cycle theory and,
  147, 148-49
Movement techniques. *See* Maneuver
  techniques
MTR. *See* Military-technical revolution
National Guard, 104
National Liberation Army (ELN), 20
National Military Strategy (U.S.;
  February 1995), 61

National power, information
revolutions expanding concept of, 9
172, 192-93
National Research Council, 49
National Training Center, 101, 135
Naval warfare, potential changes in,
37-38
NCOs. *See* Non-commissioned officers
Neo-Nazi groups, 245, 292
Networks, 11, 12, 254
civilian, 198
microsensor, 248, 267
military, 90, 129
military reliance on civilian, 187, 198
vulnerabilities of, 17, 195, 198, 201
See also Internet; Public switched
network; WarNet
New York Times, 270
Nixon, Richard, 48
Non-commissioned officers (NCOs)
responsibilities divided with
commissioned officers, 105-6, 112-13
See also Commanders, Leader
development, Officers, Soldiers,
Training
Non-lethal weapons (NLWs), 70, 129
Information Warfare tactics as, 333
in operations other than war, 244,
248, 261, 264
in Somalia, 264
See also Operations other than war;
Soft-kill systems; Somalia
Nuclear weapons capability
emerging RMA and, 43, 344
Information technologies'
vulnerability to, 16-17
spread of, 24
Observe-orient-decide-act (OODA),
143-46, 148, 152, 153, 166
See also Decision-cycle dominance
Offensive systems
of 21st century force, 213-17
information warfare favoring, 33
Internet and, 302-3
See also Weapons systems,
Information Age

Officers, 100, 102, 138-39
public affairs training for, 324-25
responsibilities divided with
noncommissioned officers, 85-86,
105-6, 112-13
training for information age
operations, 350-52
See also Commanders, Leader
development, Non-commissioned
officers, Soldiers, Training
O'Neill, Richard P., 172-73, 187-201,
332, 335
OODA. *See* Observe-orient-decide-act
OOTW. *See* Operations other than war
Operations Directorate (J-3), 191
Operations other than war (OOTW),
107, 244, 247-77
command and control issues in,
270-73
few modifications necessary for,
256-57
firepower limitations in, 262-64
force protection in, 260-62
importance of technology in, 249-251
intelligence support in, 265-68
leveraging technology in, 249-251
patience required for, 249-50, 258
political aspect of, 258, 270-71
psychological operations in, 268-70
scarce American resources for, 255-56,
257
sophisticated vs. rudimentary
technologies in, 249, 250-51
warfighting advantage increasing, 248
See also Low-intensity conflicts
Organizational hierarchies, flattening
of, 96, 272, 347, 348, 353
Organized crime
international, 20-21, 25-26
Owens, Admiral William A., 87
Paladin howitzer, 85, 121, 123-26, 128,
130-31, 135, 136, 137-38, 182,
348-50
Palletized Load System (PLS), 124-25
Panama, 264
Paralyzing operations, 39

Pattern-recognition software, 198
Pentagon
  competing with media outlets, 246, 322-23, 324-30
  low-intensity conflicts studied by, 248
  See also Department of Defense
Peru, 254
Pfaltzgraff, Robert L., 4, 9-27, 332
PKK. See Kurdish Workers' Party
PLGR. See Precise Lightweight GPS Receiver
PLS. See Palletized Load System
Political process
  on Internet, 279, 285-90
  in operations other than war, 270-72
Post-industrial societies, vulnerabilities of, 13-14, 15-16, 17-18
Precise Lightweight GPS Receiver (PLGR), 125-26
Precision operations, 171-72, 180-85, 233-34, 349
  collateral damage avoided through, 180, 181-82, 256
  fratricide reduced by, 183
  Pre-industrial societies, information technology accessible to, 12-13
  See also Agrarian societies; low-technology forces
Presence, virtual, 337
Privacy
  electronic invasions of, 52-53
  encryption and, 339
  national security interests and, 49, 54, 339
PSN. See Public switched network
Psychological operations (PSYOP), 25, 64, 67, 307-17
  emerging RMA and, 307-12
  Internet and, 270, 302
  multimedia, 269-70
  in operations other than war, 267-70
  as part of strategy, 245-46, 315-16, 329-30
  viewed as outdated enterprise, 308
  within decision-cycle theory, 147-48, 150

PSYOP. See Psychological operations
Public affairs bureaucracy (Defense Department), 324-28
Public switched network (PSN), 190
Publishing. See Direct broadcast of information
Radar, infrared, 235
Rangers, in Somalia, 249 262, 270, 328
  See also Somalia, Muhammad Aideed
Rattray, Gregory J., 331-54
RDA. See Research, development, and acquisition
Real-time information, 108, 134, 158, 160, 178, 181, 182, 210, 230, 245, 256, 272, 292
  See also Intelligence, Television
Reconnaissance patrol, in war vs. in operations short of war, 259
Reconnaissance, surveillance, and target acquisition (RSTA) forces, 218-19
Religious groups, terrorism by, 21-22, 23
Research, development, and acquisition (RDA), budget for, 235-36
Research and development, industry replacing government as leader in, 190
Revolution in security affairs (RSA), 172, 192-93, 331-43, 353
Revolution in military affairs (RMA), 4, 5, 29, 82, 171, 172, 192, 343-48
  battlespace expanded by, 344
  concept of national power expanded by, 172, 192-93
  definition of, 5, 30-31
  emerging information-based RMA, 31-33
  future security environment and, 41-45, 331-43
  implications for force structure, 40-41
  and Operations Other Than War, 247-48
  potential capabilities resulting from, 33-41
  psychological operations and, 307-13

Risk management models, 194-99, 236-37

RMA. *See* Revolution in military affairs

Robotic helpers. *See* Soldiers, automation replacing

Rose, John P., 173-74, 225-39, 349

Rothenberg, Laurence E., 331-54

Royal Air Force, 180

RSTA. *See* Reconnaissance, surveillance, and target acquisition forces

Rubanov, Vladimir, 71-73

Russia, 6-7, 20, 21, 24, 31, 61-79, 279, 332
  censorship bypassed in, 291
  clandestine sales of fissionable material in, 24
  cult of secrecy in, 71-72
  foreign information experience studied by, 63
  information anxieties of, 61-62, 64-68, 74-77
  information parity sought by, 70-74
  information warriors in, 57
  radio broadcasts in, 310-11
  as a peer competitor to the United States, 334
  satellite systems of, 340

SAMs. *See* Surface-to-air missiles

Satellites
  used for attack, 34, 36, 37, 39
  commercial use of, 340-41
  imagery capability of, 90, 91, 229, 254
  increasing vulnerability of, 33, 38-39
  media and, 246, 253, 323-24
  See also Global Positioning System (GPS); Communications

Schwartau, Winn, 6, 47-60, 333, 335

Scud, 151, 290
  See also Theater ballistic missile threat

SDI. *See* Strategic Defense Initiative

Secessionist movements, 21, 25, 26

Secretary of Defense, Office of, 248
  See also Defense Department

Security environment, 3-7, 9-27, 187-89, 210

computer systems and, 49, 284
  emerging RMA and, 41-45, 331-43
  in operations other than war, 260-62
  See also, Revolution in Security Affairs; Revolution in Military Affairs

Sendero Luminoso, 254

Sensor-to-shooter concept, 95

Shaping operations, 39

Shelters, electrothermochromatic, 36

Shershev, General-Major, 76

Shultz, Richard H., Jr., 4, 9-27, 332

Signature reduction, 33

Sikhs, 25

Simon, Bob, 323

Simultaneous attack methods, 214-15

SINCGARS. *See* Single-channel ground and airborne radio systems

Single-channel Ground and Airborne Radio Systems (SINCGARS), 121
  Paladin howitzer and, 123
  support vehicles and, 124

Situational awareness, 14-15, 84, 86, 93, 96-97, 100-119, 230
  filter design and, 109-12
  in higher and lower echelons, 100, 105-6, 112-13
  See also Battlespace transparency; Decision-cycle dominance; Dominant Battlefield Knowledge; WarNet

Small Wars Manual (1940), 247, 251, 255, 260
  on intelligence operations, 265
  on political strategy, 270
  on proper application of force, 262
  on psychological operations, 267

Snipers, countering, 257, 261

Social Security Administration, 52

Soft kill systems, 38
  See also Non-lethal weapons

Soldiers
  automation replacing, 33, 35-36, 126, 176
  division of responsibilities between, 105-6, 112-13
  in flatter organizational structures, 84, 347-48
  greater knowledge required of, 83-84, 95-96, 132, 205, 351-52
  training for, 100-4, 113-14, 131-36, 238
  See also Commanders, Leader development, Non-commissioned officers (NCOs), Officers, Training
Somalia, 90, 175, 265
  media coverage of, 253, 326, 328
  non-lethal weapons in, 264
  psychological operations in, 268
  Rangers in, 249, 262, 270, 328
  snipers in, 256-57
  technology in, 228, 249, 251-52, 257
  See also Aideed, Rangers
Soviet Union. *See* Russia
Space, increasing military importance of, 5, 28, 32, 38-39, 42, 43
  See also Satellites
States
  ungovernability crises of, 18-19, 22-23
  weakening of, 10-11
Stealth
  air power and, 34, 36-37, 41
  ground forces and, 34
  long-range strike systems and, 40
  naval power and, 37
Stock Exchange (New York), new vulnerability of, 4, 10
STOW-E. *See* Synthetic Theater of War-Europe
Strategic Defense Initiative (SDI), Russian perspective of, 67
Sub-state actors, 3-4, 11, 18-19, 22-24, 26, 332, 334
  See also Ethnic conflict; Fringe groups; Organized crime, international; Hackers; Neo-Nazis; Terrorists; Religious groups, terrorism by; Secessionists; States

Sullivan, Gordon R., 122, 139
Sun Tzu, 175
Supplies, movement of. *See* Logistics
Surface-to-air missiles (SAMs), 249, 252, 256, 261, 262
  See also Air defense
Swett, Charles, 244-45, 279-306, 339-40
Synthetic Theater of War-Europe (STOW-E), 104
System of systems, 33, 87-88, 95
  See also Owens, Admiral William A.
TACFIRE, 104, 125
Tactical engagement simulation (TES), 104
Tactics, 128, 203-04,
  of substate actors, 19, 21-22
  Information Age and, 34, 62, 178, 180, 206, 223, 348, 351-52
  See also Tactics, Techniques, and Procedures (TTP)
Tactics, Techniques, and Procedures (TTP), 85, 103, 106
  and filters, 111
  in coalitions, 100
  Information Age and, 112-13, 121-22, 127, 132, 135, 139-40, 156, 158
Tactical situational awareness. *See* Situational awareness
Tasking, dynamic, 95-96
TBM. *See* Theater ballistic missile
Technology. *See* Information technologies; Weapons systems, Information Age
Telegraph, 177, 230
Television, 247, 253, 310-11
Terrorism, 19-26, 332
  conventional weaponry and, 23, 24
  information-based, 6, 49, 68-70, 188
  See also Air traffic control system, Banks, Federal Reserve System, Federal Aviation Administration, Stock Exchange
TES. *See* Tactical engagement simulation
Theater ballistic missile (TBM) threat, 153, 233

Theater warfare
  hider-finder balance and, 40
  information warfare expanding
    boundaries of, 10, 33
  See also Battlespace
3rd Infantry Division Artillery (Fort
    Stewart), 85, 121-27, 133-35, 348
Thomas, Timothy L., 6-7, 61-79, 332
Toffler, Alvin, 5, 150, 334
Toffler, Heidi, 5, 334
Training
  advanced weapons systems and, 85,
    131-36, 351-52
  needed for improving situational
    awareness, 100-06, 109, 111-15
  in public affairs, 324-25
  See also Commanders; Leader
    development; Officers; Non-
    commissioned officers (NCOs);
    Soldiers; Tactics, Techniques, and
    Procedures (TTP)
Trans-national groups. *See* sub-state
    actors
Transparency. *See* Battlespace
  Transparency; Situational awareness
UAVs. *See* Unmanned aerial vehicles
United States
  history of modern warfare in, 176-78
  information warfare's financial impact
    upon, 51-52
  as inviting target for information
    warfare, 56
  maintaining military dominance of,
    44-45
  PSYOP's advantages and
    disadvantages to, 311-12
  Russian perspectives of, 63
  See also post-industrial societies
Unmanned Aerial Vehicles (UAVs), 35-
    36, 37, 87, 206, 210, 215, 244, 248,
    267, 272, 345
  force protection aided by, 261
Urbanization, 254
U.S. Army Europe (USAREUR), 105-6
USSR. *See* Russia
van Creveld, Martin, 10
Vehicles, increasing speed of, 208

Vickers, Michael G., 5, 29-46, 333, 334,
    343-44, 350
Video imagery
  false messages conveyed through, 269-
    70
  prevalence of, 253
  replacing text-oriented e-mail, 296-97
  See also Real-time information;
    Satellites; Television
Vietnam, 25, 178, 249, 253, 285, 308,
    322, 328
Viruses, computer, 39, 62, 63, 69-70,
    74, 284
  Internet security and, 284
  Russian perspectives of, 69-70
Visual-blind confrontations, 160,
    164-66, 345-46
Visual-visual confrontations, 160,
    161-64, 345-46
Volant Solo. See Commando Solo
  Force XXI's use of, 205-12
  implications of, 85-86, 348-49
  non-lethal, 264-65
  See also Offensive systems
Waller, Douglas, 246, 321-30, 341
Wall Street Journal, 290
WarNet, 84, 88-97, 345, 348
  direct broadcast provided by, 91-93
  vulnerability of, 93, 96-97
  warfighter training needed for, 93, 94
  See also Battlespace transparency;
    Decision-cycle dominance;
    Dominant, Battlefield Knowledge;
    Situational awareness
Washington Post, 227
Weapons sytems, Information Age
  collateral damage reduced by, 180,
    181-82, 256
  as command and control aids, 272
  downsizing resulting from, 252
  for force protection in OOTW, 261-62
  Force XXI's use of, 205-12
  implications of, 85-86, 348-49
  modernization of, 349-50
  non-lethal, 264-65
  See also Horizontal Technology
    Integration (HTI)

Webber, Jo-Ann C., 225-39
Wood, John R., 85-86, 121-41, 348-49, 351-52
World War I, information transfer in, 177
World War II
  British vs. American bombing techniques in, 180
  Blitzkrieg and, 149, 192
  commander's decision cycle in, 230
  information transfer in, 177, 321-22

World Wide Web, 282, 297
Wylie, J. C., 200
Yamamoto, Admiral, 199
Zapatista National Liberation Army (EZLN), 245, 254, 292